# RIVER OF
# FORGOTTEN
# DAYS

# RIVER OF FORGOTTEN DAYS

*A Journey down the Mississippi
in Search of La Salle*

## DANIEL SPURR

*Henry Holt and Company   New York*

Henry Holt and Company, Inc.
*Publishers since 1866*
115 West 18th Street
New York, New York 10011

Henry Holt® is a registered
trademark of Henry Holt and Company, Inc.

Published in Canada by Fitzhenry & Whiteside Ltd.,
195 Allstate Parkway, Markham, Ontario L3R 4T8.

Library of Congress Cataloging-in-Publication Data
Spurr, Daniel, date.
River of forgotten days: a journey down the Mississippi
in search of La Salle / Daniel Spurr.—1st ed.
p.      cm.
Includes index.
ISBN 0-8050-4632-1 (hb)
1. Mississippi River—Description and travel.    2. Great Lakes
Region—Description and travel.    3. Spurr, Daniel, date—
Journeys—Mississippi River.    4. La Salle, Robert Cavelier, sieur
de, 1643–1687.      I. Title.
F355.S68      1998                                          97-31163
917.704'33—dc21                                            CIP

Henry Holt books are available for special
promotions and premiums. For details contact:
Director, Special Markets.

First Edition 1998

Designed by Paula R. Szafranski

Cartography by Jeffrey L. Ward

Printed in the United States of America
All first editions are printed on acid-free paper. ∞

1   3   5   7   9   10   8   6   4   2

*For Andra*

# Contents

# *Acknowledgments*

Thanks to all who lent a hand along the trail:

Gene Correll, who first showed me the pleasures of cruising in small boats, and who brought me across Lake Michigan to the Ports des Morts, where this quest for La Salle was born.

Don Helger of Don's Service, and Dan and Kathleen at A&D Trailers, both in Tiverton, Rhode Island, who busted their butts getting *Pearl* ready for the Mississippi.

Dale Nouse, the kind of friend one hopes for but seldom finds, who encouraged this project, helped set it up, and gave wise advice about the manuscript.

My son, Stephen, and daughter, Adriana, for sharing in the adventure; without them it would have meant less.

Lee Politsch, who keeps the mystery alive, and for opening to me his archives, as well as his home.

Barto Arnold, for having me aboard *Anomaly*.

Mel Guidrick of Lafitte, Louisiana, last stop on the Barataria Waterway, who provided assistance and a place to rest when there was none left.

Stanton Murray, for taking care of us and our equipment in New Orleans.

Robert Weddle, learned man, who graciously reviewed and corrected the manuscript.

All the good people along the river who stopped to transport us and our fuel jugs.

—Dan Spurr
Newport, Rhode Island

# River of
# Forgotten
# Days

# An Idea of Pre-America

*"Nothing exists but atoms and the void"—so wrote Democritus. And it is "void" that underlies the Eastern teachings—not emptiness or absence, but the Uncreated that preceded all creation, the beginningless potential of all things.*

—Peter Matthiessen, *The Snow Leopard*

How it came upon me is not quite clear. But take ahold it did, many years ago, when every Friday at five I fled the fields of maize surrounding my southern Michigan home for the wilderness of Lakes Michigan, Huron, and Superior. It was the unending stands of pine and fir, the granite and quartz of the Laurentian Shield that kept me coming back. That and the emptiness. What I wanted was a sense of the land before the roads and railways, way back, when the whites were first coming up the rivers looking for fur, copper, and the Northwest Passage.

My earliest recollection of Longfellow's "shining Big-Sea-Water" was on a now forgotten shore of Lake Michigan. That great oblong sweet-water sea that the French voyageurs called Lac des Illinois and the Indians Machihiganing. Age six. Family vacation. There was no sand on this particular stretch. Rather, the beach was covered with smooth rocks the size of baseballs and dinosaur eggs. Sometimes you could find a Petoskey stone. The gift shops sold them guised as paperweights and good-luck charms. Silvery driftwood littered the glacis between the trees and the water. The washed-up pieces were polished by the surf to a slippery smoothness, the points of the splinters and roots rounded over like amputated fingers. It gave them a melted, artistic look. Found objects. Gift shops sold these, too. Mother saw one she liked and gave it to Father, who took it home and from it made a lamp. Its triangular shape resembled a large angelfish, the fish's eye the hole where a knot had fallen out. A quiet-spoken forester, Father had an unusual affinity for wood. I remember him drilling into the lighter heartwood and inserting a brass pipe to route the electrical cord. For years the lamp sat on an end table in the living room. No one knows where the "fish lamp" is now. Somewhere along the way it was tossed or given away, disappeared from the family consciousness. All but mine.

The ocean, when I first stood at its edge, had a different effect than the lake. There was the same endless expanse, the same rhythmic succession of waves falling over themselves to my feet, but it smelled of rotting seaweed and tasted of salt—the primordial solution, the stuff of life, its ratio of salt to water the same as that of the fluid that fills the human body.

When I learned to sail, I dreamed of crossing oceans in small boats. I lamented that there were no longer uncharted rivers or lands to discover. There was only the Uncreated.

The seven oceans, I figured, were the last frontier. But I lived in the Midwest and for many years the great freshwater lakes were my surrogate seas. Still, I was disappointed that there were no sharks, giant squids, whales, anemones, lionfish, or starfish. Just dead alewives, a few sturgeon and pike, and restocked coho salmon. The lakes seemed second-rate, so I looked for reasons to elevate these inland seas, to make them wondrous, more dangerous, more worthy of my own life.

Witness: When a storm sweeps down from Canada, the waters turn treacherous. Ships go down. The *Edmund Fitzgerald*, its bow on one wave and stern on another, folded in the middle and sank to the bottom of Whitefish Bay in Lake Superior, Hiawatha's Gitche Gumee.

Always the lakes are cold. On a changeable day in the last century, a mailman took the morning ferry from Wisconsin's Bruce Peninsula to Washington Island and returned that evening by horse and sleigh.

To transform the lakes, the trick, for me, was to go back in time, peel away the layers of civilization, and create wilderness in my own imagination. What I called pre-America, a place of lakes and rivers and virgin forests where there were no marinas, no navigation buoys, no 911 emergency telephone numbers, no 7-Elevens, nothing save clear water and, all around it, an endless field of green treetops.


From Giovanni Caboto's (John Cabot's) reconnaissance of the East Coast in 1497 and extending 409 years to Roald Amundsen's first navigation by a European of the Northwest Passage, the New World was to the great world powers an obstacle between oceans.

The Spanish, well established in Mexico, had during the sixteenth century reconnoitered Florida and much of the South: Juan, Ponce de León, who in 1513 was the first to land on the prominent peninsula, and later Alonso Alvarez de Pineda, Pánfilo de Narváez, and Hernando de Soto, who in 1541 was the first European to cross the Mississippi above its mouth and whose charts and accounts of the river would stand unchanged for 141 years. The English held the East Coast. They came first to Roanoke Island, Virginia, where the first European in America was born: Virginia Dare, who later disappeared with all the other inhabitants. No trace ever found. In 1607 Captain John Smith led a group to Jamestown, Virginia, and later, of course, in 1620, the Pilgrims sailed into Plymouth, Massachusetts, spreading themselves coastwise north and south. In 1524 the Italian navigator Giovanni da Verrazano saw from his ship New York harbor; in 1609 Henry Hudson sailed up the river that now bears his name; and in 1624 the merchant Dutch settled on the island of Manhattan. The French, too, were competitors in the transatlantic race to explore the New World: Jacques Cartier sailed up the St. Lawrence River in 1534, and in 1562 Jean Ribault settled at Port Royal, just north of St. Augustine, Florida. Samuel de Champlain began his exploration of Canada in 1603 and became lieutenant governor in 1612. A year later it was he who, for the historical record, was the first white to behold the great water-filled cavities of the Great Lakes, gouged from the earth ten thousand years earlier by fingers of ice clawing the northward retreat. And it was the coureurs de bois and voyageurs—back country trappers—who first heard of and became intrigued by Native American stories of the Mississippi. But where it began, where it flowed, and where it entered, no white knew. (I have used "white" as a reminder that the New World's "discovery" was a European context; the Amerinds, who had lived here since the Pleistocene geologic era, knew all along where the Mississippi discharged itself.)

Of all the explorers of North America, the one I became fixed on, quite by chance, was René-Robert Cavelier, Sieur de La Salle. There

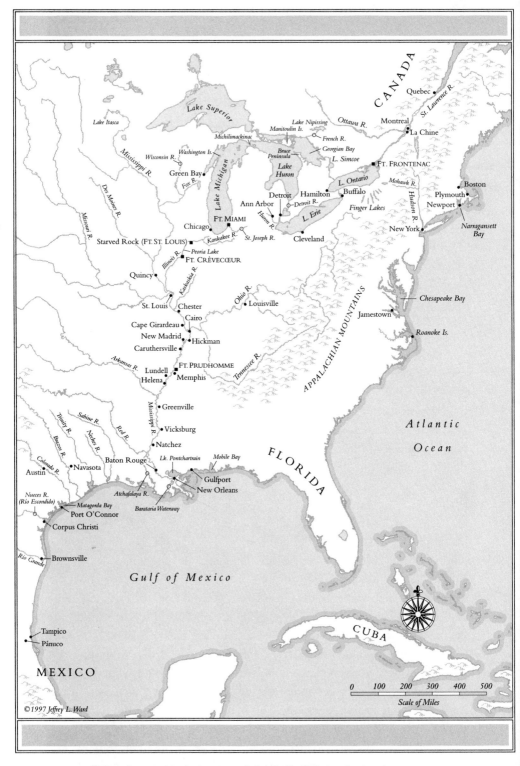

*Map of eastern North America and the Gulf of Mexico showing the waters traversed and forts established by La Salle during the years 1667–1687, as well as contemporary place-names of cities, rivers, lakes, and bays visited by the author.*

were in him four notable qualities that explain my interest: first, the dog-gedness that enabled him to *walk* thousands of miles back and forth across the North American wilderness; second, certain mysteries surrounding his discoveries that to this day beg for resolution (for example, was he, and not Louis Jolliet, the discoverer of the northern Mississippi?); third, the elements of a Greek tragedy in which the protagonist's fatal flaw unmakes his heroic acts (La Salle was murdered in Texas by his own men); and last, my own feelings of injustice that La Salle's achievements have been over-looked and undercredited (he was the first European to travel the Missis-sippi from the Great Lakes to the Gulf of Mexico, and his discovery led eventually to the Spanish settlement of Texas and the French ownership of Louisiana). Indeed, he planned to build a string of forts on the Missis-sippi, and even considered a military attack on the Spanish silver mines in Mexico.

La Salle was not a sailor but, rather, a paddler of canoes, a slogger of swamps. The pen-and-ink drawings of him, mostly by artists who lived much later, are at such variance as to offer little clue to his true appearance, and one begins to suspect that the real picture is unattainable. Much as one cannot trust depictions of Christ with brown flowing tresses, blue eyes, and a beatific countenance (the sort of offense that one imagines inspired Paolo Pasolini's *Gospel According to St. Matthew*).

In one portrait La Salle appears boyish, with twinkling eyes and a smirky grin that is much too playful for his serious nature. He has a long nose and long hair. A pencil-thin moustache curls upward at the corner of his mouth. In the wilderness, a crimson coat was his trademark and much impressed the Indians. It was worn only on special occasions, not the least of which were negotiations with Indians. But mostly La Salle's dress was appropriate to the conditions: linen shirt, knee breeches, leather leggings, and headband. More recent artists sometimes show his dark hair pulled back in a ponytail, his build average, his visage trail-hardened, the eyes critical and dark.

The son of a Rouen merchant, La Salle studied with the Jesuits for ten years before deciding against a life of subservience and devotion. He was eager to travel, but his superiors dismissed his various requests to perform missionary work in China or teach mathematics in Portugal. Impatient, he left the Society of Jesus and for the rest of his life would regard it with sus-picion, if not downright enmity. Exactly why is part of his enigma, for he remained a pious man. Returning home, he discovered that he was no

*René-Robert Cavelier, Sieur de La Salle, 1643–1687, first European to follow the Mississippi River to its mouth in the Gulf of Mexico.* (MICHIGAN HISTORICAL COLLECTIONS, UNIVERSITY OF MICHIGAN)

more disposed to the life of a Norman bourgeois than of a religious. Given a small annuity by his brothers and sisters, in the summer of 1667 he sailed for Quebec.

There is little existing evidence in the way of letters or journals from which to clarify his motivations, but one can guess that he found the political and social structures of Europe too confining, probably even distasteful, and the picture of the North American wilderness too promising of adventure and glory for him to stay in France. Though much was generally known of La Salle's immediate destination—Quebec, Montreal, and their surrounds—much remained to be learned of the lands and lakes, rivers, and peoples that lay beyond these settlements. Quite possibly, the mystery of that darkness appealed to his religious sense: the possibility of his shedding light on the land as well as learning of God's purpose for him.

Just what his initial plans were are unclear as well, though the surest means of making money was in the fur trade, which supplied European hatmakers with pelts. Buying furs from the Indians and selling them to European markets satisfied his twofold aim of gaining income and learning about the out-country. This interest in the western reaches of New France presupposes at least a curious nature, and as his time in New France passed and his ideas coalesced, it also furnishes an important clue to his ambitions: Monetary wealth did not seem to stir him, but was a means to an end. It is evident that La Salle had a high opinion of himself, and perhaps the wilderness was for him the historical tabula rasa upon which he saw the quickest means of writing his name—not as a trader, but as leader of a new colony.

La Salle, like virtually every explorer of the Americas since Christopher Columbus, believed that somewhere to the west was a route to another sea. Though he had studied navigation, in particular the means of determining latitude and longitude by measuring the angles of heavenly bodies, only latitude was possible to determine with any degree of accuracy. (Not until 1761 could longitude be accurately calculated, by measuring the difference in time between a given meridian and the Prime Meridian in Greenwich; in that year the Englishman John Harrison invented the chronometer, a timepiece accurate to half a minute a year.) So handicapped, sixteenth- and early-seventeenth-century cartographers had only the vaguest notion of North America's breadth. Early maps show the continent much compressed, which accounts for the conjecture that the Mississippi might empty into the Gulf of California. The inability to accurately determine longitude misled many of the early explorers, including La Salle, who ultimately would die for want of it.

Consider, for instance, Jean Nicolet. On canoeing across Green Bay in 1635, he was so convinced that China lay on the western shore and that on landing he would be met by mandarins, he dressed in a stunning coat of Chinese damask embroidered with birds and flowers and carried a pistol in each hand, only to be confronted by dumbfounded Winnebagos. They good-naturedly threw a party in his honor, roasting for the occasion 120 beavers.

The elusive Northwest Passage to China and India was an idea driven by commerce, of course, because money is at the root of discovery. In this instance, a sea route to Asia would make rich the purveyors of spice and tea and silk. For a time, the English were content to keep a coastwise mentality regarding the Appalachian Mountains as the natural border of the colonies. The French, on the other hand, pressed westward up the St. Lawrence and into the lakes, never in large numbers but rather in small parties of voyageurs, coureurs de bois, and "black robes," as the Indians loosely called the missionary friars. Their business was animal skins, mostly beaver, for the making of hats. Even the Jesuits, whose aim was to Christianize the savages and also to establish a sovereign religious state west of New France (essentially the present-day provinces of Quebec and Ontario), were in it for money. To this end they traded with Indians and schemed to undermine their white competitors, including La Salle. Willing to martyr themselves, they advanced fearlessly into the unknown, looking for the fabled route to the Pacific.

From the Indians word filtered to the whites of a great river to the west that flowed to the sea. The Algonquian speakers' name for it is variously translated as the Big River, Big Water, or Father of Waters. Messipi. This, the whites believed, must be the Northwest Passage.

By the time La Salle arrived in New France, most European settlers accepted the idea of the Mississippi's existence, but few whites had ever seen it.[1] And what was known of its course in the North was not necessarily connected with what was known of its course in the South. Hence, no one knew whether the northern river discharged its mighty flow into the Vermilion Sea (Gulf of California), the Sea of Virginia (Chesapeake Bay), or the Spanish Sea (Gulf of Mexico). It is unlikely that La Salle was aware of such issues prior to his arrival, but he soon became acquainted with the mysterious river via the Indians whom he invited to winter at his seigneury (an estate) outside Montreal, where the St. Lawrence widens into Lake St. Louis. He extended his hospitality with the express purpose of gaining knowledge—of the Indians' language and customs, the nature of the woodland animals, and, most important, the lay of the land.

At some point, La Salle would imperfectly connect the Messipi to the large southern river discovered by Soto, who had crossed the river in 1541 near present-day Lundell, Arkansas. The conquistador had won a fortune for himself by helping Pizarro sack Peru, but found no luck in the wilderness of pre-America. Wealthy and famous, he was not content to while away the years as a favorite at the court of Charles V. Time still for more looting and killing. He sought and was granted appointment as governor of Cuba and Florida. His instructions, honoring his desire, were to explore the peninsula and gulf coastline that had earlier repelled Pineda and Narváez. In 1539, after a year gathering his expedition in Cuba, he landed on the Florida peninsula, so beginning a three-year march through the southern states. It was to be the antithesis of his successes in Peru. The cavalry mired in swamp. The Southeast Indians did not stand and fight like the Peruvians, but rather shot their arrows and fell back into the forest—aboriginal guerrillas. Some modern artists imagine Soto in armor, his beautiful horse strutting, his men attentive and strong. In reality, they all were dirty and hungry, their clothes torn or gone, many forced to wear buckskins or grass kilts. Worse, the gold the conquistadors sought did not exist. Still, Soto pressed on, north through Florida into Georgia, then west across Alabama and Mississippi. Unconstrained by levees, the river then was nearly two miles wide, seeping over the land. The significance of his discovery was lost on him, for he saw it only as an obstacle between himself and the minerals that must surely lie across the next plain. Unlike his successors, who thought the fabled Mississippi might be the route to Asia. On site, Soto obviously knew better—that it was just a river of mud going nowhere near the Orient.

La Salle, without Soto's knowledge, was so taken by his nascent vision of establishing France in the continent's middle land, that he became obsessed with being the first to find a route to China, so much so that his seigneury came to be known as La Chine (now spelled Lachine). The way out, whether to the Atlantic, the Pacific, or the Gulf of Mexico, was the big river. The Messipi. To succeed, he was compelled to find its mouth.

Without sponsorship or political allies, however, La Salle was on his own. A discovery of economic importance surely would elevate his chances of finding favor at the court of the Sun King, Louis XIV. But discovery required an expedition—men, canoes, firearms, tools, and food—and he had not the funds for such an undertaking. During his first few years in the country, his fortunes improved as a result of his bringing in furs to sell and, more important, selling his ideas to investors. Still, he needed more money. Daringly, he asked: Why limit cargo to the tiny birch-bark canoe? Why not a ship whose capacity is a thousandfold that of a canoe, the profits from which could easily fund an expedition to the Messipi?

He was a dealer trying to score the proverbial Big One. That's what he was doing aboard the *Griffon* anchored off Washington Island, Wisconsin, in the fall of 1679, at the entrance to Green Bay, opposite the tip of the

Door Peninsula. The place the French called the Baye des Puans, or Bay of the Stinkers, after a tribe of Indians who lived in an area of the bay that reputedly smelled like the ocean. Already the bay region was occupied by French missionaries. Father Claude Jean Allouez had explored the rivers to the bay's west, the Fox and Wisconsin. It was the Catholic fathers who had given the name Port des Morts to the channel between the island and the Door. Death's Door. For La Salle, it was prophetic.

When I arrived on a small sailboat during the summer of 1975, Washington Island had the largest population of Icelanders in the United States. Probably still does. Mostly, they grow potatoes. Summer is celebrated with fish boils on the shore. One of my crew, an Italian who once had catered a private dinner for Luciano Pavarotti and Francis Ford Coppola, fell ill after tasting his own red sauce. He drank a voluminous quantity of whiskey, then repaired to a nearby motel to grapple with the fever. That evening, the rest of us walked up the dusty road and tapped on his window. To make himself sweat, he'd turned up the heat; we felt it radiating from the pane. "Go away!" he moaned. Dementia was suspected. In the morning, Mom's Taxi delivered him back to the dock. We knew he was recovered when he bitched about the jitney's bill.

With him he'd brought some tourist brochures from the motel lobby. One contained a thumbnail sketch of La Salle and the *Griffon*, the first ship on the upper Great Lakes. It was, as the story unfolded, also its first ghost ship.

I was hooked.

Standing there, our little boat bobbing at the dock before me, I looked out across the Port des Morts and imagined La Salle watching his sixty-five-foot barque sail over the horizon, and unbeknown to him, into oblivion. This image of him has never left me.

If there was any providence in the loss of the ship, it was that La Salle was not aboard. Impatient to find his river, he'd decided instead to set south by canoe.

La Salle's eloquent biographer, Francis Parkman, a Harvard man of the last century whose eagerness for adventures in the West is reminiscent of Teddy Roosevelt's Brahmin-in-battle bully-bully during the Spanish-American War, wrote of the *Griffon*'s departure from Green Bay:

The parting was not auspicious. The lake, glassy and calm in the afternoon, was convulsed at night with a sudden storm, when the canoes were midway between the island and the main shore. It was with difficulty that they could keep together, the men shouting to each other through the darkness.[2]

Meanwhile, La Salle and his men paddled the western perimeter of Lake Michigan. Three hundred years ago. No Milwaukee. No Chicago. That first week he ate only a porcupine killed by his Mohegan guide and pumpkins and Indian corn given as a gift by the Potawatomis. They were friendly, but other nations, like the Iroquois, who lost no love on the French, were anxious to rip out his heart and eat it. A compliment to his courage, perhaps, but nevertheless a good reason to sleep lightly.

Eventually, following a succession of failures and intrigues and many miles of tramping in the forest and wading in wetlands, La Salle succeeded in 1682 in becoming the first white to travel the length of the Mississippi, proving that its delta lay in the Gulf of Mexico—not California, not Virginia.

It was not this feat alone that so impressed me, but that on surveying the gulf and proclaiming for his king the vast watershed of the Mississippi, he turned and paddled back, upstream, to Montreal. And of this and his many hardships, trekking overland in midwinter with but a pouch of corn and a musket, he seemingly thought nothing. In life, he claimed for Louis XIV a tract of land twenty-six times larger than the state of New York. After La Salle's death, the Louisiana Purchase, for which Thomas Jefferson paid two cents per one hundred acres, doubled the size of the United States. The tireless, tragic La Salle had impact.

Consumed with a vision of New France and of himself, hardened beyond comprehension, he was in these respects—I realized as I wrote these words—just like my father:

Discipline, old boy, discipline. You'll never get anywhere if you don't set goals. Strap a stick to your back and from the tip suspend a carrot so that it dangles just beyond your reach. Pace yourself. Steady at the helm. Someday, when your arm is a little longer and you've learned to time the carrot's swing, you just might wrap your fingers around that orange root . . . just might . . .

But no, my reach, as Robert Browning put it, always exceeded my grasp.

The crossing from Michigan to Green Bay had temporarily satisfied the need to risk myself, but also it made me want to create more of my imaginary pre-America.

And this idea was not all cold lakes and northern woodlands. Three years after sailing to Green Bay I would see the idea in the vast floodplain of the gulf, when in 1978 I learned through my father (then teaching at the University of Texas) that the Texas Historical Commission planned a search of Matagorda Bay for the *Belle* and *Aimable*, two of the ships La Salle sailed from France back to the New World in 1684, two years after his historic descent of the river. My father put me in contact with J. Barto Arnold III, the state marine archaeologist, with whom I arranged to spend some time.

In the summer of 1978 I rented a car in Austin and drove to the coast. Down out of the east Texas hill country to the coastal plain, broad and flat, green with crops, lined with sloughs. Occasionally I passed one of the old missions. Before La Salle, the Gulf Coast had been largely ignored by the Spanish; after his discovery, fearing further intrusions from France, they staked their claim, sending troops to build presidios and friars to convert the Indians. Spanish influence ended with Mexico's independence, in 1821.

Barto's headquarters were in Port O'Connor, now a kick bucket of shrimpers and staging docks for offshore oil rigs. The town dead-ended, the coastal plain all around, itself a kind of sea.

I took a room at the only motel, a low, nondescript ranch with a tin roof and cream-colored shades. Practically the only structure in town that wasn't built on stilts, probably because it came after the last hurricane and the builders couldn't know what they hadn't lived. Nearby was the town movie theater, closed, possibly forever. From the marquis of the small brick building someone had removed the hook of the J and selected letters from the name JAMISON THEATER, so that it spelled IAM N HEAT. Below, it said AIR CONDITIONED; walking past, I noted on the side of the building a small window unit hanging precipitously.

A grass runway paralleled the main street; sometime this century the small plane replaced the quarter horse. Engineers could fly from Houston to Port O'Connor, hop a crew boat or helicopter, be on the rig by mid-morning, and be home for supper. And they did, despite the Federal Aviation Administration's having painted a large and condemning yellow X across the strip.

I waited at the old Air Force dock, standing back in the shade, smoking my pipe. The ditch of the Gulf Intracoastal Waterway came in from the east, from Matagorda Bay, and disappeared in the west. Everywhere were piles of oyster shells brought up by the dredges, mountains of them across the channel, so many they were free for the taking, should you want to lay a truckload on your drive and crush them into chips—one side dull and brushed, the inside smooth as alabaster.

The two-cycle cough of an outboard lifted my eyes. A red inflatable boat planed down the waterway; the crew, blond, bandit-looking divers with long, tangled hair; the hired hands, alternating boy-girl with research assistants in bikinis. Eight pairs of sunglasses staring forward. Behind followed Barto's boat, the thirty-four-foot aluminum crewboat *Anomaly*, the name echoing the thing he was looking for—that suspicious hit on the magnetometer called an anomaly.

Barto hopped onto the dock, looking neat and boyish: His hair cut short, blue-jean cutoffs, gym socks, and a green baseball cap with the logo of a helicopter service. So I was thinking about archaeologists in general and Barto in particular and how when you put an academic in Port O'Connor (or, for that matter, my professorial father in a Diamond Match Company logging camp) you fear for him and wonder how he can walk past a bar or down a dock without some shrimper (or logger) putting an elbow in his chest. Just for the way he looks.

Maybe Barto's credentials spoke louder: assistant archaeologist on the *San Esteban*, the 1554 wreck the state seized in 1967 from the Gary, Indiana, treasure-hunting outfit Platoro. That dig had compelled the state legislature to create the Texas Antiquities Committee, later joined to the Texas Historical Commission, for which Barto was now the chief underwater digger. For weeks all they'd turned out of the bay bottom were pieces of shrimp boats and fifty-five gallon oil drums. This day, their fortunes turned.

"Found a nineteenth-century trading schooner near Greens Bayou,"

Barto said, referring to an area of Matagorda Bay just inside the barrier island.

He pointed to several long, cylindrical objects lashed to the deck, heavily encrusted with sand, pebbles, barnacles, and oyster shells. One looked as though it might have been a musket or rifle—old, but not old enough to be La Salle's.

To keep the artifacts from rusting, I helped some of the crew wrap each one in wet towels and stuff them into plastic bags. Later, lab personnel would X-ray each to determine how much metal was inside the concretion. If a little, the concretion would be split open and used as a mold to cast a replica of the original piece—a musket, nail, crossbow trigger, or astrolabe. If, on the other hand, there was sufficient metal to salvage, the concretion would be chipped away and the artifact placed in a chemical bath charged with a low voltage of electricity. It might take a year to remove all the chlorides.

That evening I walked down the street to Barto's trailer. Carefully, he unfolded his charts before me, both the modern ones produced from surveys done by the National Oceanographic and Atmospheric Administration and the Defense Mapping Agency, and copies of the ancient maps. Barto put great stock in the map made by Jean-Baptiste Minet, La Salle's engineer on the *Belle*. It clearly shows the *Aimable* where it sank in Pass Cavallo, the entrance to Matagorda Bay, and the anchored *Belle*, hooked inside Matagorda Peninsula. It also shows Captain Beaujeu's escort ship, the *Joly*, standing offshore, which is fitting because Minet abandoned La Salle to sail home with Beaujeu. Branded as a deserter, he was sent to the Bastille, which though unkind, was at least life.

Once the Spanish got wind that La Salle was garrisoned near New Spain, they hurried to find and exterminate the intruder. From Mexico six land and five sea voyages were launched. The Rivas-Iriarte sea expedition of 1687 was the first to sight the *Belle*, canted in the mud. The expedition's diarist, Enríquez Barroto, described the ship's location and what the Spanish took from her, most notably five cannon. By the time the land army led by Alonso de León found nearby Fort St. Louis, the *Belle* was gone, sucked under by time and weather.

"The *Belle* is most certainly located near Greens Bayou, inside Matagorda Peninsula," said Barto. "We've concentrated our efforts there

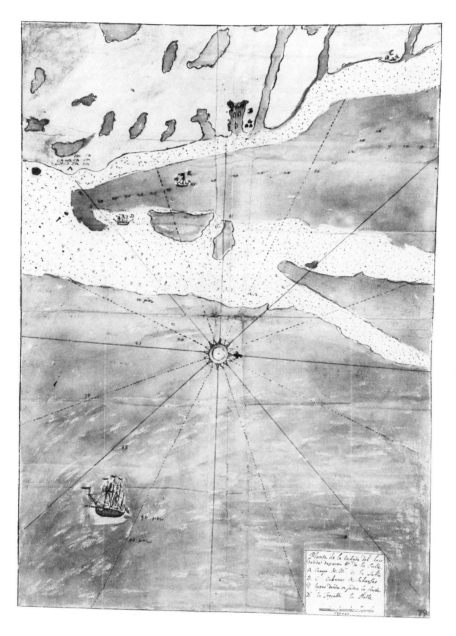

*Map of Matagorda Bay drawn by the engineer Jean-Baptiste Minet before he sailed for France in 1685 with Captain Beaujeu aboard the* Joly. *A,* La Salle's *camp; B and C, Indian camps; D, the place where the* Aimable *was lost; E, the* Belle *anchored safely inside the bay. The* Joly *lies offshore.* (J. P. Bryan Collection, University of Texas Archives)

because the water is quiet and shallow and a number of the anomalies are classic shipwrecks."

The next morning the crew loaded scuba gear, electronic equipment, buoys, and lunches aboard the *Anomaly*. I tossed my sandwich and a Lone Star beer into the cooler.

Barto steered for Pass Cavallo, to look for the *Aimable*. She was, after all, by far the larger of the two ships, and went down with four cannon, 1,620 cannon balls, 400 grenades, a forge, 5,000 pounds of lead, and 4,000 pounds of iron, more than enough to register a whopping hit on the magnetometer. The *Belle* had been stripped by the desperate crew, who ferried what they could in dugout canoes, and Indians, who wanted cloth and iron to make arrowheads. The Spanish, when they found it, took everything else that wasn't awash.

For hours the *Anomaly* crisscrossed the channel, rolling in the troughs, and the queasy crew was quiet, waiting for a hit on the magnetometer that would not come.

As we motored back, Barto left the wheelhouse and stepped on deck. He rummaged through the cooler looking for his vitamin E. Instead, he found my Lone Star, which he held high above his head like Moses showing the Ten Commandments. "I told you guys, no beer on this ship!" Then he heaved the can far into the bay. The crew chuckled, elbowing each other.

During a down day, Steve Harrigan and David Moorman from *Texas Monthly* magazine called. They had borrowed a canoe to paddle down Garcitas Creek, which feeds into Matagorda Bay from the north, for a look at the site of Fort St. Louis that La Salle built upon its bank. This was good news, because the owner of the ranch on whose property the fort's remains are located did not cotton to strangers. I'd called him the previous winter, only to be told, "The walk's a mile and a half through dense brush, it's full of rattlers, and there's nothin' to see when you get there." Steve had fared no better talking to the owner's wife: "If my husband weren't so upset about the garage door sticking, he might take you down."

The fort had once been excavated in the 1950s by a team from the University of Texas. The first digs uncovered some simple wares from the presidio, Nuestra Señora de Loreto, built on top of the fort by the Spanish in 1722. Beneath were found indications of the French palisade and here and there some shards of plates and bowls, French and Spanish commingled. Kathleen Gilmore, who supervised a later dig in 1972–73, recommended that the state purchase the land as a first step toward making it a National Historic Site, but nothing came of it. The ruin was the sole basis for the inclusion of France in the Texas motto, "Under Six Flags." Now it was overgrown with weeds and grass.

We launched the canoe above the site, under the bridge on Highway 616. As we descended, deer nibbled at roots on the banks, cattle drank, turtles sunned on half-sunken logs, herons stood frozen, scarlet tanagers took wing, and large gars leaped and crashed about us. Along the banks was a preponderance of live oaks, the creek itself was slow and winding, and save for the occasional high tension wire overhead, nothing much seemed changed from the way it had looked to La Salle. In the time of pre-America.

The bluff upon which the fort and presidio were built was easy to distinguish. We drove the canoe aground, and consulted. I recalled that just this week a young girl in Port O'Connor had died from a rattlesnake bite. David suddenly remembered a story of a man stepping into a snakepit and dying before he could pull his foot out. Indeed, one of La Salle's men, the Sieur Le Gros, had died of a snakebite in 1687. Liotot, the surgeon, amputated his leg, though he had never before performed the operation. Le Gros died two days later.

Steve said, "You're worried about snakes? Hell, it's the ranchers you should look out for. In east Texas they greet you with shotguns. Shoot first and ask questions later—territorial prerogatives and all that."

Such arguments were compelling; we did not go ashore.

Much of the next morning was spent locating an anomaly that had piqued Barto's interest. A buoy was set at the mark. One of the divers was handed the water pick, a twenty-foot pipe powered by a small engine and pump that sucks water from the bay and propels it out the mouth, which allows the pipe to penetrate the bottom. Several layers of clay prompted Barto to digress on the nature of subprofiles, the movement of the peninsula, and neoboreal wet periods. On the diver's second thrust he struck an object. The *Anomaly*'s aluminum hull acted like a speaker, magnifying the clunking sound below.

The diver surfaced and said, "I can see it, Barto."

Barto turned quickly. "What is it?"

"Looks like a Lone Star beer can, boss."

"Hell, for four hundred gammas, it better be a case!"

The *Anomaly* had anchors off the bow and aft quarters and a large aluminum, right-angle tube was bolted over one of the two propellers. With the engine running, the propellor wash was directed downward, blowing away the sand. After each blast, divers moved in to feel the bottom of the hole. Visibility was zero. A hard crust of shells. Then metal . . . it's . . . yes . . . a boiler.

So ended that day, like every other that summer. Too many false hits on the magnetometer, too much heat and salt and oyster shells, and a lot of cheap shrimp dinners.

The day I left Port O'Connor, Barto had vanished and the crew had dispersed for the weekend. I was walking down the street when I ran into a fellow named Gerry, a local who sold welding equipment in the Yucatan. Banks, he said, planned to develop the town for tourism. Sportfishing was the draw.

" 'Cept for 'bout three rich ace number one pricks, nobody here wants to see it developed. You ever eaten in Stryker's Cafe? Well, I seen lots of nights when Mr. Stryker looks out over the counter 'bout eight o'clock, don't see anyone he knows, and just says, 'I ain't cooking no more food.' And he don't. And down at the marina? It took me two years of hanging around for the old woman who runs the place jus' to talk to me. That's how long you're a stranger here."

Gerry eyed me. "What's yer name again? Oh, I heard about you in town!"

Grinning, he tossed an imaginary object over his shoulder and yelled, "Lone Star!"


Over the next seventeen years I continued the search for La Salle and pre-America. I visited the principal landmarks of his many journeys: saw where he fortified Starved Rock on the Illinois River; inspected the cove on Russell Island in Lake Huron's Georgian Bay, where it is supposed that the *Griffon* sank after leaving Green Bay; and stood among the elms of Michigan's Huron River repicturing his fashioning in the dead of winter a canoe of elm bark. But there came a time when I, like La Salle, had to connect the Great Lakes to the gulf. Down the river. Messipi. It had always been there, slumbering, waiting for me, ever since the Pleistocene. A river alive, a creature of another kind with secrets to share. Its silence was the song of the wilderness. I could not hear it at home, could hear it only if I rode upon its fast and muddy waters and immersed myself in the silted current, blindly swimming with the catfish, bass, carp, perch, and buffalo fish.

In August of 1995, that's what I set out to do: submerge myself in America's great river.

# CHAPTER 2

# The Place of the Griffon

*The voice of my ancestors said to me, the shining water that moves in the streams and rivers is not simply water, but the blood of your grandfather's grandfather. Each ghostly reflection in the clear waters of the lakes tells of memories in the life of our people.*

*When the last Red Man and Woman have vanished with their wilderness, and their memory is only the shadow of a cloud moving across the prairie, will the shores and forest still be here? Will there be any of the spirit of my people left?*

*My ancestors said to me, This we know: The earth does not belong to us. We belong to the earth.*

*The voice of my grandmother said to me, Teach your children what you have been taught. The earth is our mother. What befalls the earth befalls all the sons and daughters of the earth.*

—Chief Seattle, Chief of the Duwamish and
Suquamish tribes, *Brother Eagle, Sister Sky*

The river trip would be a pilgrimage of sorts, a natural ascension from that most American rite of passage—the nonstop transcontinental car ride. (After high school, I'd driven coast to coast, nonstop, with a California fever for woodies and surfer girls, only to blunder into the Watts riots. Fires at the end of the street. My driver's door ripped from its hinges. I came home with very different ideas about the endless summer, my prospects, the nature of hope. . . .)

Beyond the interest I had as an amateur historian, I also wanted to do something adventurous with my seven-year-old son. Now middle-aged and living in Newport, Rhode Island, I felt a sense of urgency, both for myself and for him. I was sick of listening to the syncopatic repetitions of electronic Nintendo games, to the sound of skateboards doing "rail slides" at the top of a makeshift quarter pipe; of surmounting the defenses of his tree fort to discover which of my tools he and his posse had lifted from my shop and carried into the trees like thieving monkeys.

Not that they were bad boys. On the contrary, there was much good in their experimentation: learning how to build things using rudimentary engineering; developing athletic skills; and undergoing a basic socialization that is necessary, even if unpleasant to adults.

I was fully aware that things are never the way they were, no more when I was a kid than when my father was: Yesteryear always seems simpler, more honest, truer to our conception of how growing up ought to be. Closer to wilderness, though we do not often recognize that aspect of the longing. Someday, I hoped, Steve would say to his children the same thing about the nature of his youth.

That's the way it is: We're all walking down the same long, lonesome trail, with mothers and fathers before us, sons and daughters behind, all destined to learn, live, and die.

Living in a city makes it easy to miss much of what the world holds. Beaver dams actually exist beyond books and television nature shows; they are real, and one can see them if one expends the effort. There is more to the ocean than surfing and suntans—basking sunfish the size of reef sharks; mahi mahi, which on dying turn every color of the rainbow; pelagic seabirds, which seldom touch the earth, living most of their lives airborne over the waves; the most fantastic colors of sky and patterns of water—but you cannot experience them sitting before the gas fireplace in the family room of your four-bedroom gambrel.

Likewise, the history of pre-America was made not in the halls of capitol buildings, but in patches of meadow and bands of forest and on the turning river where there is scarcely a landmark to guide one's return.

What I'm getting at is this: Both my wife, Andra, and I were growing fearful that Steve would find too much pleasure in hanging out by the mailbox, kicking stones, acquiring values from Beavis and Butt-head. I did not mean to shield him from this natural part of growing up, but I meant to show him alternatives of dramatic contrast, places where for miles there is not even a car or road or building or person to break the spell. I would take my son to the wilderness, or whatever semblance of it I could find, hoping for myself nourishment and renewal, and for him, an awakening. The experience would, I hoped, bring a change in Steve, not overnight, but imperceptibly over the weeks and months and years to follow, so that someday, perhaps when he is on the threshold of some turning point, he would turn inward to himself and say, "Remember when Dad took me down the Mississippi? Now *that*, that was . . ."

Come August, we would buy a small boat and launch it on the Illinois, where the Kankakee enters, for that was the route of La Salle, who began the final, riverine portion of his journey near St. Joseph, Michigan, a short distance from the headwaters of the Kankakee. Two hundred seventy-three miles downstream from the Kankakee we'd meet the Mississippi, just above St. Louis, then run a thousand miles to the gulf.

But now it was spring break, and perhaps as a precursor of his teen years, Steve wanted desperately to visit Florida, not for beer and bikinis, but for an appearance on *Family Double Dare*, a Nickelodeon television show staged in Orlando.

"You can win a hundred dollars!" he pleaded.

"Fat chance," I said.

My notion of a good father-son trip was plainly different from his; we'd visit his half sister, Adriana, in Ann Arbor, returning to her the futon she'd left in our attic while studying in Rome during her last year at the Rhode Island School of Design. The frame had been left with a friend, a spindly cinematographer named Snarf, who'd passed it on to Janna, who'd painted it lavender and, on graduation, brought it in pieces to our door. Unlike many of the RISD girls, whose pale, white skins, black capes, and billowing silk pants made a ghostly negative, Janna was blonde and cheery—like my Adriana—and I was happy to see her.

The bed, which I strapped to the roof of our 1985 Mercury, was as good an excuse as any for a road trip. Yet I had another motive, for between Rhode Island and Michigan there were ancient footprints to cast and spirits to consult. Groundwork for the Mississippi. We would go back to 1679, before Green Bay, and pick up the trail of La Salle fresh from his baptism in the wilderness, fresh from his discovery of the Ohio and Illinois rivers, needful of money to find the Mississippi. Back to the beginnings of his grand enterprise, when he resolved to build the *Griffon*, a ship so large that in its hold he could transport more furs than a hundred canoes.

On a Sunday in March we drove west through the Berkshires of western Massachusetts, the sun in our eyes, crossed the Hudson at Albany, then followed the Mohawk River up its valley. The road climbed to an elevation of 1,729 feet, where a New York Thruway sign informs transcontinental travelers that the next-highest elevation along this route is a village in South Dakota. Coming down, we coasted along broad plateaus of yellow grasses streaked with the snow that was shaded by the steeper slopes, down past the Finger Lakes—Seneca, Cayuga, Skaneateles, Owasco, Otisco, Keuka, and Canandaigua—all freshwater pools collected in the glacial scourings of the latter Pleistocene.

In the sixteenth century, Hiawatha (actually, a priestly title combining the meanings of imam, roshi, and archbishop) assembled in this region a confederation of the Seneca, Cayuga, Mohawk, Oneida, and Onondaga tribes. Known collectively as the Five Nations, or the League of the Long House, they also were called the Iroquois, bitter enemies of the French. The origin of their enmity was a fight in 1609 against Samuel de Champlain, who introduced them to the astonishing killing power of firearms, and later, was fanned by the incursion of French fur traders into the Mohawk Valley and the land of the Illinois. Champlain, his successor Louis de Buade Frontenac, and the independent-minded Jesuits were simply bad for the Indian economy. The rage of the offended Iroquois extended to white and red alike, and would make tremors for a hundred years.

Contact with the Europeans revolutionized Indian culture. Coveting the trinkets, alcohol, and weapons offered in trade, they abandoned their old ways almost overnight. Bows and arrows were set aside for muskets, stone and copper knives and axes for better ones made of iron. Marquis Childs wrote in his 1982 history of the Mississippi River:

> The traders taught the Indians to make bullets from the lead of the Galena district. Blankets replaced hides, iron and copper kettles the old friable pottery. Porcelain beads took the place of wampum, laboriously fashioned from clam shells, as currency. The copper or stone amulet was discarded for bangles, bracelets, and nose rings from Paris. Imported paints adorned the naked Indians with patterns more exotic than primitive colors from the earth allowed. These changes took place within less than a decade after the arrival of the trader in the Indian community.[1]

Numbed by the road, Steve fell asleep, affording me a rare opportunity to reflect, to contemplate my life from a larger aspect. My few travels these days were short range, and it was easy to resent my domestic labors, which distracted me from nobler pursuits. But of course I was accountable for my decisions—to raise a family, to maintain a home, and to work hard to prop up these fragile structures. Still, I felt that opportunities were escaping me; if I wanted to make some achievement of my life, I ought to act quickly. My shortcomings as a writer and editor, I rationalized, could be explained by a perception of self-righteousness: A father at sea is no father at all; most great works owe themselves to the single-mindedness of their creators. My father once told me that his father, an eminent geologist with a volcano and moon crater named for him, was a recluse and misanthrope. In successive generations, the trait began to recede: My father was simply antisocial, and I, merely a loner.

At sunset we berthed in Buffalo, at the Sheraton Inn attached to the Galleria Mall. That evening and the next morning we swam in the tropical atrium, Steve diving for a locker key; he was far more efficient underwater than on the surface, the rhythmic synchrony of rotational breathing having thus far eluded him.

As we toweled ourselves off we took breakfast in our room. Steve ordered bacon and toast, which he photographed with a disposable camera; he then refused to eat any of it, not because his first still life was too precious, but because the food was no longer of use. If he had been hungry thirty minutes ago, when I'd called room service, he wasn't now. And that, according to his logic, was that.

We returned to the road at ten, taking I-190 downtown. There, along the city waterfront, the map showed La Salle Park at the foot of Hudson Street. The cartographer had stippled the tract green and white, suggesting trees and bushes, paths, rocks, and panoramic vistas. As we exited the freeway, there were no signs to direct us, no clear way in through the littered alleyways beneath the overpass. Beyond a chain-link fence I could see a brown expanse of dried grass, dominated by the city's water filtration plant and the Francis G. Ward Pumping Station.

Wrongly, I had expected a commemoration, a plaque or statue like that which honors Oliver Hazard Perry in Newport, where just a few years ago, on wintry Sunday mornings, I had trekked around the empty city streets, Steve strapped into the Gerry Carrier on my back, always stopping to study the heroic bronze figure leaning forward in a half step, sword poised. Steve would stand in the stirrups, thrusting his head backward to more squarely gauge the efficacy of the sword, and I, for balance, would grip the wrought-iron fence, staring at the inscription below: "We have met the enemy, and they are ours."

La Salle, who spoke sparsely and precisely, apparently failed to deliver the quotable quote, for there was no visible connection between this scruffy plot and the explorer for which it was named.

I felt more optimistic about the next site, not ten miles north of here, where La Salle built his ship, the *Griffon*, a two-masted barque to passage what later became known as Lakes Erie, Huron, and Michigan.

Just above the Peace Bridge to Canada, Lake Erie narrows into the Niagara River like the twisted end of a sausage, and the current begins, imperceptible here, but farther down it charges and froths with frightening violence. Following the current northward along the Black Rock Canal, which separates the city from the sewage treatment plant on Squaw Island,

*A woodcut of Niagara Falls, published in Louis Hennepin's* Nouvelle Découverte *in 1698.* (Courtesy of the Burton Historical Collection of the Detroit Public Library)

we passed more pipelines, chemical pools, steam vents, and, lakeward, two white monolithic structures voraciously sucking in lake water. At the shore, signs warned boaters of the dangers—subtle maelstroms and down wellings that could spell disaster to the unwary operator of a lightweight canoe or runabout.

The town of Lackawanna was behind us now, Tonawanda before. Ever the ice-covered lake to the west, glistening as it melted in the unseasonable heat of a seventy-degree March day.

Here, as elsewhere, I was looking for the landscape of pre-America, the virgin topography from three hundred years ago, when the skies were unsullied by smoke and industrial gases, the skyline unblemished by brick tenements, and the treetops rolled across the land in long waves, the uncut stands of pine and spruce broken only by the occasional meadow and prairie, clearings where the Indians grew maize and squash, burned the scrub, shot pheasant and drove deer to the water. I would have preferred to see what was seen by the voyageurs coming into the country—the louts, scalawags, and debtors who had sailed from Marseilles in the seventeenth century, borne on barques and brigantines into the maw of the St. Lawrence to disembark, as did La Salle in 1666, at the rapids near the present city of Montreal, poised for discovery at his seigneury, La Chine, land granted to him by Monsieur de Queylus, father superior of the Sulpician Order in Montreal, on condition that at each change of ownership, a medal of silver weighing one mark would be rendered to the holy brothers.

But there was little to support my backward-looking vision: The trees have been swept away by the scythe of civilization, the soil overlaid with concrete and macadam, the horizon serrated by angled forms of cinder block and brick; only the straightedge of the lake horizon remains the same, a changeling in color and temperament, perhaps, but constant in its command of the landscape. On this day there were not even the silhouettes of lakers steaming for the Welland Canal to jolt the illusion that this is how it was for La Salle and the native peoples of pre-America. (In truth, the Indians are not indigenous, having migrated from Asia, albeit thousands of years before the whites. In any case, man did not spring from this earth.)

The land is not so immutable: There is some consolation in the speculation that man's work, if suddenly abandoned, would eventually crumble, the storm-pushed ice piling into the streets, the lake-effect snow collapsing rooftops, the tendrils and roots of saplings, dandelions, and goldenrod bursting through the frost heaves, snaking along the gutter dirt, and taking hold. Perhaps, in another three hundred years, the city would simply disappear beneath the cumulative strata, leaving merely a mosaic of road slabs and a few relic automobiles to enthrall future archaeologists: we the peoples of Troy and Pompeii and Buffalo, overwhelmed by sand and ash and time. And I wished that it were so.

I told Steve about how the country was in 1679: the Indians, the trappers and the Catholic priests, the abundant game, the vast spread of white pine, the absence of everything he sees now. He seemed to be trying to make the same picture, but failing.

The reason, I soon gathered, was that he was now hungry, a prediction I had earlier made, to no effect. If I said "I told you so," he would look at me as if to say "So what?" We stopped at a convenience store, where I conceded to a strip of vacuum-packed beef jerky, deciding it superior to Nerds, Starbursts, and Swizzles, and probably not unlike the leathery buffalo meat La Salle carried to supplement the staple corn.

Our road soon turned inland from the river, parallel to a short run of elevated highway called the La Salle Expressway, which edges the section of Niagara Falls also named La Salle. Abeam of it is Cayuga Island, separated from the mainland by the Little Niagara River. Though it was swollen with melted snow, one could, with a good arm, still heave a chunk of ice across to the other shore.

Twenty years ago I'd brought my first wife, Margaret, and two children, Adriana and Peter, to some place near here, on the outskirts of Niagara Falls, detouring from a cross-country drive. It was a father's fancy, what Adria would later describe as a "Dad thing." What I remember was a large concrete storm sewer discharging a trickle of brown fluid into the lake, but that is not what I saw this day. Had my earlier research been faulty or were my recollections crossed and muddled by other intervening scenes? It seemed unlikely I could have mistaken Cayuga Creek for a culvert, and I wondered if the senses are indeed this unreliable. At the heart of my questioning, what is at issue, of course, is memory.

> *All that we see or seem*
> *Is but a dream within a dream.*[2]

Given these errors, I would not be surprised to return in another twenty years, from another dream, to find something equally unlike this, an "else" of disconcerting strangeness.

The road map of the city of Niagara Falls proved more revealing and reliable than life or memory: a nearby field and boat ramp named Griffon Park, and across the river, Jayne Park on the near side of Cayuga Island, which is laid out with a crosshatching of quiet residential streets named Champlain, Hennepin, Joliet, and Griffon, intersected, oddly, by Eighty-ninth Street, Ninety-first Street, and Ninety-third Street, their impersonality offending my map of the sacred.

I pulled into Griffon Park, again finding no sign indicating it to be such. Just a boat ramp and a small, flat field, roughened with an anarchy of tuffets and weeds until the first mowing. A Roto-Rooter van was parked at the head of the incline, the operator arranging his equipment, fussing with parts, killing time.

We stared at the briskly moving water, then turned to the road. No cars passed. The few establishments between the bank and River Road were closed, some until sunset, others perhaps forever: Al Schoen's Garage, specializing in motor tune-ups, boarded up now with sheets of delaminated plywood; Cocktails Etcetera, a purple-painted building with one car parked out front on the rutted dirt shoulder; Ganci's Pizzeria, checkered curtains drawn; and La Salle Collision, with plenty of work in the side lot but no ready sign of help to effect the repairs. It seemed as if the neighborhood already had been abandoned, as if the elements were poised to begin the disintegration of these crude and humble works.

In the car we motored slowly across Cayuga Creek, then turned left over a second short bridge onto Cayuga Island to Jayne Park, the only public place from which to view the juncture of the creek and Little Niagara River.

The historian Francis Parkman, in *La Salle and the Discovery of the Great West*, says it was here that La Salle orchestrated the building of the *Griffon*, the first ship on the upper lakes and their first ghost ship, disappearing as it did on the return leg of its maiden voyage to Green Bay. But at the outset, all was hope. The men ferried supplies from La Chine across Lake Ontario, portaging across the falls with the loads on their backs—anchors, cloth, and tools. The *Griffon* would measure only about sixty-five feet overall, displace forty-five tons, and carry two masts (still, she was about fourteen feet longer than the *Belle*, which sailed across the Atlantic from France to the Gulf of Mexico). On the transom would be carved a winged lion with the head of an eagle, a griffon—the armorial bearings of the house of Frontenac. What the building party needed was a quiet backwater and a supply of timber.

Parkman wrote:

> It is clear . . . that the portage was on the east side [*of the falls*],
> whence it would be safe to conclude that the vessel was built on
> the same side. Hennepin [*a Recollet friar who accompanied La Salle and
> later published a journal of his travels*] says that she was built at the
> mouth of a stream [*rivière*] entering the Niagara two leagues above
> the Falls. Excepting one or two small brooks, there is no stream on
> the west side but Chippewa Creek, which Hennepin had visited
> and correctly placed at about a league from the cataract. His dis-
> tances on the Niagara are usually correct. On the east side, there is
> a stream which perfectly answers the conditions. This is Cayuga
> Creek, two leagues above the Falls. Immediately in front of it is an
> island about a mile long, separated from the shore by a narrow and
> deep arm of the Niagara, into which Cayuga Creek discharges
> itself. The place is so obviously suited to building and launching of
> a vessel that, in the early part of this century [*the nineteenth*], the
> government of the United States chose it for the construction of a
> schooner to carry supplies to the garrisons of the Upper Lakes. The
> neighboring village now bears the name of La Salle.[3]

No matter that in 1842 the 12,000-year-old falls were receding at the
rate of 3.7 feet per year, the yearly rate slowing to 2.3 feet by 1906 (Parkman
published his history in 1869). Today, Horseshoe Fall erodes about 5 feet
per year, and the American Fall, with less flow, just 6 inches. Still, when
erosion of the shale and sandstone river floor moves the American Fall back
two miles, its height will come down from its present 184 feet to about 100;
when five miles have been consumed—a straight-line calculation brings us
to the year 54,795 (7,275 for Horseshoe Fall)—the falls will be nothing
more than rapids, running with a volume of 212,000 cubic feet per second.
Kayakers will traverse slalom courses from Lake Erie to Lake Ontario. It was
a sad thought and there was not even a breeze to console me.

Then again, one could find solace in the demise of the honeymoon
hotels and their too-large signs that crowd the basin. With the Niagara
River bed rising, some scientists theorize that in 3,500 years it will be
higher than Lake Erie. If this happens, the Great Lakes will theoretically
discharge through the Mississippi or perhaps into Hudson Bay, as did their
immense ancestor, Lake Agassiz, during the Ice Age.

Steve and I stood under the chestnut trees spaced along the bank of Cayuga Island, the Little Niagara flowing at our feet, looking back to the mouth of the creek. The spring ice that still clung to the bank was punky and falling away in jagged plates, borne swiftly from view toward the falls. The trees were dun and still.

On the mainland shore, a line of houses, once seasonal cottages with screened-in porches overhanging the water, documented an obscure though fundamental change in American life and economy: Like the hermit crab, a swelling population fills anything empty and makes it its own. Most of the houses had docks, though at this time of year there was no sign of the runabouts and pontoons that in a few months would be launched at the park ramp and station themselves along the canopied waterway: water-skiing, laughter, freckle-faced kids, picnics, hot dogs—but not today.

Weather did not stay La Salle, who launched the *Griffon* in February. Cold, the men sang the Te Deum, and fired cannon, and the company—

The building of the Griffon, *published in Louis Hennepin's* Nouvelle Découverte *in 1698*. (Courtesy of the Burton Historical Collection of the Detroit Public Library)

*The* Griffon *was constructed here, across from Jayne Park, at the junction of Cayuga Creek and the Little Niagara River, a few miles above the falls.*

Frenchmen and Indians—drank brandy and shouted their joy. La Salle, who did not conceal his dislike for the black-robed Jesuits, declared he would make the griffon fly above the crows.

Venturing onto a shelf of dirty ice, Steve drove down his heel with a sudden violence that I found mildly disturbing, as if it presaged some future criminal streak; he picked up a broken-off piece of ice and shoved it into the current, where it lodged on a fallen branch. Grabbing a long and slender stick, he reached out to free it, whereupon it, and he, entered the continuum of the cycle of water, beginning as rain falling on the hills, flowing to the creeks, rivers, and lakes to the saltwater sea, evaporating and reentering the loop as it goes. Wet to the knees, grinning broadly, he let out a whoop—the only sound save the faint trickle of water.

Though the park was a logical habitat, there were no squirrels that I could see, nor crows nor pigeons nor the sound of them, and it seemed, but for ourselves, that the place was devoid of life, even spirits. It was not the place La Salle described as

   . . . nearly all so beautiful and so fertile, so free from forests and so
   full of meadows, brooks and rivers; so abounding in fish, game

and venison, that one can find there in plenty, and with little trouble, all that is needful . . .[4]

I walked the length of Jayne Park hoping for a revelation, a sign evincing Father Louis Hennepin's antique sketch of the site where La Salle's men shaped virgin timber with adzes and fired the forge, and the feathered savages, bows in hand, chased deer across the meadow. But there were no glimpses of pre-America, nor was I able to call up from the earth the spirits of the men who long ago had stood here, hammer in hand, one eye on the nail, the other on the western horizon.

A plastic bag snagged on Steve's stick, an empty Budweiser can rolled under my foot. We left the bank and walked to the center of the park where, amid a circle of low branch-broken arborvitae, their exposed roots scuffed and raw, there were bits of cotton batting, some strewn cardboard, and pieces of a chair. The abandoned still life was reminiscent of the discarded furniture I'd seen bums in the early 1980s drag into the bushes of a Haight-Ashbury park, near where my sister Jean still lives, just up Central Avenue from the Jimmie Hendrix Electric Church Foundation. All here was scattered, as if the occupants had been rousted with clubs. I did not show Steve the trophy condom hooked on a branch above the leafy bed.

Pogo: *We have met the enemy and he is us.*[5]

Breaking the sadness, a mother wheeled her baby in a small carriage along Joliet Avenue. She was movement and life and I moved toward her to ask about the place (What would I say? "Do you know René-Robert Cavelier, Sieur de La Salle?"), but she did not wish to see me, hurrying her step, afraid I supposed of the wild-eyed stranger mucking about in the riparian compost.

We left the park, heading for the bridge to Ontario, drifting like fallen leaves toward the cataract, hoping for something splendid and uplifting. On the way, I noted the La Salle Yacht Club, Lake La Salle, the La Salle Branch of the Niagara Falls Public Library, and the La Salle Senior High School. Just when I thought that history had indeed remembered the explorer, I noticed the St. John de La Salle parish school and church, and it seemed that today, as then, the Church had sought to undermine the explorer's achievements, confusing him with a saint of the same name.

Steve looked pensive, as if assembling ideas that had come to him on the stream. He handed me the quilled cover of a fallen chestnut, which crumbled to dust over the seat. I brushed it to the floor.

"I don't believe in spirits," he said suddenly, surprising me with the formidable connections he had made, for I had not spoken of these things. "Do you?"

"Depends," I said.

"Gran and Auntie Gay make me go to church."

"My parents used to make me go to Sunday school."

"What did you do?"

"Read books about Jesus."

"I don't believe in him either, but I probably would if I went to church more."

"Would you like to?"

"No. It's boring. And I still don't believe in spirits."

CHAPTER 3

# Oma Kuna

*You've got to get obsessed and stay obsessed.*

—John Irving, *The Hotel New Hampshire*

A dream sequence that begins in a hospital—I am moving down the halls through crisscrossing white uniforms that enter through doors on one side and disappear through doors on the other, and am stultified by the white noise of machines, the air vents pushing a breeze at me—segues to this:

*We're running down the big river at twenty knots, the two corners of our wake peeling away from the transom, recurving, joining briefly at the vanishing point before the foam disperses like a contrail.*

*The shoreline is dark, thick with trees and vines; the sky threatens rain. Cretins with ignoble designs, unseen among the willows, watch us pass, waiting for an opportunity to . . . what?*

*A washboard chop slaps the hull. The motor hums.*

*Suddenly there is impact.*

*We have struck something hard and immovable—perhaps a tree, fallen upstream when the spring floods eroded the bank beneath it, now waterlogged, unable to float or sink. The boat lurches up and over, hesi-*

*tating like a horse jumping a fence. My head hits the windshield. Blood dribbles into my eye. The hull settles into the water, heaving, gored in the gut.*

*The engine has sheered from the transom, leaving a gaping hole through which water flows and ebbs, wetting my feet. We are dead meat, dead in the water. At the mercy of the river and the creatures concealed along its flank.*

*Around the bend steams a tow, pushing a raft of barges the size of two football fields. Black smoke rushes from the tug's exhaust. The current carries us, powerless, inexorably into its path, sweeping us under the overhang of steel.*

*How could I have been such a fool?*

Returned from Niagara Falls nearly five months, I awoke and looked at the night-table clock. Three A.M. Andra slept soundly at my side, the dog on the floor, in the next room Stephen. For a time I tossed, anxious that I had committed myself to a wildly ambitious small-boat trip for which I was ill prepared. Summer was slipping away and our August 9 departure was just a week away.

Damning the hour, I put my feet on the floor, slipped on a T-shirt and pair of shorts, closed the bedroom doors, and in the kitchen brewed a cup of tea. On a piece of Steve's drawing paper I began my list, at the head of which was a boat—first things first.

Soon I would call Tango to walk the beach that lies over the hill from our home, there where each day we see first light advancing across the wild roses and sea grass that cover the leeward side of the dunes. These things I anticipate: If the weather is mild, as it is during a Newport summer, the air will be soft. If the breeze is onshore and the tide low, I will smell seaweed among the salt. If offshore, the scent of rose hips, though decidedly weaker than bougainvillea and frangipani, will make me think of the West Indies. Indeed, until the light fills in the puddingstone cliffs at the southern end of the beach, defining the horrific crack of Purgatory Chasm, the gentle break of water will repaint a morning years ago when Andra and I sat on Grand Anse beach among the grugru trees on the western coast of Grenada, holding hands, before the boys came to sell us black coral. Their prices were high—justified, they said, by the risks of free-diving: "Very deep, very dangerous, very beautiful, mon."

At the northern end of our home beach, near the Sachuest Wildlife

Refuge where the sandpipers congregate in the surf, their quick little legs barely outpacing the foam, Tango will chase them to flight and we will turn back. The sun will break over the dunes . . . just about now . . . and ahead, on the hill separating our house from the beach, I will see the gothic stone tower of St. George's School, beneath it the stained-glass chapel window, and I will be transported by the beautiful and strange dawning of the light, become a man walking the Lake District with his sweater and staff. This, I will think, is mine: *This blessed plot, this earth, this realm, this England.*

At middle age, when there's more to your past than future, I naturally enough found myself dwelling more on what has been than what will be. This morning, still seated at the table, I thought of my first son, Peter, Adria's brother, who died when he was twelve, struck by a train while playing on a railroad trestle. Already our order of file on the long, lonesome trail had been broken. Then I thought of my father. He, too, is gone, just a few years. This is the time of day, right now, just before sunrise, when he moved on. Necrologists say it is a popular hour for the making of that passage, because our bodily systems are at full ebb, but I think it is because the world is so quiet, so at rest, that one might slip away without being noticed.

I was not there for his last breath and am still having a hard time forgiving myself. His heart, weakened by quadruple bypass surgery sixteen years earlier, followed by the progressive debilitation of Parkinson's disease, at last gave out, failing to come round with the brightening of the drawn shade.

A week earlier, just after a thrombotic warning, Mother telephoned, saying with a steady voice that he had been admitted to the hospital, and that the prognosis was extensive rehabilitation in a nursing home. I flew to Austin the next day. One look at him and I knew he wasn't going anywhere. When he slept, which was most of the time, one could hear Chain-Stokes breathing—the labored wheeze, the death rattle.

His palsied hand gripped mine and there were tiny bubbles of saliva on his lips as he stuttered to speak, saying that no stranger was going to pin him in diapers. In character to the end: New England Puritan stoic, stiff upper lip, never let 'em know how you feel. Whereas once I hated this impenetrable veneer, I now admired and respected his need for privacy, his firm resolve. "Basically, I'm a fatalist," he had confided several times in the course of his decline. Which is not to say that he did not have his beliefs, but he was a Unitarian, defining God as the unknowable being who *might* account for the world and the way things are. He said the hymns made him feel good even if they didn't mean anything. Strange, perhaps, for a scientist, but even Einstein recognized in his seemingly cold, dark universe the hand of a Creator.

By a bad turn of timing, in a few days Andra and I were to close on our first house, and the real estate agent didn't want it delayed. The agent warned that we were dealing with "an emotional seller"—a commercial fisherman busted by an empty ocean and a failing marriage. The implication was that these circumstances had given him an attitude about land-lubbers and land values, veiling what I suspected was the real issue: the agent's commission.

For three days I sat by my father's side with my mother and sister, Jean, he looking smaller and smaller, his shoulders curved inward, consciousness coming and going as if he were making quick trips to the other side.

In the early evening the three of us left his room, taking the elevator to ground level where for a few moments we might step outside the white tiled halls and breathe unfiltered air, relieve the tedium of our watch, I to tug at my pipe. When we returned a half hour later, Father's bed was empty and Mother gasped that they'd taken him.

I strode to the nurse's station, conscious of each step, my eyes, my mouth, the swing of my arms.

The nurse said, "Doctor ordered an X ray to check his kidney functions."

"Was he awake?"

"Yes."

"Did he say anything?"

"He asked for his son."

When the escort aides wheeled him back to his room, Mother asked for time alone, and as Jean and I closed the door, we could hear her softly singing to him the love songs only he would recognize, the whispered syllables of a dim time fifty years in their past.

Later she said, "He's going in whispers."

The next morning he clutched my hand again, hoarsely speaking of a certain savings account and of a task that I must perform. I could not understand him, so I lied, assuring that it would be tended to as soon as he slept. To cover all his possible meanings, I told him not to worry, that I would take care of Mother, and at that he loosened his fingers and fell back into the half sleep, half coma that eases one onward toward the shipping dock like a carton on a conveyor belt, onward through the portal.

Assured that he was stable and likely to linger in this manner for days, possibly weeks, I flew to Rhode Island for the house closing, scheduled for the next morning.

Just as Andra and I were leaving for the lawyer's office, the phone rang.

Later, in the meeting room, the real estate agent, relieved to see me present, stood and offered her hand. "We're so glad you could make it. I understand your father is ill. Do hope he's going to be okay."

"Thank you," I said. "He died this morning."

At the funeral, following Edna St. Vincent Millay's "Renascence" and Alfred, Lord Tennyson's "Crossing the Bar," Jean read, as he had stipulated, William Cullen Bryant's "Thanatopsis":

> To him who in the love of Nature holds
> Communion with her visible forms, she speaks
> A various language; for his gayer hours
> She has a voice of gladness, and a smile
> And eloquence of beauty, and she glides
> Into his darker musings, with a mild
> And healing sympathy, that steals away
> Their sharpness, ere he is aware. When thoughts
> Of the last bitter hour come like a blight
> Over thy spirit, and sad images
> Of the stern agony, and shroud, and pall,
> And breathless darkness, and the narrow house,
> Make thee to shudder, and grow sick at heart;—
> Go forth, under the open sky, and list
> To Nature's teachings, while from all around—
> Earth and her waters, and the depths of air—
> Comes a still voice—

Home from my walk, I stood over my sleeping Stephen, looking at him as any father would, even as my father must have looked at me:

*This is my son, mine own Telemachus,*
*To whom I leave the sceptre and the isle—*

I wanted for him what any father would want, what my father wanted for me: happiness, health, education, experience. More, I wanted him to live longer than Peter, certainly longer than me. I could not give him years that were not due him, but was determined to provide what I could of the rest. In some ways, the form of this father-to-son transference would be different, for I endeavored to avoid repeating the mistakes of the past, though at times I feared I could not help being other than what I am, and what I am is more of my father than I sometimes care to admit. Therefore, I would do like my father and listen to the *still voice*.

It was late July and still we had no boat to take us down the Mississippi. Each day I scoured the classified advertisements. My requirements forced the exclusion of any boat too large to trailer or too small to sleep aboard. At last an ad appeared that showed some promise, the key word being "versatile."

As Steve and I walked over the rise at the edge of the sand parking lot, then down the Third Beach ramp, I saw her and my heart sank. She was *Pearl*, a twenty-foot Proline fishing boat with a squarish cuddy cabin painted mud brown. The rhomboidal windows looked like the eyes of a jack-o'-lantern crudely cut with a bread knife. On the transom was a faded blue Evinrude 150-horsepower outboard motor. At the rear of the cockpit a homemade plywood seat had been screwed to the floor, draped with a dirty gray vinyl cushion that was secured with straps and brass cup eyes. A piece of threadbare indoor-outdoor carpeting, unraveling at the edges, covered the fiberglass floor. A small anchor, its shank bent like a broken arm, tethered the bow to the beach. A large and bearded man sat on one of the two mildewed seats.

We waded into the water, Steve raising his arms to John MacDonald, who hoisted him easily into the cockpit.

"You come aboard, too," he said to me. "I'll get the anchor through the hatch."

Bending forward into the tiny cabin, his head tucked and his shoulders rounded inward, he reappeared through the too-small deck hatch as if from a recently surfaced submarine.

In the cockpit, I watched him start the engine, back away from the shallows, lower the tilt mechanism, then spin the old cast-aluminum-spoked wheel toward open water.

Quickly she rose up on plane, skimming smoothly past the bouldered shore toward the mouth of the Sakonnet River, the eastern arm of Narragansett Bay, whose broad horizon lay before us. *Pearl*'s rather sprightly performance belied her clunky looks, and I was relieved, more for the owner than myself, because at first glance I didn't think I would buy her.

MacDonald maneuvered through several wide turns, jumping waves so that I might feel the cushioning effect of the veed forward hull sections, then alternately slowed and accelerated, to demonstrate the absence of any bad behaviors.

*Pearl* was without a doubt the homeliest boat I had ever seen, almost laughable next to the sleeker, more modern boats moored nearby. But sitting at the stern, watching John and Steve talk, I realized that the two-berth cabin, protected helm, and large cockpit made her well suited to my purpose. She would not offend the watermen on the Mississippi or the denizen bogeymen of my dream. If Huck and Tom were alive today, making a little money painting fences, repairing lawn mowers, or running trot lines across the back channels, this was the sort of boat they might conspire to buy for another run at adventure. With just a week before departure, I could not afford to widen the search. *Pearl,* a cartoon, was the one and only choice.

Off the bow, the water suddenly pooled and a large, dark shape broke the surface.

"Turtle!" Steve yelled.

I said, "Leatherback."

"He must be feeding at the river mouth," MacDonald said.

"Fish?" Steve asked.

"Yup."

"Why don't you troll?"

"I would if I had my rod."

"Why not *that* rod?" Steve pointed to the rack tucked under the gunwale.

"That's a casting rod."

Steve didn't see that it mattered.

We followed the turtle for several minutes, observing its large head rise up for air, then lower under the surface film as the animal sounded, the powerful flippers banking the Volkswagen beetle–shaped body deeper into the blue.

Later, after we struck a deal, MacDonald said that in all his years as a commercial and recreational fisherman, he had never seen a sea turtle.

"Perhaps," he declared, "this is your *oma kuna*. Some years ago my brother became friendly with the royal family of Hawaii. One day, before he left the islands, they told him to go to the beach, and that if he saw turtles, his journey would be a safe one. So he went to the beach, and sure enough, he saw a turtle. When he returned to his friends, they told him that the turtle was his *oma kuna*, a sort of guardian spirit. Mine is a whale, but that is another story."

When the next day I handed MacDonald a check, he studied it for a protracted moment, squinting, as if I'd requested his daughter's hand. Maybe it was retail training—making sure all the blanks were filled—but later I saw that he was detaching himself from the vessel and all that it had come to signify. More than automobiles, boats can do that, especially to the boy in the man to whom it reveals itself . . . as the fort, the cave, the cabin in the woods, the ultimate escape machine, the womb without a head requiring address.

He turned to me and said gravely: "*Pearl* is yours."

I was admitted to the clan, the rite consummated. A vessel of some sacredness was conferred on me. *Pearl,* MacDonald then explained, was named for his grandmother. Much revered, she had taught him the ways and beliefs of her kind and his, the Scots.

I said that she must have been a special lady, to which he nodded yes, that he had returned to Rhode Island after many years away. The American walkabout had taken him to Key West, Flagstaff, and Crater Lake, and now he'd come home so that his children might know her and through her know him. Things he could not teach, because they were not yet his.

The luck presaged by my patron-saint turtle did not immediately manifest itself. There remained just seven days to have the motor checked and the boat provisioned. That MacDonald could not find the title was merely a precursor. Complications loaded up like carbon on a spark plug. *Pearl* was more than twenty years old, her engine half that—proof that boats are depreciating assets that rot, shatter, and rust in what is quaintly termed the "marine environment."

Luck drove *Pearl* to Tiverton, to Don's Service, for the investigation of a small oil leak staining the cavitation plate. I gave Don Helger a day to complete the diagnosis and repair, then drove over to discuss any additional work that might be necessary for the trip.

Crossing the Sakonnet River Bridge, I saw in the distance the roof of Don's Service overlooking Nannaquaket Pond and, opposite the oyster-shell drive, the rambling structures of Helger's produce and ice-cream stand and farther still, the white clapboard lift-windows of Helger's turkey farm. A compound made, a family arm in arm against the outer forces. No wonder MacDonald liked Don Helger, the slender young man wearing a white knit shirt and black baseball cap.

"How far are you going?"

"Chicago to New Orleans—fourteen hundred miles."

He frowned. "This is not good. Do you have to take a *used* engine?"

I explained that I had little choice, the cost of a new engine being twice what I had paid for the boat, motor, and trailer combined.

"I'm going," I said. "Tell me what to do."

"Next summer?"

I shook my head.

"I'd do the head gaskets, impeller, recircs, rotors, that sort of thing—anything likely to fail."

He removed his cap and scratched his head, which was balding. Prematurely, like my father's, whose hair had been gone by the time he was twenty-five. "It's an eighty-five. If the power tilt quits with the engine up, you're screwed. Unless you can turn the pressure-relief valve, but that looks corroded, and if we bugger it God help us. You wouldn't even be able to raise and lower the motor by hand. When are you leaving?"

"Monday."

"Impossible. This is our busiest time of the year. Two weeks soonest."

"There's no choice," I said. "We're not coming back up the river so I've got to drop the boat on the Illinois by Wednesday so we can drive the car and trailer to New Orleans by Friday [where we would leave them] to make our airline reservations Saturday back to Chicago. My daughter arrives in St. Louis on the twentieth. I'm locked."

He backed away from the counter, grimacing at the ceiling. He scratched the back of his head.

Then Don turned and said, "This is Wednesday. I'll put my best mechanic on it. I don't know if he can do everything by Friday, but we will try."

Freeing myself for a month-long trip down the Illinois and Mississippi rivers was no simple task.

While I waited for Don I made lists, which I endlessly revised: one-burner butane stove, life jackets, insect repellent, cooler, sun protection, fishing gear . . . what about stereo, CDs, rain gear, wine? The pile in the bedroom climbed and caved out, tripping me when I got up in the middle of the night to second-guess myself. Too much gear would needlessly slow *Pearl*; forgetting a critical piece—first-aid kit, spark-plug wrench, spare parts—could have sinister consequences. Of course, these parts and accessories meant nothing if the boat was not ready.

Figuring a physical presence would punctuate my urgency, on Friday I again drove to Don's Service. It was five o'clock, the mechanics were cleaning their tools, and there was no sign of *Pearl* in the shop or yard. Wayne, the shop foreman, said the mechanics were performing a water test.

"Don't usually have the time to do it, but we like to. You learn a lot more than running it in a drum. First time out she didn't feel right. We checked the bilge and found it full of water. I thought maybe the bottom was punky. A lot of old fiberglass boats are, you know. Turns out the tubes inside the transom drains were pulled away from the hull and leaking. The guys had the plugs on the inside, so we put them on the outside—no problem. But you gotta remember which side they go on.

"Plus," he said, "you got the wrong prop. Tried a fifteen-seventeen. Runs great." He skipped one hand off the other to illustrate the favorable results of this new synchronicity. "Also gave you low-compression head gaskets. It'll take a little off your performance, but last a lot longer. Where you're going, you want reliability more than revs."

When the mechanics returned I paid the bill, hitched the trailer to the car, and drove to A&D Trailers in search of a spare tire. Everything seemed nice until the speedometer reached fifty miles per hour. Suddenly the boat and trailer began swaying from side to side, the cart wagging the horse in oscillations of increasing intensity, nearly wrenching the car off the road. I released my foot from the accelerator and looked through the rearview mirror at the following traffic, which had dropped back several hundred feet.

At A&D, owners Dan and Kathleen produced a spare that would fit, showing me both sidewalls, sticking their fingers deep into the treads, bouncing it on the floor. Expensive, but worthy. The trailer, they said tactfully, was an unusual assemblage of junkyard parts, a hybrid of several brands mounted on a truck axle. Tough but bastard. Yes, yes, I would buy the tire, but there were more serious problems, to wit, the sway. MacDonald, I told them, had moved the trailer axle forward to neutralize the tongue weight, enabling him to manhandle the trailer around his property without a dolly wheel.

Dan nodded knowingly. He dropped the tire and kneeled to inspect the axle, springs, U-bolts, and lights.

"When are you leaving?"

"Monday."

"No you're not."

"That's what Don said."

"You need at least ten percent on the tongue. That means the axle's gotta be moved back at least a foot. The U-bolts will have to be cut off with a torch. These aluminum brackets might fall apart and fabricating new ones out of steel is gonna take at least a day. The wiring on the lights is corroded and the first pothole you hit, these leaf springs are gonna pop. If that ain't bad enough, there's no fenders. You go through Connecticut and the troopers will impound your whole rig. Three hundred bucks minimum. Shit you not."

"Is this a job I can do?"

"Sure. If you can get the boat off the trailer, use a torch, do the welds. I can sell you the U-bolts and springs. Want to see them?" He made a move toward a rack of bent metal, the springs of annealed alloy, flat black, shopworn, dusty, very auto, stressed to resist straightening, proof that for every action there is an equal and opposite reaction.

Quickly I said no. "When can *you* do the work?"

"A week, maybe two."

I gave Dan the same explanation I had given Don, the itinerary and all the consequential reservations.

Dan drew in a deep, purposeful breath, as if he were preparing for a dive, then exhaled slowly and turned to his wife.

"Told Joe I'd start his trailer Monday . . . unless something came up. Maybe this could be that something . . ." Looking at me he said, "Tell you what. I'll start at six-thirty Monday morning and won't quit until it's done. Best I can do."

On the drive home the driver's-side power window arrested itself in midframe. I could not conceive driving to Chicago, New Orleans, and home with a half-closed window—inviting thieves and rain, confounding all parties at the tollbooths.

In a rain, I disassembled the door, only to discover the inevitable—I could not repair it. Thank God I hadn't tried to fix the trailer!

Dale Nouse and I had worked together off and on for fifteen years, first at *Cruising World* magazine, where he was editor, and now as my assistant at *Practical Sailor*, a twice-monthly newsletter. At seventy-four, he was remarkably fit and trim, though now he tired more easily and worked half days in my home office. During the past week he had fingered through the three books of navigation charts published by the U.S. Army Corps of Engineers, penciling in annotations to reflect his principal concern: procuring fuel. He determined the longest distance between obvious fuel stations to be 188 miles; considering that *Pearl* carried just forty-two gallons of gasoline, Dale thought we would have a major problem keeping the tank wet. I had asked MacDonald for a mileage estimate, but like most skippers who putter about, he had no idea. Not until we were actually running on the river would I be able to determine how far a tank would take us. By then, my only recourse would be to buy portable cans.

At 8 A.M. Dale drove across the yard and parked his white Saab 9000S (his last car, he warned) against the split-rail fence. He stepped out dressed in khaki shorts, white kneesocks, deck shoes, and a straw hat. Tall and balding, he looked very much like Daddy Warbucks on safari. In his hand he carried a small canvas bag with a selection of trick tools, including a ratchet screwdriver, right-angle drill bit, and double-jointed wrench.

"Any job is easy if you have the right tool," he always said.

The critical accessory was a vinyl Bimini top to shield us from the sun and rain. This was installed easily on the fittings left from an old canvas cover, now in tatters. Afterward, we gutted the boat, vacuumed and scrubbed, then arranged all of the stockpiled gear in the front yard, packing the pieces one by one to see how much would fit and where: rain awning, flashlights, battery-operated fans, sleeping bags, fishing rods and tackle, tools, and life jackets.

The outside air was hot, still as a cave. Dale made tomato sandwiches. Throughout the day we drank sodas and juice, sweating it as fast as we could swallow. At day's end he drove me to the auto dealer. Two hundred dollars for a rebuilt power window motor module, which at that point seemed a pittance.

Anticipating an early-morning departure, I hitched the trailer to the car. All that remained was to raise the outboard motor into towing position: elevate to near horizontal, flip down a spring-loaded bar against the transom bracket, then lower the motor until the lower unit rested upon the bar, all to take the load off of the tilt motor, the fragility and criticality of which Don Helger had warned me.

I inserted the ignition key and pressed the tilt button—nothing. No juice in the wires. Why, I could not comprehend.

I looked at Dale, who was occupying himself with the zen-like job of splicing fender lines. I took a deep breath and called Don.

Before dawn I felt Tango's wet nose on the palm of my outstretched hand. Soon we were on the beach, she roaming from the surf to the dunes, sniffing, peeing, searching for the putrid remains of a minke whale that a month earlier had washed ashore. Just as she lowered a shoulder to roll in the blackened skin, I called and she froze, staring at me as if to decide whether satisfying the primal urge was worth a whupping. I started toward her and she launched upward on hind legs, racing past me, showing me who was fastest, straight into the surf. There she flopped down. If there were no waves, she would swim, not just lie there and let the water wash over. I would miss these walks and told her so.

Andra squinted into the camera, took several steps to her left, then snapped a photograph of Steve standing by the boat, the morning sun making his blond hair white. Yesterday he had cut his hand on an oyster shell, and already he was picking at the stitches beneath the dressing.

Dale walked around the boat and trailer, saying nothing. I could not tell if he was simply curious about some aspect of the rig or looking for a trailing line or loose nut.

With a kiss and a toot of the horn, we were gone. At the first corner I pushed the window button. The window did not move. Backing up, I hailed Andra, who simply laughed. Like La Salle, beset by misfortune at every turn, I felt I was being tested, my worthiness tried.

"I'm calling Saccucci's. No. Forget it. I'm going to park right in front of their shop and sit there until it's fixed."

Andra smiled. "I'll warn them."

I do not know what she said to the "service representative," but we were met by a mechanic who ambled down to the street with a handful of tools, disassembled the door, and replaced a length of wire that for some unknown reason would not carry electricity. A mystery, he said. Not to me. I had figured it out. Same thing happens to outboards, brains, and hearts: The spark goes out.

By ten we were leaving town, breaking free from the gravity of home.

At a convenience mart, I stopped for a cup of coffee. On the counter the morning paper carried an item headlined "Rare Leatherback Found Dead on Beach."

*Oma kuna* my ass.

# *Westward*

*It's not strangers we don't like, just people we don't know.*

—Jonathan Raban, *Old Glory*

Steve, usually so animated and chatty, was uncharacteristically quiet, sitting in place, his legs and feet angled off the seat, well distanced from the floor despite his earlier proclamation that soon they will touch. He had yet to grasp the various conventions of measuring time—seconds, days, especially years—and during his next growth spurt he fully expected to elongate himself an astonishing six inches, perhaps over a long weekend.

But his self-absorption could not last long: Already he had played Game Boy to boredom, drawn his way out of a dozen mazes with a broken number two pencil, read a chapter in *Frog and Toad*, and eaten a roll of spearmint LifeSavers, two Twinkies, and a bag of Hot Fries. On the dash he'd found an envelope from his grandmother, inside a fifty-dollar bill designated for "something special." He appropriated it as his own, and despite my better judgment, I let him stuff it in his wallet. But he could not leave it there, continually pulling it out for study and soliloquy on what it might buy: Sega, pocket television, a boom box . . .

Soon he would talk of fish, asking me to list each freshwater species I had ever caught (it is short: many perch, a few blue gills and sunfish, one catfish). What is the biggest freshwater fish you've ever caught? How many pounds? How many inches? Did you eat it? When my answers no longer satisfied him, failing to make little pictures in his mind, he would ask me to tell a John and Jim story, characters I invented some years ago for bedtime amusement.

In the first of three I would tell today, John and Jim, who live on the coast of Maine, are fishing in the ocean on their father's lobster boat, drifting next to a clanging buoy marking Smith's Ledge. A Chinese junk ghosts by in the fog, which they approach, tie to, then daringly board. Its decks are empty, the vessel apparently steering itself. Jim, always the more prudent, reluctantly follows John belowdecks. In the corner of a dark cabin filled with incense sits a Fu Manchu, legs crossed, hands folded on his lap, eyes closed in an opium sleep (though I tell Steve he is just tired). About the cabin are trinkets of jade and articles of silk. Opening his eyes, the Chinaman tells the boys that he had grown old and is sailing home to die. In exchange for their assistance in manning the vessel, he promises to reward them with treasure. In one hand he holds a pile of pearls, in the other assorted emeralds, rubies, and sapphires. Both he extends to them. The boys demur, citing the importance of school and the penalty for truancy. Then there appears on the bulkhead behind the Chinaman what seems to be a painting of a dragon. As they study it, the form lifts from the flat surface, undulating sinisterly as it becomes three-dimensional. Its red eyes begin to glow, hypnotizing the boys. They answer the Chinaman's questions sleepily. Recognizing that they are losing control of their wills, they urge one another to escape. But they cannot, so powerful is the spell.

Again the Chinaman asks them to crew his boat.

Feeling drugged and helpless, John and Jim are about to relent when a wave rocks the boat, tipping over a vase. The sound breaks the dragon's hold. The boys dash to the deck, leaping back aboard their lobster boat. They cast off and back away, watching as the junk sails on through the fog, on blindly toward Smith's Ledge, which it strikes with a terrible force. The bow rears, then follows the stern, sliding backward under the surface. Through a sunken portlight the red eyes of the dragon still glow. Leaning over the rail, Jim watches the ghostly shape of the sinking junk. The eyes draw him down. Just as Jim is about to dive overboard, John grabs him around the waist.

The sequence is dreamlike and the boys look at one another as if to assure themselves that what they have seen is real.

Jim kneels to tie his shoelaces. He discovers a pearl fallen in the cuff of his pants. John starts the engine, and they hurry home. They take the pearl to a local jeweler for appraisal.

Steve interrupted: "Dad, can John and Jim see *over* the counter?"

I turned with surprise. His face was down, studying the composition of a crushed Hot Fry. He wanted his heroes to drive boats and cars, to go off on long adventures and outwit master criminals, and I had always assumed they were teenagers, similar to the Hardy Boys or Tom Swift. It had never occurred to me that Steve imagined them as his own age.

"Depends how old they are," I said.

"How old *are* they?"

"How old do you *want* them to be?"

"Seven."

Approaching the Massachusetts Turnpike, the forested hills heaving up before us, I wondered if this was the way things looked three hundred years ago, wondered what it was like to sail toward an undiscovered coast, not knowing whether one would find the gilded temples of China, savages ripping out the entrails of deer and beaver, or nothing human at all, just the limitless forest, the pine-needle floor, dappled sunlight shining through the broken canopy, the sound of birds on the wing, the buzz of insects in your ear.

Steve awoke, blinking at the sun.

"How much longer?"

"A few hours," I lied. I wasn't even sure where we'd stop beyond somewhere in upper New York State.

I asked if he remembered the Massachusetts Turnpike; he raised himself to look out the window, his eyes scanning the roadside blur, and he did not.

We drove on in silence, retracing our route of last spring, through the Mohawk Valley, below the Adirondacks. Despite the modifications made to the trailer, on the flats I could only hold fifty miles per hour, steadying the rig as we ran through the Montezuma Refuge—channeled wetlands of grass and purple flowers, empty now of the snow and Canadian geese that had blanketed them last spring.

This day, encumbered by the resistance of the load behind us, we progressed no farther than the town of Victor, near Rochester, just west of the Finger Lakes in upstate New York. We'd made 420 miles. All day I had felt the tug of the boat and trailer. The car had labored, too weak to power the air conditioner on the uphill grades. With temperatures and humidity both in the nineties, we opened all of the windows. The force of the wind loosened the headliner, which flapped so violently that it hung from the ceiling like laundry, obscuring the rear window. When Steve pulled out his fifty-dollar bill, I closed all the windows for fear the draft would suck it from his hand.

We checked into a Microtel a mile off the New York Thruway. Steve happily discovered Nintendo programmed on the television set. Seven ninety-five room charge. There oughta be a law.

(My father foresaw the dangers of television even as the first sets began to appear in our neighbors' homes. When the parents of my best friend, Jim Dunlap, bought one circa 1955, Father said he'd wait for color. When, after a year or two, it dawned on me that this technological difficulty was not going to be hurdled next week, next month, or even next year, I pressed harder. The reversal occurred one evening at our home, during a cocktail party, when Mr. Dunlap, having consumed several Manhattans, joked about how much time I spent in *his* den, watching *his* television. The punch line was the passing of his hat around the room, taking a collection to buy the Spurrs their own look at the wasteland. Father broke down the next day and purchased a black-and-white Magnavox with wooden case. We owned it long after the advent of color, until one day it blew a tube and Father was told by the service center that having it repaired was stupid.)

Fortunately, Steve was hungry, and near the Microtel, across a field, was a Chili's restaurant. Walking, I skirted a water-filled culvert. Steve's blond hair was like a sunspot, disappearing down the grade.

"Frogs!"

"You see one?"

"No. But there might be."

During the early-morning hours, a fog came over the land. When we threw our bags into the backseat of the car you could see the moisture on the hood, feel it on the handles. I drove slowly down the expressway, the few other cars appearing and disappearing from the circle around us. Then a long black skid mark paralleling a blood line veering onto the shoulder, ending at a smashed horse trailer and, just beyond, in the V of the median, a dead horse. A backhoe, left by a maintenance worker, who'd presumably used it to drag the carcass off the road, was parked a few feet away.

Steve did not understand how this could happen. Death smeared across the highway. We talked about it until breakfast.

"Could be anything," I said. "Flat tire. Speeding. Maybe in the fog another car hit the trailer."

"Maybe," Steve said, "a bomb went off."

As we rolled over the gentle hills of northeastern Ohio, the temperature did not moderate and still the air conditioner was moribund. We wore shorts and T-shirts, which clung to our skin when the car slowed and the buffeting wind eased. The car was happier on the level grades of the Midwest, running the perimeter of Lake Erie. Here, though the Mississippi lay yet more than six hundred miles to the west, we entered its vast watershed, the network of creeks and streams that drain 1.25-million square miles of land—41 percent of the continental United States.


The years 1669–72 were for La Salle his initiation into the wilderness. Not much is known of his whereabouts or activities during this period. What is known is this: From the Indians who visited his seigneury he had learned some geography of the lakes and rivers to the west. The Senecas who had wintered at La Chine spoke of a large river that in nine months' travel would lead one to the Mississippi and thence the sea. They called it the Ohio, meaning "beautiful."

Ten years before the building of the *Griffon*, La Salle set out on July 6, 1669, with twenty-four men in seven canoes, three of which were reserved for Fathers Bréhan de Gallinée and Dollier de Casson and their attendants. At Irondequoit Bay, on the south side of Lake Ontario, they stopped to visit a Seneca village. For a month they lingered, hopeful of being furnished with guides. Events deteriorated. The Indians got drunk on brandy obtained from a Dutch trader and grew violent. Later, following an intertribal skirmish in which a Seneca boy was killed, the Seneca men brought home a member of the offending tribe to torture. La Salle and the priests were obliged to witness his six hours of torture, after which the body was cut up and eaten. All that night the people banged sticks against the bark lodges to drive away his angry ghost. Then some of the men decided the whites ought to be killed as revenge for the murder of a Seneca at Montreal some time earlier. Fortunately, the guilty had been executed in sight of a goodly number of Iroquois, who spoke on the behalf of La Salle and his party, and eventually the tension eased.

The French party moved on toward Tinaouataoua, just north of the present site of Hamilton, Ontario, at the eastern end of the lake, beyond the cataract at Niagara. There they met Adrien Jolliet,[1] who was returning from a fruitless search for copper mines in the Lake Superior region.

Jolliet shared a map he had made of the upper lakes and urged the priests to attend the Potawatomis, who he said were ripe for conversion. Gallinée and Dollier consulted and agreed that they ought to proceed north into Ontario. Frustrated by their inability to communicate over the past month with the Senecas, they saw an expediency in this plan as both of the priests and the Potawatomis spoke the language of the Ottawas.

Because it lies along the shortcut between Buffalo and Detroit, I have driven through Hamilton many times; the occasion of the La Salle-Jolliet meeting is vivid to me with my eyes closed, but difficult for me to picture when on the scene, as out of place as the building of the *Griffon* on Cayuga Creek. The overlay of streets, rows, and columns of tract houses so alters the landscape of my pre-America that it seems to disappear, become a fictional fantasy contrived by Tolkien, C. S. Lewis, or Swift.

La Salle was of a different mind. Perhaps because he chose the path less traveled, perhaps because he earnestly believed that the Ohio was the way to the Mississippi, he could not break with his plan. And so he parted from the priests, fabricating an illness to explain his departure. In fact, he was relieved to see Gallinée and Dollier go. Foremost, he preferred to operate alone, without interference from others who had their own agendas. Also, though he was a devout Christian, he did not countenance the missionary zeal to save or convert the Indians, whom he regarded as men in their natural state and therefore already pure. His critics—and there were and remain many—would say that he was arrogant and haughty, determined to keep for himself all his discoveries and their benefits.

What he did next is both illuminated and confused by Abbé Eusèbe Renaudot, who years later interviewed La Salle in Paris. Renaudot was an abbot in name only. His father, Théophraste Renaudot, published a newspaper, the *Gazette de France*, that broke tradition by running news of foreign places first and news of France last, and by selling advertising space (he is generally credited with being the first to do so). Eusèbe had taken over the newspaper and moved adroitly in both religious and political circles. According to his account, La Salle backtracked with the remainder of the party to the south shore of Lake Erie. En route, he was given a male Shawnee captive named Nika, who would remain faithful to him until their last days, which were to be separated by but a single sunrise. From there he portaged for six or seven leagues (a league varies between 2.4 to 4.6 statute miles) until he reached a river that carried him to the Ohio. Which tributary he took is not known. A modern map suggests the Allegheny, which begins in northern Pennsylvania, arcs briefly across the border into western New York, then dives toward Pittsburgh, where it meets the Ohio. To reach the Allegheny he could have taken any of several smaller streams, the Cassadaga, Brokenstraw, French, or Cussewago. We did not cross them on Interstate 90, because none of them begins at the lake, but just south six or seven leagues.

Parkman and many other historians doubt that this particular exploration progressed farther southwest than the turbulent rapids at Louisville, Kentucky.

La Salle's biographer Anka Muhlstein wrote:

> The channel was clogged with rocks, gravel, tree trunks and debris. Large alluvial deposits collected at the bends in the river, and these shifting dams created dangerous and unstable stretches churned by eddies and falls.[2]

The men, ever mindful of rattlesnakes, were also plagued by flying insects—flies, gnats, and mosquitoes. Often they were forced to portage the canoes, though the banks were difficult.

At the rapids his remaining men deserted, working their way eastward over the Appalachians to the Dutch and English colonies. La Salle affirmed this in a memorial to the governor of New France, Louis de Buade Frontenac, in 1677. Time and again, La Salle's inability to inspire the scalawags who schlepped his supplies proved to be his fatal flaw, one that never failed to compound his troubles.

But for Nika, he now was alone. What did he do?

Nearly a year later, in the summer of 1670, the well-known voyageur Nicolas Perrot, an articulate man who later wrote an account of his time in the woods, found La Salle hunting with a party of Iroquois on the Ottawa River. (Note that the Iroquois were the constant enemies of the French, but that here, as earlier at La Chine and the Seneca village, La Salle managed to befriend them, as he did nearly all the Indians he met.) Had La Salle turned around and ascended the Ohio, back to Lake Erie? Or had he continued on down the Ohio to the Mississippi, as Renaudot claims, descending the great river to the 36th parallel, where he became convinced that it discharged not into the Gulf of California, as was supposed, but into the Gulf of Mexico? And if so, how did he return? By the onerous Ohio, or perhaps by ascending the Illinois? Not until the summer of 1671, when he returned to Montreal, can his whereabouts be verified. But his appearance was brief, for he again vanished into the woods until December 18, 1672, when he made an appearance at the registry at Ville-Marie, in Montreal.

These years, 1669–72, are the missing years, and his biographers have offered a variety of theories about them. Their conclusions are important because at issue is whether, during the interregnum, La Salle discovered the Ohio, and whether he, not Adrien Jolliet's brother Louis, discovered the Illinois and Upper Mississippi.

Louis Jolliet, born in Quebec in 1641, two years before La Salle's birth, also had quit the Society of Jesus, but unlike La Salle, he remained under the Jesuits' influence until just six years before his death, when he broke off all relations. Much is made of Louis Jolliet's 1673 expedition with Father Jacques Marquette partway down the Mississippi. Though he was brave, honest, and determined, Jolliet seemed to lack the consuming forward vision that carried La Salle. It is easy to imagine the two as competitors, but so focused was La Salle, it seems he scarcely worried about the activities of others. And for Jolliet's part, his schemes were not nearly as grandiose as La Salle's plan of settling the heartland, though La Salle was so perpetually in debt and hounded by creditors that only a fool would have envied him.

In any case, La Salle did not waste the time spent in the woods. He learned numerous Indian tribes' dialects and customs and acquired the skills to survive in the wilderness—hunting deer and rabbits, making his own moccasins, reading trails, reading water. When he emerged Moses-like from the wilderness, his vision was shaped. He knew he had to make money, and to do this he needed to establish outposts from which he could pacify the Indians and thereby trade with them—places where they could bring him furs, as at Michilimackinac, already a thriving settlement at the apex of the Michigan peninsula, where the traders bought furs from the Indians and the priests endeavored to catechize their hearts and minds with the blood of Jesus, the sorrow of Mary, and the retributive power of the Father.

On the outskirts of Cleveland, a fish truck pulled in front of us and slowed; irritated, I eased out of my lane to pass, but when a car I did not see appeared in the rearview mirror, laying on the horn, I quickly retreated. The fish truck took the next exit. As we pulled abreast the driver yelled, pointing at me as if to say the next time he'd put me under.

One hundred fifty miles later, while fueling at a highway plaza near the Ohio-Indiana border, a motorcyclist, bearded and leathered, pointed at the rear of the trailer. No words, just a motion signifying: There, check it. One of the trailer's taillights dangled by its wires, the aluminum bracket having sheared at the bolt, a victim of corrosion caused by the mating of dissimilar metals. The repair required a drill, bolt, washer, and nut—items that should be native to service stations. But when we pulled in, the attendant lamented, "I have no tools." He shrugged as if he knew the operation was lame—blame it on management and the insurance company. All he could do, he said, was refer us down the road to Hutch's 24-hour Truck Service, which we found locked. A woman dressed in shorts, white sweat socks, and low-cut work boots—presumably the wife of a trucker— circled the large tin structure, banging on the many doors, swearing, "Twenty-four hours my ass!" She directed me to sweep the grounds counterclockwise while she went the other way, and when we met she asked what trouble with my rig had brought me to Hutch's. I mumbled something about the trailer, and when she realized we had but six wheels, I faded from her to the shoulder where Steve waited, thumbing the rocker switch of Donkey Kong. In the trunk I found a roll of duct tape to bind the light to the frame, then left, the woman still on tiptoes, peering through windows with cupped eyes.

Steve, for reasons that should not have astonished me, became preoccupied with farts—counting them, adjusting their resonance with his hips, inquiring of my own habits, their frequency and magnitude, wondering if they smoked. He asked to buy a Sega video game in which a character named Red & White could be made flatulent. For a time I ignored his remarks; when this failed to dissuade him I scolded; and when both tactics brought no change I experimented by laughing with him, saying that his gas smelled like a McDonald's hamburger.

I cannot imagine ever having spoken such words in the presence of my father. Even when I frowned and spoke sternly, it had only a temporary effect on Steve, who then would spell the word or choose another that rhymed ("Dad, how many times did you 'cart' today?"). These were ridiculous conversations, and exasperating, though secretly I admired his tenacity. Why, I asked myself, did Steve not respond to me with the deference I gave my father? Did the difference lie between my father and me, as fathers, or between Steve and me, as sons? Certainly, as a father I considered myself more liberal, though I still corrected "got no" to "have no," and insisted on at least a two-minute presence at the dinner table. (I had been required to sit until the last bite of beets was consumed before *I* could then clear the table, return, and, following dessert and more clearing, ask, "Please, may I be excused?") That I still remembered those excruciatingly long meals, which could not be rescheduled or interrupted even by the firing of an Apollo rocket or Michigan in the Rose Bowl, probably explains why I still loathe this useless Edwardian decorum. I understood that my father was not even allowed to eat in the same room as his parents, but was the price of my liberalness to suffer the ceaseless anality of a seven-year-old? Nothing, it seemed, could pry Steve's mind from his butt, though, to my surprise, I succeeded in planting a seed of disdain for Ronald McDonald's Happy Meals.

Nevertheless, one morning on Main Street, Elkhart, Indiana, forsaking a sit-down breakfast, I pulled into the center turn lane in front of the Golden Arches. My intention was to enter the Marathon gas station just beyond, but on seeing that the drive was roped off and the pumps ripped out of the concrete, I checked both mirrors, then inched backward so that I might negotiate the turn into what Steve now called Micky D's.

"Just the drive-through," I said, mindful of the time. "Couple of potato cakes, OJ, coffee—a Danish if you like—then off we go."

As I was speaking, still slowly backing, the car suddenly stopped. Though I had heard no sound, the nature of the event was unmistakable.

Stepping out of the car I was confronted by a heavy-set man with long sideburns. He was dressed in a black western shirt and black jeans held up by a wide belt and large copper buckle, an absurd-looking clypeus of astonishing prominence.

"What the hell you think you're doin'?!" He slammed the door of his pickup, swiping at the handle as if it were now a piece of shit.

I looked stupidly around the corner of the boat transom. The outboard propeller was firmly embedded in the truck's grille—the image one might expect to see on an avant-garde postcard, the juxtaposition of unexpected forms belying the violent grotesquerie of torn and punctured metal. Of course I already knew that my propeller had pierced his radiator. Still . . .

And his was not just any pickup, but a brand-new black double-cab Ford F-350 with amber fog lights, accessory chrome, bug deflector, and yards of custom pinstriping on the perimeter of the dimpled hood.

I could not think. "I don't know," I said.

"Five hundred miles on it!" he bellowed.

It was quickly agreed that I must notify the police from the pay phone in the McDonald's parking lot ("Yes, of course," as if the idea was reflexive, which it certainly was not). I lifted Steve from the car and carried him across the road, his skinny legs banging my thighs. The sight of the wide-eyed child apparently softened the man, for minutes later, after I deposited Steve back in his seat, he extended his hand and introduced himself.

"Goddamn! Sorry I swore in front of your son, but Jesus, five hundred miles!"

A police officer arrived, and because I freely admitted fault, he elected to forgo a diagram, instructing us to pull off the street and park at the rear of the McDonald's lot. There he asked for our driver's licenses and registrations; on seeing that the truck's owner was from New Mexico, relocating to Kansas, en route to Bristol, Michigan, to do tire setups for a NASCAR race, and me from Rhode Island, on my way to Chicago, then New Orleans, he dropped his head on his logbook and cried, "Why me? I just came on duty!"

I asked myself the same question. The dead *oma kuna* did not answer.

During the next hour I obliged the man by writing a letter of explanation to his father, who had helped finance the truck and obviously held some sway, phoned the insurance agency, and completed several police forms. Mercifully, we soon escaped to the dubious refuge of the freeway entering Gary, where a tandem trailer had flipped, reducing traffic to one lane crawling.

"Fartskers," Steve said. "Why did you hit that man's truck?"

"Dumb, dumb, dumb," I groaned.

"Hey, Dad, you're dumb and dumber!"

"Yes, I am."

"Buy me a Bud!"

Steve seemed to parrot every commercial, and had me doing it, too. I could not wait to board the boat and cast off, going anywhere where there were no highways or television, police, fast food, or video games.

# Starved Rock

*Such stillness—*
*The cries of the cicadas*
*Sink into the rocks*

—Matsuo Bashó

Ninety miles southwest of Chicago, we exited Interstate 80 and drove through the town of Ottawa. Instinctively, I aimed for the river until we found a bridge and a sign warning that "Implements of husbandry" were forbidden to cross. I was not sure if this included me, but on seeing the water beyond a row of wooden houses, I turned right, continuing for several miles until at last we came to Starved Rock Marina, the site I had chosen to launch *Pearl*.

I parked the rig in the gravel lot. On the low bank there was a restaurant, a fuel dock, and a ship's store; beyond, canted in the shallows, were many stumps and tree limbs caught on the bottom. Inland were two large tin sheds for storing boats. Nearer was the office.

I asked for the owner, Tom Novak, with whom I had spoken earlier about several matters, including used boats and slip space.

I told him that we already had purchased a boat in Rhode Island and towed it here. His countenance soured. He propped his hands on his hips.

"So you bought somebody else's boat instead of mine? What do you want from me?"

If there had been another marina nearby I would have said "Nothing." But I was worn, disabled in the heart of the heart of corn country.

"Dock space," I said.

"The girl can take care of you."

He pointed to a young woman seated behind a countertop.

I did not relish humbling myself further, but out of desperation proceeded to describe how I'd punched the propeller through the grille of a pickup truck and how, when I now spun the propeller, strange clicking noises could be heard inside the gearbox.

Conceding to examine the motor, Tom followed us outside.

Parked in a lot full of so-called "penis" boats, *Pearl* looked like a children's book illustration, the scorned ugly duckling who manages to win the race against a fleet of larger, faster craft, overcoming their cheating and conniving by virtue of her pure heart.

Laying eyes on our boat, Novak stopped dead in his tracks, adjusted his sunglasses, and said, "That's a far cry from what I was going to sell you. Looks like a *fishing* boat. You're taking *that* all the way to New Orleans?"

"Yes. I couldn't afford your boat."

I resisted the urge to tell him that his twenty-two-foot Sea Sprite, with its chopped-off transom and sinisterly sloped nose, was to me repugnant, that *Pearl* was honest even if ugly, and eminently seaworthy.

Tom put his hand on the prop and turned it. *Click. Click.* "You're a brave man. We don't work on Evinrudes. You'll have to take it to an OMC dealer. There's one the other side of Ottawa. Name is Leopold's. Use the phone inside if you want. It's a local call."

After nearly an hour of backtracking, we parked *Pearl* in a fenced yard behind Leopold's long, single-story cinder-block building. Johnson and Evinrude motors evidently were a small part of Leopold's business; as the area Honda dealer, it devoted the vast majority of floor space to every conceivable model of motorcycle and four-wheel-drive all-terrain vehicle. In an alcove was a smaller assortment of portable generators, lawn tractors, and related accessories. Implements of civilization. All designed to subdue, transform, and lay waste to my pre-America.

While waiting for the outboard motor mechanic to finish a motorcycle job, Steve fell in love with a miniature dirt bike, on sale for just fifteen hundred dollars.

"I could ride it in the yard!" he said. "Run over Mom's garden."

I shook my head. No motorcycles as long as he lived at home—same rule as my father's. I repeated this without thinking, without remembering that one of the first things I did on leaving home was to buy a 650cc Triumph Bonneville, install high pipes, and practice wheelies.

"Then I'll ask Santa and he'll give it to me."

"I don't think so."

"Santa gives you whatever you want."

"Santa checks with Mom and Dad on such questionable things as this."

"How do you know?"

"I know."

"Has he ever asked you before?"

"Yes."

"What's 'questionable'?"

I steered him outside. Soon he was running down a dirt track toward a small lake half hidden behind a row of trees. He'd be just as happy finding a frog as owning a dirt bike. Locusts flew up about him in a cloud and I could hear their metronomic refrain even against the backdrop of wheels whining on macadam. The air was damp and hot. A nearly full soft drink turned warm in my hand. Time crept on three legs.

At last the mechanic emerged from the shop door, spun the prop a few times, and declared that there was no problem in the gearbox. The noise, he said, occurred when the transmission gears were only partially engaged; by wiggling the gearshift at the helm in and out of the neutral position, we could make the noise come and go. After a brief discussion about debris in the river, I returned inside to buy yet a second spare propeller. After all, Tom Novak had warned me we'd never make it to New Orleans with just two props.

Late in the day we returned to the marina, and while Steve fished, I launched *Pearl* into the still, brown water. To either side of the ramp were large rental houseboats with vinyl patio chairs on the upper decks and swim slides off the transoms. The marina's phone number—1-708-THE ROCK—was painted in large numerals on each topside.

Several years had passed since I'd handled a powerboat in close quarters (driving a photo boat in Newport, darting past the Coast Guard 44-footers to take my clientele under the long overhangs of the legendary J-boats *Shamrock V* and *Endeavour*, old prewar America's Cup rivals resurrected by the millionairess Elizabeth Myers to joust again for the media and the old-timey yachties dressed for the occasion in blue blazers and red pants). I maneuvered deliberately, and once the boat was tied up at the transients' dock, I began emptying the car trunk of our gear, carrying the stuff across the lot and stowing it in *Pearl*'s cabin. The sound of cicadas was white noise.

I paused to drink a soda and wipe the sweat from my eyes. Across the river stood the tall mesa of Starved Rock, incongruously sprung from the fields, formed from deep loess over sedimentary bedrock known as the Driftless Section, ancient terrain that escaped the maul of glaciation. Called by the French the Rock of St. Louis, the block of St. Peter's sandstone now called Starved Rock is so named for the tribe of Illiniwek besieged and starved there in the 1760s by Potawatomis. On the bluff grew black oak, red cedar, and white pine. In a dead limb a yellow-bellied sapsucker drilled parallel rows of small holes to feed on sap and insects. Before the French, before the Illiniwek, as far back as 8000 B.C., people of the Hopewellian, Woodland, and Mississippian cultures lived here. Providing an abundance of deer and beaver, the rock made it easy to find your way home.

Now it is a state park, well cared for with a lodge and marked trails. Nearly twenty years ago I'd stopped to visit on the return leg of a car trip to Nebraska, to see firsthand how first the Indians, and later La Salle, had used the steep bluffs to their advantage to keep attackers at bay. The forest seemed everywhere atop the mesa, with only a bald, open spot overlooking the river, and I wondered if the trees looked more or less the same in their pre-American time.

My eyes fell to the shade of a tree on the near side of the river, under which a man fished from the bank. Steve wandered over to chat with him.

"What's running?" he asked.

"Running?"

Here there were no big schools of bluefish chasing pogies into the shallows, and the verb was misplaced.

"What kind of fish is that?"

"Catfish."

"Any bass?"

"No bass in this river. Just carp and catfish."

Steve saw me coming and retreated. As we turned toward *Pearl*

Robert A. *Thom's* Arrival of Jolliet and Marquette at the Village of the Kaskaskia at Starved Rock, 1673, *painted in 1967.* (ILLINOIS STATE HISTORICAL LIBRARY, SPRINGFIELD, ILLINOIS)

he whispered, "What does he mean 'no bass'? There's always bass in freshwater."

Louis Jolliet remarked to the Jesuit superior Father Dablon that the discovery of the Illinois was of equal importance as the discovery of the Mississippi, for the Illinois represented a significant shortcut between Montreal and the larger river. Neither Jolliet nor La Salle, however, came quickly to that understanding. Nor, as suggested earlier, is it clear which of them discovered it.

In 1672, Louis Jolliet and, ostensibly, Father Jacques Marquette were sent by Frontenac to find and explore the Upper Mississippi, which they did the following year by means of exiting Green Bay at the Fox River and proceeding to the Wisconsin, which empties into the Mississippi. They followed it to some point below its confluence with the Ohio, where they became convinced that it discharged not into the Pacific but into the Gulf of Mexico. Feeling no compunction to journey farther, especially as they feared capture by the Spanish in New Spain, they returned to Montreal. During this journey, they hung a right just north of the present city of St. Louis, ascending for the first time the Illinois, which flows from the northeast, fed by smaller rivers and streams in the region south of Lake Michigan. In so doing, they realized great savings in both time and distance and quickened the penetration by Europeans of the river valley. Because transportation by water was much more efficient than by land, the only obstacle between the Illinois and Lake Michigan was the Chicago portage, a land bridge between the two. This was before the Sanitary Canal, before the Sears Tower, Rush Street, Al Capone, Richard Daley, the blues, Ina's Kitchen, the barge loads of brick, cement, and asphalt, and the masses of people.

La Salle had an assignment like that of Daumont de Saint-Lusson, who was sent by Frontenac's intendant, Jean Talon, to the west in search of "some communication with the South Sea that separates this continent from China." Talon directed La Salle toward the southwest to find the "river that we can hope some day to find the opening to Mexico." On November 2, 1671, Talon informed the king that La Salle had not yet returned from the west.[1] This letter adds weight to the assertions of Abbé Renaudot that after discovering the Ohio and Mississippi, La Salle next approached the area via the northern route favored by Jolliet. He ascended the Detroit River to Lake Huron,[2] passed through the Straits of Michilimackinac, then coasted down the shore of Lake Michigan to a river that led ultimately to the Illinois.

On these points—his alleged discovery of the three rivers—La Salle's biographers break like a fault in the earth. His sympathizers—Pierre Margry, Paul Chesnel, Gabriel Gravier, John Gilmary Shea, and John Turrell—rely largely on Renaudot. His detractors—among them Céline Dupré, Hubert Howe Bancroft, and Father Jean Delanglez—accuse Abbé Renaudot of ulterior motives, for it was he, a skilled petition writer, who later (with Abbé Bernou) helped La Salle solicit the aid of Louis XIV in colonizing Louisiana.

Céline Dupré wrote that the case for La Salle's discovering the Ohio and Mississippi rests primarily on a *Récit d'un ami de l'abbé de Gallinée* ("an account written by a friend of Abbé Gallinée") and a *Mémoire* furnished by Abbé Bernou, the latter a member of Renaudot's circle.

"Eusèbe Renaudot," wrote a skeptical Dupré, "an outstanding orientalist, a polyglot and a member of the French Academy . . . famed for his erudition," was "very valuable to Louis XIV in that monarch's relations with Rome, England and Spain. Renaudot's passion for the sciences, among them geography, his religious zeal, tinged with Jansenism and hostility to the Jesuits, made him just the person to become the protector of La Salle, an explorer in perpetual conflict with the sons of Loyola [the Jesuits]." Dupré dismisses the *Récit* as an anti-Jesuit pamphlet whose objectivity therefore is "doubtful."[3]

Bernou's "Mémoire" he discounts because the priest aspired to become "the explorer's paid agent, and even dreamed of an episcopate in the territories with which La Salle might be expected to enrich the kingdom of France."[4]

Francis Parkman, choosing the middle road, mulled over the evidence for and against, finally taking the position that because La Salle himself made no mention of discovering the Mississippi, probably he did not.[5] But Parkman did give La Salle the Ohio (and probably the Illinois as well), in part because two of Jolliet's maps bear the respective inscriptions "route of the sieur de La Salle for going into Mexico" and "river down which the sieur de La Salle went on leaving Lake Erie, to go into Mexico." Dupré protested, saying that both are "interpolations having nothing to do with Jolliet, the first being of unknown origin, the second in the hand of Bernou himself."[6]

Embedded in these debates are assessments of La Salle's character. Objectivity languishes, which affirms the interpretive nature of history. Those who think La Salle beat Jolliet to the Illinois rate him a tragic-heroic visionary; those who favor Jolliet label La Salle an inexperienced, wild-eyed bungler.

Which begs the question of whether *I* would have liked La Salle. Strangely, I have seldom considered the matter. I fix on the miles covered: Anyone who could spend the better part of twenty years walking back and forth across these vast, uncharted lands is worthy of admiration. La Salle's faithful lieutenant, Henri de Tonti, walked and canoed an estimated 85,000 miles in pre-America. An average of about 3,300 miles each year. Nearly 10 miles a day . . . day in, day out. La Salle, though he died seventeen years before Tonti, was on track toward similar numbers. One stroke forward, two back—his wanderings were Sisyphean. His "rock" was not the pre-American wilderness, which he was capable of rolling to the summit, but the unattainable vision of his own creation, and that is what consumes and ultimately crushes brilliant, driven men.

But the controversy surrounding the discovery of the Mississippi extends beyond La Salle's missing years. In 1923, Father Francis Borgia

Steck, a Franciscan scholar, was asked to deliver an address at Quincy College in Quincy, Illinois, a trading post on the Mississippi River, on the 250th anniversary of Jolliet and Marquette's voyage down the Mississippi. Marquette is revered in the state, not only for his part in exploring the great river, but also for founding the first French mission on the Illinois River, at the Illinois village of Kaskaskia, where we now stood at Tom Novak's marina, and for the sentimental evocation of his slumbering death on the frozen shore of Lake Michigan. Towns and townships were named for him. So, too, rivers. Statues were erected.

After much careful research, what Father Steck learned was a shock: Marquette in all probability did none of these things. In 1928 Father Steck published the first of several obscure books detailing his findings, including *The Jolliet-Marquette Expedition 1673* and *Marquette Legends*. The conclusions seem largely overlooked by historians. Don't mess with saints or those nearly regarded as such. In the 343 laborious pages of *Marquette Legends*, Steck dissects the cases for and against Marquette's participation in the Jolliet expedition. The culprit behind all these "legends" is none other than Father Dablon, the Jesuit superior. The opportunity for revisionism was possible because Jolliet, when returning triumphantly to Montreal, overturned his canoe in the rapids. Lost were his journal and maps. Also, some members of his party, including an Indian boy entrusted to his care. Jolliet was despondent. Though he had supposedly left a copy of his journal with Marquette in Green Bay, he met with Father Dablon, who transcribed an oral account of the trip. In 1681, Melchisedech Thevenot, a Parisian publisher, printed a "narrative" of the Jolliet expedition. The narrator, in what Steck calls an "unpardonable" breach of truth, is none other than Marquette! Dablon's motive? The "misguided zeal for the glory and influence of the Order."[7] Indeed, the Jesuits were just as fanatical about their order as they were about Christianity.

The story was further complicated by the discovery, in 1844, of the so-called *Montreal Narrative*, supposedly based on the copy of Jolliet's journal left with Marquette. Everyone thought this would set the record straight. But it too was doctored, not by Father Dablon but by a collector named Jacques Viger. Worse, it turns out that the *Montreal Narrative* was written by neither Jolliet, Marquette, nor Dablon, but by a Father Martin, who arrived in Montreal in 1842. His version, Steck claims, is merely an "amplification of the Thevenot *Narrative*."

No wonder that Jolliet severed relations with the Jesuits. Not only had much credit for the expedition been attributed to Marquette, who very likely did not even accompany him, but for various other reasons he had fallen from the favor of Governor Frontenac and his successors. Jolliet died in 1700, "probably in September, the exact date being unknown. Neither is it known how he died, where he breathed his last, nor where he was laid to rest."[8]

But Father Dablon wasn't through making mischief. Because all of the Jesuit missionaries' *relations* (accounts of his activities that each missionary was obliged to write annually) were submitted to him, similar opportunities permitted Father Dablon to place Marquette at the Kaskaskia village at Starved Rock before Father Claude Allouez. The latter was, in fact, the true founder of the Kaskaskia mission.

Nothing is as it seems. Imposters are unveiled. The vain are unmasked. Or are they? The truth is lost in pre-America. Even if we could through a time machine return to yesteryear, the trees and streams could not speak. Those who know are dead and uncaring.


Once *Pearl* was fully packed and I was satisfied that the dock lines were secure, we began the drive south, taking a state highway across the river toward Interstate 39.

Steve repeated that he did not believe the fisherman at Starved Rock Marina, that there must be bass in the Illinois River. Nor could he believe the man was throwing back twenty-inch fish. I made a poor effort at defining "sport," concluding that some people just want something to do while sitting on the bank. The concept of "catch and release" seemed anathema to Steve.

As the trailer swung wide onto the entrance ramp, one of the black rubber rollers that cushion the boat flew off, a line drive shot that caromed off the pavement into the grass, rustling the stalks like a scared rabbit. I stopped the car and stood on the shoulder. Corn stretched as far as the eye could see; only a cluster of silos broke the edge between land and sky. Overhead, a crop duster banked sharply, the yellow bi-wings catching the sun. I kicked at the grass, halfheartedly looking for the roller, catching only burrs on my cuff.

There were no rooms in Bloomington. We continued south. With the engine relieved of the boat's weight, the air conditioner resurrected itself. An hour after sunset we stopped at a Super 8 motel standing by itself in the middle of a cornfield—like the farmhouse in the Talking Heads movie *True Stories*. We ate dinner at a Hardee's, then returned to our room, and called Andra. The AC was cranked. It was cold. I slept, dreaming of the river, in the absence of firsthand knowledge making it over to fit my idea of pre-America, which was obfuscated by contradictions: the current alternately languid and violent; the colors light in the mainstream, dark near shore; its nature sometimes joyous, sometimes malevolent.

Saturday, August 12, all day we aimed south down the floodplain of the Mississippi River valley, crossing the river at Cairo (pronounced KAY-row), so named because the city bridges the peninsula that breaches the Ohio and Mississippi and resembles in geography and fertility the city of Cairo, Egypt, situated on the Nile. The area, and farmlands to the south as far as Memphis, Tennessee, is known as Little Egypt.

The temperature drove past one hundred degrees and again the air conditioner was overwhelmed. The texture and color of the landscape changed subtly from corn to cotton.

We recrossed the river entering Memphis and stopped at the Best Western Riverbluff Hotel. The black desk clerk told us he had no rooms, but I had the distinct impression that he simply didn't want us staying at his hotel. A sign welcomed the Rucker Family Reunion and from the outdoor pool we heard the screams and yelps of children dunking and splashing.

Feeling suddenly alien in our own land, like a black in white America, we stopped outside the hotel on a grassy bluff and studied the river below, which roiled under the highway bridge, folding into itself in shelves and eddies. A small runabout played with the current, keeping its bow pointed upstream in the way of hovering salmon contemplating the falls before it.

"Not too muddy," Steve observed.

Downriver, the water shimmered in the last of the hazy sun, the low, green banks winding away toward the gulf. In the fading light, the surface reflected the sky and did not show the sediment the water contains—forty-two pounds per thousand cubic feet.

Turning, we saw a tall fellow in a sleeveless T and polished boots park a Harley-Davidson and dismount at the edge of the grass. He strode toward us, interested, I assumed, in the view. In his hand he carried what we took to be a gun belt, swinging it lightly. Steve stopped to watch him, caring little that he might be caught staring. (He thought himself invisible, as children do, because they are lower to the ground, because they are used to no one listening.) As the man passed I could see that the belt actually held a hammer, level, and wrench, slung ever so perfectly like a nickel-plated magnum. Have roofing job, will travel. I told Steve, but he did not believe me: "I'm sure it's a gun," he whispered.

As we pulled away, Steve warned me to look where I was going, reminding me that we still pulled the trailer. Not only was he afraid I'd back into another truck, he now speculated that the trailer tire would catch on the lip of a precipice, dragging us to our death in a deep and craggy ravine. This came as a complete surprise, for hitherto the only thing he had feared was the pinprick to remove a splinter. My God, perhaps he had a sense of mortality after all!

He also began to notice every passing police car, inquiring of our speed and any pertinent traffic laws, suggesting that I might be arrested. Which reminded me that I, too, had passed through a brief phase, at about his age, when at each passing of a cop I hid on the floor of the car. Mother issued vague reassurances, Father said they were the good guys, but I did not believe them.


We left Memphis early, not long after the sun rose steamy in the east. The air-conditioning was working well, which was difficult to understand because the temperature had been as high yesterday and the day before. We drove 380 miles, through Jackson, Mississippi, into Louisiana, entering the bayous where the highway is built over them on concrete pilings—a sort of causeway that shadows the trailers and rectangular flat-bottomed johnboats aground on the patches of hard earth below.

Today Steve counted twenty-five farts.

Joke: What is your favorite color? Blue.

What is your favorite animal? Dog.

What is your favorite number? Seven.

Punch line: Have you ever seen a blue, seven-legged dog?

Steve repeated the questions over and over, insisting that we take turns at the game, and I could not understand why he continued to find it amusing, knowing the construction.

At a roadside variety store I bought him his first pocket knife. The label said "pipe tool," and the blade was dull, but he accepted it as a knife. In the parking lot he found a piece of wood, which he whittled fervidly, covering with shavings the floor and dash.

After an hour, he proudly displayed his work: "A snake!"

In the late afternoon we made New Orleans, heading straight to the marina complex at West End, where we had arranged to leave the car and trailer with Murray Yacht Sales. Stanton Murray told us to dump the trailer behind a neighboring business, Sintes Marine Hardware. "No charge. Good friend. Do something nice for him." Murray also agreed to broker *Pearl* once she arrived in New Orleans, which pleased me greatly.

Taking a room at the Best Western All Suites Airport Motel, we unwound in the unheated Jacuzzi playing pincer crab with our toes. Afterward, in our rooms, Steve ran circles around the wall separating the living room and bedrooms, catapulting himself from mattress to mattress in a sort of wild and jerky Mick Jagger stage step. I called Andra but Steve would not talk with her, despite saying all day that he wanted to. Said he needed a hamburger, then lost interest watching *Shark Week* on television. Five minutes later he was sound asleep.

In the morning we returned to the Jacuzzi. A small frog floated dead on the surface, perhaps a relative of my *oma kuna*, and I wondered what the river held for us, with no guardian spirit.

Driving back to West End we stopped at a hardware to buy washers, then to Skipper B trailers to buy trailer rollers, which were needed before *Pearl* could be hauled. Unfortunately, the proprietor had just one roller that would fit, but promised to order two more and have them in time for our arrival several weeks hence.

At noon we visited Stanton to sign the broker's agreement. His brother-in-law Michael drove us to the airport. There, sitting on stools, we ate a slice of cheese pizza and a giant pretzel. Steve spilled a Coke over himself. I changed his clothes in the men's room, thinking we hadn't come all that far from diapers.

Airborne, we flew over the Mississippi, which from thirty thousand feet looked like an intestine, bloated and convoluted.

Cousin Tony picked us up at Chicago O'Hare. By the time he arrived, Steve was filthy from running up and down a U-shaped concrete structure supporting the upper deck. The sun hurt my eyes and I could not find my sunglasses but had a vague recollection of the airline clerk in New Orleans calling after me.

The heat, as it had been everywhere, was suffocating, so much so that

Tony and his wife, Laurie, decided to put us up at her parent's air-conditioned home in Oak Lawn. Downtown, hundreds of elderly had succumbed to heat prostration. Medical authorities were mystified. In the backyard Steve found the amputated, reddish-brown tail of a small mammal, which suggested that even here in the upscale suburbs, you never know when you might get yourself ripped apart.

It was odd for me to watch Tony, a Ph.D. who teaches comparative literature (for example, the influence of French symbolist poets on T. S. Eliot) cooking hamburgers on a charcoal grill. If he hadn't married, I doubted he'd have ever learned how to fan coals and keep the patties from sticking.

Steve and I bunked in a guest room. I slept with a sheet and blanket, happy that the morrow was the day of our departure, the true beginning of this voyage down the river that bisects America, defining East and West, the great cleft La Salle followed, the vena cava of the continent, sending, spreading, and spilling itself on the long gradient down.

# CHAPTER 6

# *Dwellers on the Threshold*

*clear the way*
*in a sacred manner*
*I come*
*the earth*
*is mine*

—Sioux tribe, anonymous, *In the Trail of the Wind:*
*American Indian Poems and Ritual Orations*

The proprietress of Cajun Bait & Tackle pushed the horn-rims back to the bridge of her nose, stepped around the glass counter, and directed me down the far aisle to a large-scale fishing chart fastened to the wall with pushpins.

"There's a little of everything in the river," she said, pointing to our location just above the Starved Rock Lock and Dam. "Northern, striped bass, catfish, carp, shiners, crappies, you name it."

Pen-and-ink fish drawings were superimposed over the backwaters, channels, and side streams of the Illinois where the species were known to hang.

The woman was proud of her river, which she knew well, and while proffering advice she sold us a fishing license, a fillet knife, number 01 hooks, steel leaders and swivels, and a variety of spoons and iridescent lures, which she selected from pegboard racks with considerable deliberation—with *our* fishing needs in mind.

Obviously, she had mistaken me for a serious angler, but at the rate I was spending money, her confusion was understandable. I passed on the chart, not having the heart to tell her I had no intention of actually *looking* for fish, that if a pike happened by the boat, hooking itself by happenstance, fine, but I wasn't tilting up the motor to gunkhole in some shallow marsh to read the water and the grasses for *signs*.

"Try up under the dam; they've been having good luck there. How much you draw? Two feet? Forget it. Better ask my husband. He's out there now. You see a Starcraft with a blue top, that's him. Just go on over and tell him I told you to. Fish move around, you know, so what I'm telling you might be true, it might not."

Outside, standing in the gravel parking lot under the hot sun, Steve tugged at my shorts: "I told you, there *are* bass in the river."

Cousin Tony, who had driven us back to Starved Rock Marina, helped bring *Pearl* around to the fuel dock, the brief moments of motion teasing him with the river dream, and he smiled the smile of a man contemplating an escape, an eye bending around the river, picturing the form in which it would next reveal itself.

We filled the tank with gas, the coolers with ice, and at 2 P.M. we cast loose the dock lines and aimed the bow tentatively into the stream. Watching Steve, I thought it a pity Pete wasn't here to share just one more adventure. On one side of a card I carried, prepared by his mother and me and handed to friends at his funeral, is a photo of him steering a cruising catamaran on the Chesapeake Bay. On the other side were these words Margaret, my first wife, had selected from *Siddhartha*:

> There shone on his face the serenity of knowledge, of one who is no longer confronted with conflict of desires, who has found salvation, who is in harmony with the stream of events, with the stream of life, full of sympathy and compassion, surrendering himself to the stream, belonging to the unity of all things.
>
> "I have waited for this hour, my friend. Now that it has arrived, let me go."
>
> With great joy and gravity he watched him, saw his steps full of peace, his face glowing, his form full of light.[1]

Steve and I were borne on a stream of water, Pete on the stream of life, where one of the milestones is death; even then, the voyage is not entirely over, though I do not think of him sitting on a cloud playing a harp, or sitting in a meadow, as illustrated by fundamentalist Christian comic books, petting a tame lion. Rather, he endures as memories of the living, and the ashes I have sprinkled into the waters we sailed together—the bays and oceans where the wide gyre of the Gulf Stream circulates, so in that very real sense Pete continues to be, as in life, on the move.

Steve says, "Dad, if Pete were still alive, would he be my baby-sitter?"

I say, "Yes," and he is pleased at the prospect of ridding girls from another aspect of his life: They don't roughhouse or say dirty things, and you can't talk *about* girls *with* girls.

Slowly I put the throttle down, feeling the latent power of the outboard as *Pearl* surged forward, nose up; then, just when it seemed she might rear on her hind end and flip over backward, her nose gently lowered, the stern lifted itself from the water, and the hull came onto plane, into its designed attitude, free and fast.

Before me on the dash I glanced at the chart, the blue water and the yellow land, the hatched lines of the railways, the parallel solid lines of two-lane highways and the wavy demarcations of the sloughs and marshes, which were everywhere about us, though obscured by the bank, for when I raised my eyes all I could see were trees and the limestone outcroppings of Starved Rock.

Several miles downstream we approached out first lock. Slowing to an idle, I called the lockkeeper on channel 24 VHF, requesting permission to enter.

"Light's green. It's all yours, Captain."

The radio exchange was casual, requiring none of the protocol insisted upon by the Coast Guard. More like CB, in which callers identify themselves with handles rather than call signs.

We passed between the two steel gates, accepting a line dropped by the keeper, who did not break stride on his businesslike way from the upstream gates to the down. Then the gates swung closed and the water began to drop, falling away beneath us as if draining into the earth, the motion imperceptible, the only sensory clue the scrolling of slimy ladder rungs recessed into the concrete wall.

Tony, who had pursued us by road, hailed us from the deck of the observation center: "Hey, Dan! Just think, all this just for you!"

"I'm a taxpayer!" I yelled back. "I paid for this!"

"Not in the state of Illinois!"

Before I could come back with a rejoinder about federal funding, the gates ahead opened and a horn blew, signaling us to leave. I started the engine and inched forward. Looking back, I saw Tony grinning and, outside the lock, the dam and waterfall from the river water swirling and churning into us, avalanching at the hull. I gunned the engine and Tony could color us gone, speeding at twenty knots over the smoothing surface.

The length of inland waterways is measured in statute miles, beginning at the river's mouth. Day marks, the traffic signs of the river, are posted on the banks to aid the tug pilots in their navigation. They are positioned at the bends and midway along the straights so that at night the navigators can sight the lights and set a course on the rhumb line between any consecutive two.

We had begun our trip at mile 233, and at just mile 226 I tucked into the channel of the Vermilion River, which joins the Illinois at an oblique angle, trickling in from the east.

Francis Parkman wrote:

> Go to the banks of the Illinois, where it flows by the village of Utica, and stand on the meadow that borders it on the north. In front glides the river, a musket-shot in width; and from the farther bank rises, with gradual slope, a range of wooded hills that hide from sight the vast prairie behind them. A mile or more on your left these gentle acclivities end abruptly in the lofty front of the great cliff, called by the French the Rock of St. Louis, looking boldly out from the forests that environ it; and, three miles distant on your right, you discern a gap in the steep bluffs that here bound the valley, marking the mouth of the river Vermilion, called Aramoni by the French. Now stand in fancy on this same spot in the early autumn of the year 1680. You are in the midst of the great town of the Illinois,—hundreds of mat-covered lodges, and thousands of congregated savages. Enter one of their dwellings: they will not think you an intruder. Some friendly squaw will lay a mat for you by the fire; you may seat yourself upon it, smoke your pipe, and study the lodge and its

inmates by the light that streams through the holes at the top. Three or four fires smoke and smolder on the ground down the middle of the long arched structure; and, as to each fire there are two families, the place is somewhat crowded when all are present. But now there is breathing room, for many are in the fields. A squaw sits weaving a mat of rushes; a warrior, naked except for his moccasins, and tattooed with fantastic devices, binds a stone arrow-head to its shaft, with the fresh sinews of a buffalo. Some lie asleep, some sit staring in vacancy, some are eating, some are squatted in lazy chat around a fire. The smoke brings water to your eyes; the fleas annoy you; small unkempt children, naked as young puppies, crawl about your knees and will not be repelled. You have seen enough. You rise and go out again into the sunlight. It is, if not a peaceful, at least a languid scene. A few voices break the stillness, mingled with the joyous chirping of crickets from the grass. Young men lie flat on their faces, basking in the sun. A group of their elders are smoking around a buffalo-skin on which they have just been playing a game of chance with cherry-stones. A lover and his mistress, perhaps, sit together under a shed of bark, without uttering a word. Not far off is the graveyard, where lie the dead of the village, some aloft on scaffolds, above the reach of wolves. In the cornfields around, you see squaws at their labor, and children driving off intruding birds; and your eye ranges over the meadows beyond, spangled with the yellow blossoms of the resinweed and the Rudbeckia, or over the bordering hills still green with the foliage of summer.[2]

We tossed an anchor off the stern, ran the bow up on the beach, cut the engine, and leaped ashore. The sandy mud was firm and brown. Steve, having invented his own variation of the half hitch, tied the bowline to a log.

Walking up the incline and stepping through the border of trees, we saw beyond to the meadows of Indian grass, side oats grama, there the switchgrass, and a little farther along wildflowers—blue stem, late boneset, and the faintly colored evening primrose stippling the yellow fields that stretched on to the next band of trees.

We'd finally escaped. I returned to the boat and opened a beer. Steve decided to "bait up."

In a stream below us swam a family of blue-winged teal and on the banks a solitary pied-billed grebe stood motionless, listening to our clamorous voices.

Time passed as slowly as my desires. Shadows of shapely white clouds moved across the plain. In the trees the insects clicked and the crows cawed.

"Nothing's biting," Steve said, which was more of an observation than a complaint. He peered over the side into the looking-glass water, which was disturbed only by the circular ripples whose epicenter was the hole made by the monofilament. Nibbles or no, he seemed satisfied to have a hook in the water, soothed by the handling of familiar instruments.

"Dad, what does a worm look like to a fish?"

"Like a worm."

"But fish don't know what worms look like."

"They don't?"

"How could they? Worms live on land. In dirt. Fish have never seen them before."

I allowed as how he was probably right, adding that fish are not very smart and, probably, if the crawler smells right, as it surely must, the fish simply considers it a safe and delectable meal. As it surely is, unless, of course, there is a hook in it.


Nothing was ever said of Steve's grandfather's Parkinson's Disease or that when it had progressed to obvious stages, he began to experience hallucinations. A fish story I would not yet tell: In the middle of the night Mother found Father gurgling on the bedroom floor, believing that he was a fish swimming under ice, flailing at the fishermen above who had spotted him and stopped to chop a hole in the transparent barrier. All his life, he'd hated hunting and fishing, loathe to pull the trigger on any other form of animal life, and in the hell of his disease, became the hunted.

I shot a .22 the summer of '58 at Camp Manitou in the northern woods of Michigan. But guns never took. Later I discovered the slingshot, a wooden Whamo with a leather pouch and long rubber. A park gardener apprehended me exploding milk bottles set on a neighbor's back porch and felling his long-stemmed flowers (the object was to make the cut so cleanly that the top half fell stem first). But it was killing a hummingbird that finally made me put my slingshot down. A lucky shot, really: I wheeled, drew, and knocked it out of the sky with a ball bearing—a deadly "steelie" whose trajectory was truer than that of a rock. The distaste my father felt for killing came round when I saw the tiny red tinge of blood on its beak. I remember staring at it on the ground, neatly camouflaged by the sticks and grass and fallen leaves, feeling sickened and shocked. I have not killed an animal since. Only mosquitoes, ticks, and flies. If I find a spider in the house, I place it outdoors.

Steve and I talked about wantonness, the preciousness of life, and other concepts necessary to a fisherboy and not wholly misunderstood.

But like Audubon, who shot birds in order to paint them, Steve liked to keep his catch.

I admonished, "Keep only what you eat."

He could not argue on moral grounds, so grabbed at the pragmatic: "But Dad, you can use the little fish for bait. Or cut 'em up for chum! What's the diff?"

"The *difference* is not whether it is acceptable to kill an animal to help kill another that can be eaten; it is whether you actually use it for bait or let it rot in a bucket for three days until your father can't stand it any longer and throws it overboard."

"Geez. That stinks."

"Not as much as chum."


The towns of La Salle, Peru, and Hennepin passed to starboard, the red bricks, white clapboards, and green shutters opening and closing behind the trees. The latter was named for the Franciscan priest, also a diarist, who accompanied La Salle on his early discoveries and who later, during an exploration of the Minnesota woods, claimed to have followed the Mississippi to the Gulf of Mexico (he did not; historians dismissed his narrative as the fabrication of a wannabe).

By 5 P.M. I began looking for a place to anchor, choosing the channel inside Lower Twin Sister Island, abreast of Swan Lake on the north side of the shore. As we had done all this day and would do all the days to come, we dwelt alone on the river that was our world, between the banks and levees and narrow walls of white and black oak, elm, black walnut, hackberry, and tamarack, which hid the surrounding landscape from us, and us from its farmers and drivers.

As soon as the hull wedged itself into the sandy bank, Steve baited up.

The sky clouded over and we heard thunder, soon feeling the gentle, cooling droplets of rain. Protected in a fashion by the Bimini canvas covering the forward half of the cockpit, we watched the houseboats from Starved Rock Marina push downstream, the sound of their air conditioners trailing after them.

The flies sought refuge with us, and we had no swatter. As dusk fell, the cicadas began their rhythmic, pulsing song. Steve alternately swam in the murky shallows and fished, catching a twelve-inch silver bass, which I put on ice.

I fitted the screens to the two hatches and when the first mosquitoes appeared we slipped below into *Pearl's* tiny cabin, lying on top of the sleeping bags. Two battery-operated fans played a light breeze over us as I read to him the first chapter of *Huckleberry Finn*.

Once Steve was asleep and the light extinguished, I lay back with my head cupped in my hands, staring at the water patterns reflected on the window above him. The days were exhausting, the heat taking whatever energy wasn't expended on Steve and navigation. Part of me wished he'd hurry and grow up, another mourned the anticipation of loss, the time when a boy begins the painful break, the quest for independence and self-identity, and Dad, he's square, the aggregation of too many bittersweet feelings, even his body smell too revealing of the boy's own animalness.

We had some years left, I knew, days like these when he would beg for a piggyback ride, tickle my armpit, lean against me in the store. And nights left, like this night, Steve lying next to me in the cabin of a very small boat, learning the ineffable truths about boats, not unlike the time, when I was eleven, that I slept beside my father inside a tree.


As a forestry professor and research scientist, my father spent winters in the classroom and summers in the woods. When his breaks did not overlap mine, I was brought along on field trips, where I listened to him teach students how to recognize various diseases, how to measure the acids in soil, and how to prune limbs for maximum yield. At home I would find him in his workshop chipping at some abstract sculpture educed from a seasoned piece of apple wood. We lived in an orchard and there is no doubt that I was subtly and indelibly conditioned to love wood. But not the way he did.

One summer, en route to a consulting job of my father's with the Weyerhaeuser Paper Company, we camped in Sequoia National Park. Without any sign of premeditation, he called me to his side and set off into the woods, leaving Mother and my sister Jean in the trailer. He was searching for a hollow tree with the stated intention of sleeping inside it. His stride was long; my feet and my mind raced to keep the pace. *Inside?* We hiked several miles from the campgrounds and at dusk rolled out our sleeping bags inside the blackened cavity of a thousand-year-old giant. The gash had been caused by lightning, a primary means of regeneration. Life from the fire. On all fours I crawled the perimeter. A bat brushed my cheek, and were it not for Father's insistence, I would have bolted. We lay down amid the pungent smell of decomposing bark and needles. The darkness was absolute. My thoughts were of the four thousand tons of wood above and around me, the fibers and capillaries, and the rings too numerous to count. At last we slept.

For my father, it was an act of intimacy and respect for the beautiful plant forms he had studied so long and so well. They were *alive* and he believed he could *know* them. Know them the way I know this boat, its motion under way and at rest, and know whether it feels right or wrong.

In the morning, Steve swam while I boiled water on the camp stove. I made tea, ate a granola bar, then cleaned the fish, which I could not fry because I could not find the vegetable oil. After the mosquitoes left, the flies returned. Shopping list: fly swatter, cooking oil, sponge, toilet paper, and towels, though the latter were hardly necessary, given the heat. Even at the day's coldest, around 4 A.M. when I might pull the sheet to my knees, the temperature still measured in the low seventies.

Steve dried in the sun while taking inventory of his tackle box. I cleaned the cockpit and made notes in the log. At nine I started the engine and let it warm up. Steve hoisted the anchor and I turned slowly into the swift current, increasing the rpm gradually for fear of shocking the cold engine into a block-splitting thrombosis. After a few minutes I pushed the throttle down and we leaped onto plane. Just as suddenly, the engine faltered, surprising me no less than if it had been my own heart. It was as if the fuel line had suddenly been pinched; the smooth drone was broken by a popping sound, and the boat fell off plane. No sooner had the bow fallen than it rose again and the engine smoothed.

Help was the nearest town, Henry, six miles downstream, situated at the end of a bridge that soon crossed the river. We tied up against the stonewall of an old lock laid into the earthen promontory that had once formed the north side of the structure.[3] Here, as elsewhere along the Illinois, gasoline was stored in a small, above-ground tank set well up the riverbank, with a long hose and nozzle snaking down to the dock. A tall, lean man in his early forties parked a pickup among the trees. He unlocked the pump, then talked of this and that and mostly nothing at all while Steve fished and I pumped. Lived here all his life, he said, which should not have surprised me, but did because I assume that everybody is from someplace else, that most people are sufficiently desperate to move out from under the weight of their hometowns to somewhere new and different. He was quite amused with Steve, commenting on the goodness of fishing and how it keeps youngsters on the straight and narrow, off the streets, and off drugs, which everywhere was regarded as the particular nemesis of our time.

After fueling we motored a few yards over to the town float, to which we tied *Pearl*; we locked the cabin and walked into town with our shopping list. The grocery and hardware stores, a block apart, were nearly empty, as were the streets of Henry, where the business names were like a directory of the folks we didn't see: Wilson Insurance Agency, Mother's Restaurant, Hafer's Pub, Hank's Hardware, William's TV. So that it seemed strangers such as us could open a door and say, "Hi, Hank. Didn't see you on the street this morning," and Hank would nod and say, "Hot enough for you?"

A block off the main street we stopped to watch two men with a chain hoist lift a dead cow from the bed of a pickup, swinging the carcass like a cable car into a dark garage. Except for the horse on the highway, Steve had never seen anything so large so dead. He held my sleeve until the shadows took it.

At the edge of town we made our last query in the hope of locating an OMC dealer, but succeeded only in purchasing a plastic cup of night crawlers from Don's Service Station—ninety-nine cents a dozen, more for the reds. Then we raced one another down the slope to the boat, Steve leaping off an embankment of railroad ties, sufficiently shortcutting the distance to win.

In the absence of an outboard mechanic to diagnose the cough in the 150, I pull-started the 7.5 backup motor, just to be safe, just in case we were swept beneath the overhang of a tow, powerless as in my dream, powerless like Pete before the train, waving uselessly for it to stop.

The sailing line marked on the chart took us across a number of narrow, shallow lakes and sloughs. From our vantage point, low on the river, the difference between them was indistinguishable. After passing Chilicothe Island, we entered Peoria Lake, really just the swelling and overflow of

*On Peoria Lake, not far from Fort Crèvecœur, Steve caught his first catfish.*

the banks accentuated by a downstream dam. There was a lake here even in La Salle's time. Halfway across, Steve blurted that he was both hungry and anxious to fish. Near the Detweiller Park light, I turned out of the main channel and aimed for a small fleet of boats on the shore, only to feel the outboard slow in the mud. Turning back to the channel, I anchored at its edge. Fifty yards away, an old man in a johnboat bobbed in the center of the channel; as we watched he netted three big ones. For Steve, each was a fist-slamming thrill.

"Let's go over there!"

"Not *in* the channel," I cautioned. "Look, here comes a big boat."

A cabin cruiser sped past the johnboat, missing it by fifteen feet. Though rocked by the waves, the fisherman seemed unfazed, and Steve was unconvinced.

"C'mon, Dad. Motor over there and ask him what he's catching."

So I did, asking myself whether it was better to stick to my position for the sake of authority or to relent in the face of compromising evidence. The voices: "I mean what I say . . . *most* of the time" vs. "Be flexible, man!"

"Bull cat," the man said, holding up a ten-pounder. "Got four of them. This one here's a buffalo."

"Buffalo what?"

"Buffalo *fish*. The water's so warm they're all down in the holes. I'm sitting over one right now."

Acting on insider advice, Steve guided me toward holes by the images on our LCD fish finder. Zeroing in on the lentic dwellers. We reanchored over a hole twenty-two feet deep, and in minutes Steve had a two-pound catfish, which he proudly held up for the fisherman, its shiny black skin glistening in the sunlight, reminding me that you don't scale a catfish, you *skin* it.

I called over, "Hey, how do you skin a catfish?"

He ignored me for a time, fussing with something in the bottom of his boat, then without looking said perfunctorily, "Cut the skin around the head, pull it off with pliers."

CHAPTER 7

# *Broken Hearts*

*The sky will weep,*
*The sky,*
*At the end of the earth;*
*The sky will weep.*

—Fox tribe, anonymous, *In the Trail of the Wind:*
*American Indian Poems and Ritual Orations*

Whether or not La Salle visited the Illinois during the missing years, he was indubitably present in their territory during the winter of 1679–80. He had some money now from a trading concession at Fort Frontenac, which with the help of the governor he had built near Kingston, Ontario, at the eastern end of Lake Ontario. In 1677, La Salle had returned to France and successfully petitioned Louis XIV for the grant. But where La Salle had asked for twenty years to build a string of forts in the western reaches of New France, the king had given him but five, "since we have nothing more at heart than the exploration of this country through which, to all appearance, a way may be found to Mexico." The king was of course thinking about the Spanish, who five years later, in 1683, would declare war on France. Relations between the two countries were strained, and the implementation of La Salle's plan would secure the river valley for France.

Though Louis XIV had given La Salle all he asked and more (the sole right to trade in buffalo hides), the five-year deadline made his exploration of the Mississippi even more urgent. He had come to the inevitable conclusion that there were no gilded pagodas towering beyond the next hilltop, and that the elusive and fabled Northwest Passage, if it existed at all, ran north to south rather than east to west. (The only true Northwest Passage, the Atlantic–Pacific sea route north of Canada, was not traversed until 1903–6, by Roald Amundsen.) Among the Illinois nation he found willing partners to further his trade, and on their lands he sought to establish himself.

The antecedent of La Salle's historic journey from lake to sea was beset with the kind of misfortune that followed him throughout his life, marking him to many as a failure. Though this first strike into Illinois territory ended short of its goal, it can be viewed as preparatory to his later success.

In the fall of 1679, at Green Bay, after watching the *Griffon* sail free of ice, carried to the horizon on a soft, westerly wind, loaded with pelts, La Salle canoed south along the western Lake Michigan shore, rounding the foot of the lake to disembark near St. Joseph, Michigan. The plan called for the *Griffon* to sail back to the Niagara River, where its cargo would be transferred for delivery and sale at Fort Frontenac. The proceeds would be used to pay La Salle's debts and to procure important supplies for his descent of the Mississippi. The *Griffon*'s Danish pilot, Luc, a large, intimidating man who had vigorously protested the small number of his crew, was to return the *Griffon* and the supplies to Michilimackinac, presumably before the onset of winter. But she was destined never to reappear. La Salle didn't know that yet, but his concern for her mounted daily. Rather than go looking for her, he determined to proceed onward toward the Mississippi. In wintertime he led his party overland through the snow to the Kankakee River and onward to the Illinois, at that juncture merely a thread of water.

Francis Parkman described the scene:

> Fed by an unceasing tribute of the spongy soil, it quickly widened to a river; and they floated on their way through a voiceless, lifeless solitude of dreary oak barrens, or boundless marshes overgrown with reeds.[1]

Ashore, the grass was scorched by Indian fires set by hunters of buffalo; their bleached skulls and carcasses were strewn across the prairie.

The scene changed again as they descended. On either hand ran ranges of woody hills, following the course of the river; and when they mounted to their tops, they saw beyond them a rolling sea of dull green prairie, a boundless pasture of the buffalo and the deer, in our own day strangely transformed,—yellow in harvest time with ripened wheat, and dotted with the roofs of a hardy and valiant yeomanry.[2]

Parkman, writing in the 1860s, noted that these changes were recent even to him, that "within the memory of men not yet old," wolves, deer, wild turkeys, swan, and pelicans had been common in this area, that in 1840 a friend of his had shot a deer from the window of a farmhouse near the present town of La Salle, and that "running wolves on horseback was his favorite amusement." Parkman lamented that the buffalo were long gone. For Steve and me, so were all the other game, save catfish and blue herons.

Not far below the Indian dwelling place at Buffalo Rock, La Salle and his party first saw the lofty cliff known today as Starved Rock, later the site of his Fort St. Louis. Below in the valley, near present-day Utica, they saw the great village of the Illinois Indians—Kaskaskias, Peorias, Kahokias, Tamaroas, and Moingona, all Algonquian speakers—and counted 460 lodges built of poles and covered with interwoven rushes, deserted at that time by the tribes, who traditionally departed for their winter hunting.

They continued southwest, entering an expanse of the river they called Pimitoui, now Peoria Lake. Just below it they saw smoke and, rounding a bend, eighty wigwams. Warned earlier that the Illinois Indians would regard them as enemies, La Salle ordered the eight canoes to move abreast in a warlike formation. The Indians set about in a panic, whooping and howling, making the *saçacoye*, or war cry, with a hand clapped across the mouth. La Salle leaped ashore, making no sign of friendship lest it be interpreted as a sign of weakness or fear. Two chiefs came forward offering the calumet, or peace pipe, which La Salle accepted. Some of the Indians showed welcome by rubbing the white men's feet with bear grease. La Salle in turn made presents of tobacco and hatchets. He then advised the chiefs that he had come to protect them and to teach them to pray to the true God. He promised to defend them against their enemy, the Iroquois, who, he told them, were themselves subjects of the Great King, Louis XIV (though hardly under his control, as the Illinois were well aware).

La Salle succeeded in winning their confidence, despite the treacherous plot of several other Frenchmen in the region, who sent to the Illinois chiefs a Mascoutin Indian named Monso who accused La Salle of spying for the Iroquois. La Salle, who suspected the troublemakers had been incited by Jesuits, spoke boldly to his hosts, saying that if he was in fact their enemy, he could have killed them in their sleep. And where were his accusers anyway?—vanished in the night!

In January 1680, when a thaw broke up the river ice, he left the camp of the Illinois and traveled downstream a half league to a low knoll on the southern bank with deep, marshy ravines on two sides. By digging a trench connecting the ravines, the men managed to isolate their knoll, which they further fortified with sharply sloping edges. A twenty-five-foot-tall palisade was constructed, as well as houses for the friars, a portable

*Drawings by Arthur Lagron, a railroad worker who in 1913 investigated probable locations of Fort Crèvecœur, were the basis for this sketch.* (ILLINOIS STATE HISTORICAL LIBRARY, SPRINGFIELD, ILLINOIS)

forge, and their ammunition. This was the first European community in the state of Illinois. Still distraught over the presumed loss of the *Griffon*, La Salle named the fortification Fort Crèvecœur, or "broken heart." "The name," wrote Parkman, "tells of disaster and suffering, but does not do justice to the iron-hearted constancy of the sufferer."[3]

Below the lake there is today a reconstruction of Fort Crèvecœur, owned by a private company and open to the public. It does not appear to be an entirely accurate effort, but close enough to give a sense of the formidable challenge such projects were to men laboring with crude tools. La Salle described its construction as follows:

> Two wide and deep ravines shut in two other sides and one-half of the fourth, which I caused to be closed completely by a ditch joining the two ravines. I caused the outer edge of the ravines to be bordered with good "chevaux-de-frise [*a fortification of projecting spikes*]," the slopes of the hillock to be cut down all around, and with the earth thus excavated I caused to be built on top a parapet capable of covering a man, the whole covered from the foot of the hillock to the top of the parapet with long beams, the lower ends of which were in a groove between great pieces of wood which extended all around the foot of the elevation; and I caused the top of these beams to be fastened by other long cross-beams held in place by tenons and mortises with other pieces of wood that projected through the parapet.
>
> In front of this work I caused to be planted, everywhere, some pointed stakes twenty-five feet high, one foot in diameter, driven three feet in the ground, pegged to the cross-beams that fastened the top of the beams and provided with a fraise at the top two and a half feet long to prevent surprise.
>
> I did not change the shape of this plateau which though irregular, was sufficiently well flanked against the savages. I caused two lodgments to be built for my men in two of the flanking angles in order that they be ready in case of attack; the middle was made of large pieces of musket-proof timber; in the third angle the forge, made of the same material, was placed along the curtain which faced the wood. The lodging of the Recollets [*friars*] was in the fourth angle, and I had my tent and that of the sieur de Tonti stationed in the center of the place.[4]

Archaeologists have not been able to locate or identify any direct evidence of the actual fort. La Salle described it as being built on a "hillock about 540 feet from the bank of the river; up to the foot of the hillock the river expanded every time that there fell a heavy rain."

In 1913, Arthur Lagron, an employee of the Peoria & Pekin Union Railway, examined a number of sites and concluded that the fort was just east of Wesley Slough, where today a dirt road crosses the Pekin & Pekin Union Railway yard. To one side is a parking lot for staging trailers, to the other several commercial buildings, light brown and nondescript. Perhaps it is fitting that now, as then, the occupants are engaged in the transportation of commodities, but the real heartbreak is the cheap utilitarianism of the site's plan—the absence of any architectural and landscaping aesthetic that everywhere across the land is a desecration of pre-America.

After lunch we passed through the lock at the dam. Maneuvering up and down the riverfront of Peoria, the largest city on the Illinois, was the first of many floating casinos we would see. The next year, a report for the Better Government Association would find that riverboat gambling was draining as much as $500 million a year from the state's economy. The legislators who approved the gambling measure had counted on picking the pockets of out-of-state tourists. The study found, however, that 84 percent of the casino patrons were residents of Illinois, and virtually none stayed overnight. A coauthor of the report, Ricardo C. Gazel, said, "Gambling does not create new wealth for an economy unless the players come from elsewhere." It seems the city fathers never figured it would take more than a casino boat to entice Iowans and Michiganders to Peoria.

By early afternoon it was time again to refuel, which we did at the Pekin Boat Club, a private organization perched on a bluff overlooking the river. A banner hanging from the clubhouse's deck proclaimed it the home of "Miss Illinois River Bottom: 1989, 1991." It was 2 P.M., Wednesday, and there were a few women and more men drinking at the bar. The locked door could be opened only by a key or code; I knocked until the Budweiser drinker nearest the door took notice. He requested the gas-pump key from the bartender and followed me back down the hill to the dock. I mentioned Fort Crèvecœur, to which he said, "We go there sometimes. The fall is fun when they have Rendezvous—a lot of mountaineers all dressed up."

Naturally we found Steve fishing; he held up a small catfish for our commendation.

My calculations of fuel consumption, which would become so important on the Lower Mississippi, indicated that we were averaging about two and a half miles per gallon, giving us a range, with present tankage, of about 125 miles. Not enough for the long runs in Missouri and Louisiana. Somewhere I'd have to buy jugs.

Thirteen miles downstream we tucked in behind Coon Hollow Island, anchoring away from the shore in a vain attempt to lose the mosquitoes. Anvil-shaped thunderheads piled up in the west and Bloomington radio reported storms.

As daylight waned, great blue herons stalked the shallows and black terns flitted against the graying of the sky, swooping to the water, looking for minnows, or perhaps simply engaging in a joyous rite of sunset, playing in the cool of dusk, all members of the flock.

I cleaned Steve's catfish, pulling the skin off with a pair of pliers, as instructed, then running the thin fillet knife down the spine to slice the meat from the ribs. I dropped the pieces in a plastic baggie with a cornmeal mix, then dumped the lot into the frying pan until the white meat flaked. The taste was good, with none of the fishy flavor we'd sometimes experienced in restaurants.

Steve made daily examinations of the eight stitches in his hand, the number of which was important, because the more there are, the more grievous the wound, the more pride in the suffering. Despite instructions to keep it dry, he had insisted on swimming, first wrapping his hand in a baggie held to his wrist with a rubber band. It hadn't worked very well, and after each dunking he went below to remove the wet dressing and rummage through his three medical kits in search of gauze, tape, and scissors, wrapping and unwrapping until he was either satisfied or bored or both.

That night he was restless, waking to the turnings of his dreams, sitting up to holler "Catfish!" and "Hook!" Once, he cuddled near to me and rubbed my chest, running his fingers through my hairs as if I were his dog, Tango.

Throughout the night the mosquitoes that inevitably penetrated our defenses buzzed in my ear. Before dawn an approaching tow shone its spotlight on *Pearl*, bathing the cabin in light. Sitting upright, I watched through the portlight as the pilot trained the high-intensity beam up and down the shore. Fully awake, I decided to start my day as well, and slipped under the netting into the cockpit, where I brewed a cup of tea and watched the sky lighten.

Later, when the sun was above the treetops, Steve enjoyed his morning swim. He balanced on the submerged anchor line, holding it in his toes. I heard him whisper "Dad!" and, looking, saw his lips barely above the water. At first it seemed he wanted me to check out some maneuver, and I resumed my chart work. He called again, gurgling, and suddenly I realized he was having difficulty keeping his head up. Hopping over the side, I reached into the silt-filled water and lifted him, discovering only then that he had wound the anchor line in a tightening loop around his ankle. I toweled him dry with a T-shirt (I'd forgotten to buy towels in Henry), and flashbacked to 1960, to a bungalow resort outside Papeete, Tahiti, when an outgoing current had carried me from the sunken Japanese ship on which my father and I were skindiving. He had had to carry me to shore on his back. Like Jack Kennedy after the sinking of *PT-109*. Some years later, for reasons that were clearer to him than to me, he sent me to a psychiatrist, with whom I discussed the incident. At the end of the session the shrink told me that I could not always count on my father to bail me out of trouble, that he could not always do so, and that I must learn to be responsible for my own actions. Offended, I vowed thereafter not to speak to him, and after six months of our staring at each other during our weekly fifty-minute "hours," the psychiatrist, and my parents, gave up.

Without the supplies carried by the *Griffon*, La Salle felt compelled to leave Fort Crèvecœur and return to Fort Frontenac to reprovision. He sent Father Louis Hennepin to explore the Illinois to its mouth. The missionary was reluctant to oblige but eventually agreed. La Salle commanded Henri de Tonti to hold the fort with but a dozen Frenchmen. Tonti, the son of an Italian financier who had designed the *tontine* (an early form of life insurance in which a group pays equally into a joint pot that is distributed to the last remaining survivor), had had his military career terminated when a grenade exploded in his hand. In its place he wore an iron fitting that he often covered with a glove. Having moved to France with his father, he became the protégé of the Prince de Conti, who did not know what to do with the young man. The matter resolved itself when Abbé Renaudot suggested that Conti introduce Tonti, whom he described as "honorable" and "amiable," to La Salle. Tonti and La Salle took an immediate liking to each other. In the years that followed, Tonti was one of the few men La Salle trusted, executing his orders faithfully and fearlessly. That the Indians respected his iron fist, which in skirmishes he sometimes used to smash heads, only added to his worth. The artist Lonnie Eugene Stewart, in a 1990 painting that commemorates the founding of Peoria, shows him dressed in a white coat with blue cuffs and gold belt, black leather boots to the knees, and a three-cornered hat. Like La Salle, he may well have occasionally dressed up (usually to impress Indians), but such garb was impractical for canoeing and hiking.

To replace the large forge, rigging, and anchors lost with the *Griffon*, which he needed for constructing and equipping a riverboat, on March 1, 1680, La Salle set out across the isthmus of Michigan with Nika and four Frenchmen. To one of his creditors he wrote:

> Though the thaws of approaching spring greatly increased the difficulty of the way, interrupted as it was everywhere by marshes and rivers, to say nothing of the length of the journey, which is about five hundred leagues in a direct line, and the danger of meeting Indians of four or five different nations, through whose country we were to pass, as well as an Iroquois army, which we knew was coming that way; though we must suffer all the time from hunger; sleep on the open ground, and often without food; watch by night and march by day, loaded with baggage, such as blanket, clothing, kettle, hatchet, gun, powder, lead, and skins to make moccasins; sometimes pushing through thickets, sometimes climbing rocks covered with ice and snow, sometimes wading whole days through marshes where the water was waist-deep or even more, at a season when the snow was not entirely melted,— though I knew all this, it did not prevent me from resolving to go on foot to Fort Frontenac to learn for myself what had become of my vessel, and bring back the things we needed.[5]

Carrying their canoes along the bank of the Illinois, La Salle and his party again passed Starved Rock. Thinking the mesalike top an excellent place where a few Frenchmen might repel Indian attackers, he sent word back to Tonti at Fort Crèvecœur to examine the mesa and to fortify it.

In an 1848 painting, George Catlin portrays La Salle and his men

La Salle Returns to Fort Frontenac by Sled, March 1680, *by George Catlin, painted in 1847–48.* (PAUL MELLON COLLECTION, © 1997 BOARD OF TRUSTEES, NATIONAL GALLERY OF ART, WASHINGTON, D.C.)

pulling a sled through knee-deep snow. They move along the bank of a lake, the fir trees bowed from the weight of snow on their boughs and the ice along the shore frozen in wave-shaped arcs. Such hardship and beauty lie at the heart of my fascination, the two imposing on each other a character of pre-America that is preternatural and in many places lost.

Eight days after leaving Starved Rock they saw the shimmering blue waters of Lake Michigan and soon arrived at Fort Miami at the mouth of the St. Joseph River. There the loss of the *Griffon* was confirmed. In all probability, La Salle had already resigned himself to this egregious setback. Still, in his heart of hearts he must have held out hope that somehow she had survived. As always, he was undeterred, revising again his heady plan.

Continuing toward Fort Frontenac on the 25th of March, La Salle wrote:

> The rain . . . lasted all day and . . . the woods, . . . were so interlaced with thorns and brambles that in two days and a half our clothes were all torn and our faces so covered that we hardly knew each other.[6]

Later, the woods became more open and the party found ample game, including bear, deer, and turkey. The carcasses they left behind marked their whereabouts to roving Indian parties, which came upon them as they slept.

> On the evening of the twenty-eighth, having made our fire by the edge of a prairie, we were surrounded by them; but as the man on guard waked us, and we posted ourselves behind trees with our guns, these savages, who are called Wapoos, took us for Iroquois, and thinking that there must be a great many of us, . . . they ran off without shooting their arrows, and gave the alarm to their comrades, so that we were two days without meeting anybody.[7]

Correctly inferring the cause of their fright, La Salle drew on the trunks of trees with charcoal the usual marks of an Iroquois war party, with signs for prisoners and scalps, to reinforce the Wapoos' suspicion that La Salle and his men were indeed Iroquois.

The artful plan nearly backfired when a band of Mascoutins, who were pursuing Iroquois, readied one morning to attack them, until upon seeing La Salle they recognized the Frenchmen as their "friends and brothers."

On April 4, according to a letter from La Salle to a friend, two of his men fell ill, and to meet this emergency he went in search of a river on which the others could safely transport the stricken men to Montreal. The river they found was the Huron, on whose banks, some miles west of Ann Arbor, Michigan, I once lived. Many times I canoed its rapids and walked the animal paths above its banks, thinking that if I could close out the sound of cars and trains, I might in the twilight see La Salle and his men steaming bark from the elms to cover the crude frame of a canoe, pressing sap into the seams, then gently launching into the stream and slipping silently away.

Milton Charboneau, an area resident given to wearing coonskin hats and paddling the old rivers to trace Indian highways ("I want to see where the Indians lived, and to prove that even in this day, all these river systems they used are still possible to travel"), believes La Salle built this canoe a few miles upstream from my old house. This site is just below Portage Lake, in the shadow of Peach Mountain, a vantage point where, according to La Salle, two portages and two rivers could be seen.

Of course, it was impossible to determine the precise place where La Salle built the canoe, nor was it particularly important other than for the peculiar wont of men to stand on a spot and know that years before others of some note stood there in the same manner, making a history, making it sacred to those of us fated to be followers in time.

So if the spot where I sat as a young man with my dog Caesar beside the railroad trestle above the Delhi Rapids was not "the spot," it did not matter. I knew La Salle had passed beneath me, passed the rushes on the bank where, years later, my son Peter, flung by the train, landed dead in the leafy fold like a pheasant or dog gone down to the river to die, now one of several ghosts that hallowed this place.


Driving down the Illinois River, this welling wetness was the tears of a father, tears for a son that could not be felt for a father, whose death was far more timely. Not just for Peter, but also for Steve, who would not know until he too became a father why I sometimes looked at him so, in some strange way making him and Peter one in their son-ness to me so that the grieving for one, despite becoming a hope for another, was a sadness for both.

CHAPTER 8

# The Wreck of the Griffon

*I leaned over and caught my breath. There she was, resting quietly in the clean blue water; opened out and settled peacefully. There was no scepticism now. No doubt. Below me, resting serenely beneath the waters of this inner cove, was the Griffon, the little barque whose loss broke La Salle's heart. Now she was a skeleton of oak in a light blue grave.*

—Harrison John MacLean, *The Fate of the* Griffon

After covering a thousand miles over a period of sixty-five days, La Salle and his haggard followers finally completed their cross-country trek and on May 6, 1680, entered the gates of Fort Frontenac. Waiting was a woman—the only woman, perhaps, to whom he showed affection—Madeleine de Roybon d'Allonne. Three years younger than La Salle, Mademoiselle d'Allonne was born in Montargis, France, and had come to New France alone, perhaps to find a husband. From La Salle she had obtained land around the fort and presumably managed some sort of income, as she was able to make him several loans. But whatever the nature and degree of his interest in her, the wilderness called more loudly.

On the tenth of August, 1680, La Salle was reprovisioned and returned to the Illinois, hoping to reach Tonti before any more disasters befell the mission. On the Illinois, the party found the prairies alive with game and killed many buffalo, which were cavorting in the waters. But this was not the scene at Fort St. Louis at Starved Rock, which, according to La Salle's instructions, Tonti had fortified, nor at the nearby Illinois village, which had vanished. The meadow was blackened by fire. Human skulls were stuck on poles, and wolves picked at the remains. Crows and buzzards darkened the sky. La Salle recognized the hand of the Iroquois, who already had destroyed the nations of the Hurons, the Neutrals, and the Eries. Though fragments of French clothing were found, there was no sign of Tonti.

Leaving some of his party hidden on a midstream island, La Salle and a few others paddled downstream, witnessing along the banks the signs of the fleeing Illinois and pursuing Iroquois. At Fort Crèvecœur he found the vessel still in the stocks, its iron nails and spikes drawn out. On one of the planks were written the words "Nous sommes tous sauvages: ce 15 — 1680" ("We are all savages on this 15 A . . . 1680"), written by men who deserted after Tonti left to secure Starved Rock. La Salle followed the river to its juncture with the Mississippi but found no sign of the loyal Tonti, and so turned his back on the river of his dreams, and returned upstream to rejoin those who waited on the island. Then, feeling it futile to again turn south, he returned to Fort Miami, on Lake Michigan. Months later, Tonti and La Salle were reunited at Michilimackinac, at the upper tip of Michigan's lower peninsula, and the enterprise was begun anew.


Over the years, eleven Great Lakes wrecks were thought to be that of the *Griffon*, but none was authenticated. Each discovery created a bit of a stir in archaeological circles and in the newspapers, because, after all, she was the first ship on the upper lakes and had come to symbolize both La Salle's achievements and failures. These wrecks included one found in 1848 in the sand near Hamburg, New York, on Lake Erie (later determined to be a British man-of-war circa 1768); one discovered in 1934 off Birch Island, near Hessel, Michigan, a town on the north shore of Lake Huron, not far from the Straits of Mackinac (but found by divers to be 120 feet long, more than twice the length of the *Griffon*); some cannon and timbers found near Eighteen Mile Creek on Lake Erie; and another wreck discovered in 1927 on the rocky shore at the western end of Manitoulin Island, just east of the other supposed site at Hessel. The 1927 discovery seemed promising because six skeletons were found in a nearby cave, one with a large skull that proponents figured might belong to the pilot, Luc, a man of very large proportions. The presence of threaded bolts, however, quickly debunked any claims that she was the *Griffon*.

*Painting of the* Griffon, *La Salle's ship built on the shores of Lake Erie in Cayuga Creek, near Buffalo. She is shown here slipping along the lake shore at dawn. The* Griffon *sank on the return leg of its maiden fur-trading voyage to Green Bay, in 1679. Several wrecks have been claimed to be that of the* Griffon, *but none has been authenticated.* (PAINTING BY RAYMOND MASSEY, MEMBER, THE AMERICAN SOCIETY OF MARINE ARTISTS)

The most recent wreck to show promise was found in 1952, on Russell Island, just north of the Bruce Peninsula, which defines the western rim of Georgian Bay in Lake Huron. While researching shipwrecks, the *Toronto Telegram* journalist Harrison John MacLean met a local man named Orrie Vail who told him of a particular wreck known to his family for many years and escorted him to the Russell Island site. Archaeologists removed and studied timbers found resting in the cold, clear waters of the cove, as well as a number of nails and other fasteners thought to be used only by French carpenters during the latter half of the seventeenth century.

During the summer of 1976, a year after sailing through Green Bay's Port des Morts and learning of the *Griffon*'s ill-fated maiden voyage, I undertook the first of many attempts to apprehend La Salle, still believing in the idea that one can know something by placing himself in its proximity.

So I bought a nineteen-foot English twin-keeler, which was ideal for exploring the islands of Georgian Bay because it was both trailerable and stable. With me were Cousin Tony and our culinary friend, Frank Viviano. Together we trailered the boat to Tobermory, Ontario, a small fishing village at the tip of the Bruce Peninsula. The outcroppings of granite, known as the Laurentian Shield, were crowned with cedar and the dark green of evergreens. Devoid of industry, the town was slowly awaking to tourism; the water was clear, the air sweet with the smell of fir. Along the waterfront skin divers sat on benches and squeezed into wet suits. Face masks and air tanks were thrown randomly into rubber rafts half launched. Townspeople—predominantly Irish and Scots—stood in the background, conversing with folded arms. Cruise boats, like the converted fishing craft *Ahab*, signed on passengers for picnicking at Flowerpot Island.

We launched the *Compass Rose* and motored around the point from Tobermory to Big Tub, a mile-long indentation where there was a government wharf but no store. We anchored in eighteen feet on a limestone bottom. The anchor flukes needed coaxing to bite. Evening. Except for starlight on the water, all that was visible were the anchor lights of other boats, swinging in the rigging.

Below us, underwater, were the muted beacons of three lights, turning, all the while coming closer, until they illuminated the shapes of divers. Surfacing, the divers informed us we were anchored above *The City of Grand Rapids*, an old side-wheeler driven into the cove on fire. Then they dove again, their lights disappearing through the ship's hold, revealing a dozen open portlights. In the morning the *Compass Rose* had swung around, and below us the full length of the wreck was visible, the ragged hole in her deck behind the hold, the starboard rail gone, the decks clean of any growth. With a little work, it seemed she might sail again.

Borne on a fresh east wind, we sailed north several miles toward Russell Island, doused the sails at the cove entrance, and cautiously motored inside. The bottom, which was easily discerned, appeared as fossilized mud, pockmarked with quarter-size craters. After anchoring we rowed ashore in the dinghy and walked ankle-deep in water about the site, where, as we knew from photos in MacLean's book, the *Griffon*'s keel had rested for nearly three hundred years. Like a bird I stalked the shallows, shading my eyes from the reflections, searching for a nail or bolt, any small piece to connect me. Though I did not realize it at the time, this futility was to pre-echo the conclusions of two decades' quest for tangible proof of La Salle's presence in North America, for an artifact of any sort that I could actually get my hands on . . . until many years later, on a day in Texas, where La Salle's and my own stories end.

MacLean believed that the *Griffon* had been hauled into the shallow water by men on the shore pulling ropes; perhaps she'd been scuttled by the crew, who made off with her valuable cargo of pelts. Then again, she might have been burned by jealous Indians, who saw the French as a threat to their trade. For his part, La Salle, after interrogating a young Indian, believed that the pilot, Luc, had offloaded the furs, treacherously sunk the ship, then headed west to the Mississippi and into present-day Minnesota to join the chief of the coureurs de bois, Du Lhut. The Indian, La Salle wrote, had seen a white man answering the description of Luc, who was held prisoner by a tribe living beyond the Mississippi.

On my return home, I wrote to the National Museum of Canada to ask why they had not authenticated the Russell Island wreck (or Griffon Cove wreck, as some call it) as being that of the *Griffon*. F. J. Thorpe, the chief of the History Division, wrote in response:

> Underwater archeologists of the National Historic Parks and Sites Branch, Parks Canada, Department of Indian Affairs and Northern Development, believe the Tobermory wreck to be the remains of a shallow-draft British gunboat of a type commonly used in the war of 1812–1814, rather than the deep-draft vessel *Le Griffon* is known to have been. The matter has been discussed at meetings of the National Historic Sites and Monuments Board of Canada, which decided that the evidence favouring the Tobermory wreck as that of the *Griffon* was not proven.

Later, I tracked down the nautical archaeologist Paul Hundley's 1980 Texas A&M University master's thesis, "The Construction of the Griffon Cove Wreck," in which he concluded, on the basis of analysis of the timbers and artifacts, that it was "a smaller, local variation of a Mackinaw boat that had been abandoned in the mid-1800s."

This disappointing conclusion forces one to take greater stock in Father Louis Hennepin's journal, according to which Indians told La Salle they had seen the *Griffon*, not long after it had left Green Bay, "tossing in an extraordinary manner, unable to resist the tempest, so that in a short time they lost sight of her, and they believe that she was either driven on some sand bank, or that she foundered." This occurred in northern Lake Michigan, by all counts 150 to 200 miles from Russell Island. MacLean had noted references to the finding of hatch covers and other flotsam on Mackinaw Island not long after the *Griffon*'s departure from Green Bay, but dismissed them. Furthermore, in 1722 the author Charles LeRoy wrote that the *Griffon* had sailed only five or six leagues from its anchorage before being driven into a bay. There, Indians boarded the vessel, killed the crew, and set all afire.

MacLean, like other amateur archaeologists for a century before him, thought he had the *Griffon* in his hands, only to lose her to the critical analysis of experts.

Presumably, the first ghost ship of the Great Lakes remains just that, a ghost ship, which means it is still there, somewhere in or on the lake, waiting, like the river, for me.

And the big river drew nearer with each bend in the Illinois. We were intentionally pokey, seeing no point in arriving at the St. Louis marinas before my daughter, Adria. We'd been on the river three days and had but one to go. If we'd wanted to, we could have covered the entire length of the Illinois in twelve hours, pedal to the metal, but what was the point? If we wanted to sense La Salle, we couldn't go slowly enough.

Steve, his nasty oyster-shell gash still bandaged, would not allow me to cut his stitches with any of the tools at our disposal—nail clippers, wire cutters, or pocket knife. He preferred to pick at them with a small scissors from his first-aid kit, poking one blade underneath, then cautiously snipping until the cord frayed. When he held the last stitch between his thumb and finger, which we both inspected closely, he said gravely, "It's like graduation or something."

When I saw him growing bored, I slowed, finding anchorage in Bath Chute at mile 113. He quickly lost a lure that became snagged on a bottom log and was agitated. We moved on to Hamm's Boat Harbor, tying to a half-sunken fuel dock. On the hill above us, across a muddy lot, was a small restaurant that sold double cheeseburgers for $1.75. Beneath the glass-covered bar were photos of hunters and dead animals, sleds and giant catfish caught along the nearby banks, reminding Steve that we needed more worms. When we inquired about bait, the bartender told us he had none, but made a call into town and advised us that one of his regular patrons would bring a box when he came for lunch. Soon, a man in a Caterpillar baseball hat and red plaid shirt dropped a cardboard Chinese take-out container on our table. He accepted a few dollars but no tip, preferring to complain of the heat, to which I said come January we'd be whining about the cold, and he allowed as how he'd like that better.

On the restaurant radio, the sound of Cool FM announced that "revenues at the Illinois State Fair were down twenty percent, but presidential hopeful Bob Dole came to visit anyway."

In midafternoon, we stopped at Sugar Creek Island, again to fish and swim, our eyes bloodshot from the muddy water. Later we passed through the La Grange lock and were once more in need of fuel; my eye was caught by a fuel pump standing at the end of a long dock. This turned out to be a shell, the real tank high on a hill near the old stone farmhouse. A nearby marker was inscribed "Ulysses S. Grant camped here on July 6, 1861, with the 21st Illinois Volunteers."

The Riverboat Trading Company was run by Tucker Floyd, who with his wife, Diane, and children, Tiffanee, Tanya, and Tawni, had recently moved from Quincy. He worked about the rented building with a mania, looking rather like Richard Dreyfuss, more, *acting* like Dreyfuss in *Close Encounters of the Third Kind*, so eager was he to restore the old building to his vision of the grand riverside inn of yesteryear that he imagined. Today's project was the unearthing of a stone walk, buried six inches under the lawn.

"Look at those stones, will you? See how they fit?" He swept the dirt away with a broom. "The guy who laid them knew what he was doing!"

Steve and I sat at the air-conditioned bar, empty now, drinking a Sprite and a beer. Tucker said he was anxious to attract boaters to his establishment, and so would drive us to town for errands. As we had no clean clothes, I accepted the offer to do laundry in Bluffs, ten miles inland. An hour later, Diane Floyd, a short, buxom blonde built like a barrel, motioned us to her station wagon. As we passed through mile after mile of cornfield, she told us of the ill luck that had brought her to the river, to wit, her husband's crazy dream of living on the water, watching the world go by, catering to people of means and note.

"Look what's around you?" she exclaimed, waving her hand out the window. "There's nothing! Ninety people in town. Hell, we left all our friends for this pipe dream? When I sit on the bank at dusk and watch a tow go by, it sometimes seems all worthwhile, but shit, during the day . . ."

She dropped us at a Laundromat, as deserted as the dirty, depressing intersection of heat and corn on which it sat. Huge flies buzzed against the windows. The ineffectual fan turned slowly. The soap machine took two quarters but delivered no product. The air smelled of fertilizer. I changed money at the Napa auto parts store down the street. We walked across the railroad tracks to drink sodas in the comparative coolness of a family restaurant (the bar next door displayed a sign that said "Positively No Children Allowed"). Once the clothes were dry, I called Diane. We waited a half hour, then were hailed by another woman in a small truck.

"I'm supposed to pick you up."

"Lucky me." Her smile said you could talk to her like that—flattery appreciated.

Jere Nelson said Diane had suddenly gotten busy in the kitchen and had asked her for the favor of fetching us. Jere had started the *Trader* weekly newspaper six years before, with an investment of $100. Horatio Alger, rags to riches, and she was proud. Delivered them herself. Stacks of issues tied with string fluttered in the bed of the truck. She handed me a stack, including several that were years old, suggesting I share them with friends.

Pointing to an article and photo of the Marquette statue some ways downriver, she said this was the best story she'd ever written, one that really meant something. I scanned the paper as she drove:

Item—A list of new books at the Beardstown Library.

Item—Griggsville News: "The High School Tornado cheerleaders were waitressing at the Pizza Hut Monday evening, June 7th. They received money for each medium and large pizza that was sold, plus their tips. They would like to say Thank You to everyone who stopped by for a pizza to show their support."

A one-sixth-page ad—"Wholesale-Retail. Davis Fish Market. Buffalo—Carp—Catfish. Now taking picnic orders!"

Item—The Coonridge Digest, by Freida Marie Crump: "Greetin's from the Ridge to the Graduates of 1993! Don't get too discouraged. Things usually ain't near as bad as they seem. Many of you are gonna be among the first graduates of your school who will hold your ceremonies without the benefit of prayer. This is partially due to livin' in a free country where nearly everything is allowed but the public expression of your faith and partly due to the cowardice of those runnin' your society."

Item—"Jeff Merrill plays the funny lovable Hillybilly Fisherman, Elmer Barnes, on 'The Gospel Bill Show.' Jeff was born again as a young child and helped work in the church his father pastored while growing up. Jeff has been with Willie George Ministries since September of 1985. After graduating from Bible School in May of 1987, he has continued to work for Willie George in a helps capacity. Jeff has traveled to churches across the nation ministring God's Word. The call is supported at home by his wife, Tina and their two young children, Bethany De and Joshua Paul. Each service in an Elmer Rally contains singing, stories, illustrated sermons, skits, live puppets and special music."

Item—"Sandwich Safety. According to Jananne Finck, Nutrition and Wellness Educator with the Springfield Extension Center, it's important to keep a few food safety tips in mind to ensure the sandwich and other perishable foods don't spoil."


A few miles from the river, Jere Nelson pointed to her home, which was also a secondhand store, convenience mart, and miniature golf course, though the latter had been flattened a year ago by a tornado; the plywood figures of Snow White and Pinocchio were still prostrate in the weeds.

We ate dinner at Tucker Floyd's inn. On the menu: 30-ounce T-bone, 4-pc. Fried Chicken (All White .50¢ extra), Blackened Alligator (Farm Raised from Louisiana), Catfish, Buffalo Fish. Two bites into a burger, Steve was called outside by Tucker, who even in darkness was still uncovering the buried stones and wished to show him the tree frogs clinging to the windows by the porch lights, catching up bugs with long tongues. In fact, the entire lawn was covered with frogs. Steve, who hadn't had this much fun since hooking the catfish on Peoria Lake, gathered up all the frogs that he could and burst into the restaurant looking for a container. A woman recoiled at the sight of so many frogs so near to escaping Steve's grasp.

"Special on frog legs tonight, madam," I said.

Failing to convince me to give him the water glasses from our table, he sped back outdoors and retrieved a net from the boat, inside which several dozen frogs spent the night on the lawn of the Riverboat Trading Company (I wouldn't have them aboard). In the morning, which could not have come soon enough, Tucker called us from the deck of the inn, offering coffee and juice, which he served us standing in front of a wall-size cooler of beer and ice. The point, and opportunity, was not lost on me. Following our purchase, Tucker bid us on our way.

Our last night on the Illinois brought us to the Pere Marquette State Park, a few miles above its junction with the Mississippi River. There was a marina with rows of neat wooden docks, deserted this Friday except for one runabout next to which a young man and woman floated in inflatable donuts, lazily drinking beers in cozies.

The air was dead still and the humidity stifling. Steve tethered the beanbag to a stern cleat, threw it overboard, and hopped in, and I followed. The water was nearly as warm as the air. Shortly, a thirty-five-foot sportfishing boat approached the dock without any lines ready. I guided the boat in and held it by hand until they could tie up. The captain advised me that once on the Mississippi I should refuel on the Missouri side as gasoline was much less expensive there than on the Illinois side—"When you're taking on several hundred gallons, twenty cents makes a *big* difference!" He and his crew of two young men took off up the hill, and when they hadn't returned in an hour, I began to wonder what attractions of the park they had found so entertaining, especially as they hadn't seemed the type to hike trails or linger at the butterfly exhibit.

Steve and I dressed and followed; we spent a few minutes in a log cabin outbuilding that housed an exhibit of park flora and fauna, then continued on up the hill until we came upon a magnificent lodge with a restaurant, bar, video games, swimming pool, weight room, and accommodations. The crew of the sportfishing boat were seated at the bar. We took a room, fetched some things from the boat, and treated ourselves to a night ashore. The great room was styled after a north woods hunting lodge, with cathedral ceilings and exposed beams from which hung large, hand-woven tapestries with a leaf motif. We relaxed in cool leather chairs set in clusters about the room's centerpiece, a life-size chess board. Children, directed by their tickled parents, posed for pictures with their favorite player. Steve said, "Teach me to play," and I promised that I would. A piano player sang "That's Why the Lady Is a Tramp" and "Chattanooga Choo-Choo." The old folks danced. I did not sweat.

Steve ordered catfish, but it tasted fishy and he would not eat it. He could barely keep his eyes open, and I had to play I Spy to keep him awake. In our room he quickly fell asleep. I too was exhausted, yet apprehensive about meeting the Mississippi tomorrow. For a few minutes only I read *Quimby's* cruising guide, which said that the vast majority of cruisers leave the Mississippi at Cairo, ascend the Ohio River to the Tennessee, then make their way to the gulf via the elaborately civil and expensive Tennessee-Tombigbee Waterway. Of my intended route it said:

> The Lower Mississippi is a dangerous river, not having the slack-water pools provided by locks and dams on the Upper River. Not all fuel stops listed herein are full harbors. There is little pleasure boating except around cities and at the time of spring and fall traffic of northern boats. The river runs between levees 14 to 40 feet high and towns mostly are behind levees, which may be up to a few miles back from the river. Old plantation mansions are not visible from the river. In fact, many are very isolated and deeply buried in inland woods.
>
> U.S. Army Engineers advise that banks and shores on islands shouldn't be used to tie to because they can cave in. The channel shifts here unlike the Upper River, where it is more stable. Sandbars also can be unstable—check to see if you can walk on them. Beware of floating debris and, in the shallows, submerged snags.
>
> Engineers say treat the Lower River with respect. It can be up to 1/2 mile wide in low water and when bankful up to 1-3/4 miles wide. Big ocean-going ships use the river up to Baton Rouge, and the smaller miniships go occasionally to Natchez.
>
> Inquire among boaters who have been on the Lower Mississippi. Call a harbor operator listed in the Guide for advice. CARRY EXTRA GAS.[1]

# CHAPTER 9

# *The Keeper of the Stone*

*crane: "my way is best"*
*worm: "my way is best"*
*stone: "stone"*

—reps, *Gold and Fish Signatures*

One day many years ago, sometime around the turn of the century (nobody is quite sure just what year it was), Sam Cook walked down the slope behind his farm. The house sat on the highest point of land in Ellington Township, Adams County, Illinois. The view was westward over the fields toward the Mississippi. In the gully below ran the clear spring waters of Cedar Creek. And on the knoll across the creek was an ancient Indian campsite. Long before the advent of foundries and breweries that would constitute the waterfront economy of nearby Quincy, Illinois; long before the arrival of Father Francis Steck, who taught at the college there and whose research would lead him to conclude that Marquette did not accompany Jolliet down the Mississippi; long before the first steamboat; long before the whites ventured down the great river in the birch-bark canoes whose use they had adopted—Indians hunted on this site, cooked, and made shelter. Locals found a shallow fire-pit lined with rock slabs and filled with charcoal. Once in a while Cook found other signs. It was the arrowheads he especially liked, and they were most readily spotted following a rain, such as there had been the previous night.

This day he would find something unlike anything he had seen before. Cook almost missed it, lying as it was underwater, its image blurred by the falls and froth flowing over. He turned, stooped, and picked up a piece of limestone measuring about eight inches wide, eleven inches long, and one and a half inches thick. An adhesive mixture of mud and sand obscured parts of the numerals on its surface. He studied the strange markings, then hurried up the hill home. Several carpenters and painters were working on the farmhouse, and Cook called to them. One of the men took a screwdriver and cleaned the mud from the deep etchings.

What they saw were the letters *IHS*, with a cross standing atop the bar of the *H*, and the numbers 1671. In the center of the stone was a larger, half-fallen cross, and in one corner a small hole. Once it was cleaned he took it inside, and there it remained for the next fifty years—a conversation piece.

And there it might have remained were it not for Leroy J. T. "Lee" Politsch. In 1956, Politsch heard about the stone from Charles Griep, the father of his friend Bob. Lee, born in 1922, had lived his entire life in Quincy, most of those years with his parents in an apartment above the hardware store they owned. The elder Politsch, Charlie, sold paint and tools, cutlery, fishing tackle, and housewares, which in his earlier years of business were brought upriver to Quincy by packet boat from St. Louis. He also traded in furs, which trappers brought to the backdoor: twenty to fifty cents for a colored house cat, more for opossum, raccoon, coyote, muskrat, weasel, mink, and civet cat. Premium was twenty dollars for dark extra-large mink.

When he was old enough, Lee helped work the store. He liked it there among the wooden shelves full of clever mechanisms. His life was safe, nurtured, confined. "I was always a homebody," he said.

Fate would make him far more of a homebody than he could ever wish or dream: On graduation from high school in 1940, he was stricken with polio. He spent eight months in bed, taking daily treatments in a Hubbard Tank. Eventually, during the opening days of World War II, he recovered sufficiently to be conscripted for military service. But he did not have full mobility of his legs and was assigned to the Army Air Force Photo School at

Lowry Field in Denver. After graduation he was sent to the Sioux City Air Force Base, where he spent thirty-three months repairing land cameras, requisitioning photographic supplies, and assisting in the training of B-17 and B-24 bomber crews. After his discharge he returned to help his father in the store. It was the only place he ever truly wanted to be. But his imagination traveled further afield. Perhaps because he was never able to walk or run like his friends, he developed an abiding interest in the history of the area in which he lived. Or perhaps it was owing to Henry Schild, from whom Charlie Politsch had bought the business. As a lad, Mr. Schild had fought in the Civil War. He never really wanted to be anywhere else, either, and was welcome—even to his last days—to hang around the store. And when Lee or anyone else would listen, he told about *his* war, fought with the 27th Illinois Volunteer Infantry, fought with horses, muzzle loaders, and cannon.

In the stone, Lee found a means of bringing history to life. When Lee heard about Mr. Cook's curious discovery, he arranged to meet Sam's son, Ed, in whose possession the stone now resided. Perceiving the magnitude of Lee's interest, Ed made him a loan of it. Lee treasured it as he might a special bow or canoe, which were his other loves. He kept it in his office, wrapped and concealed in the bottom of a wire wastebasket.

*Lee Politsch holding the Ellington Stone, which he believes was engraved by Robert de La Salle in 1671, proving that La Salle preceded Louis Jolliet on the Upper Mississippi River by two years.* (JOE LIESEN, COURTESY OF THE QUINCY HERALD-WHIG)

For the next forty years he would strive to prove that the creator of the stone was none other than Robert de La Salle. The more postpolio syndrome slowed him, the harder he worked. He wrote and called archaeologists, historians, authors, and professors, anyone who might hold a helpful tidbit of information, anyone who could give momentum to his cause.

The project was important because the first recorded visit of Europeans to the Upper Mississippi is generally attributed to Louis Jolliet and Father Jacques Marquette, who paddled down from Green Bay, via the Fox and Wisconsin rivers), in 1673, two years *after* the date on the stone, 1671, which is one of La Salle's "missing years," lying beyond the veil of time.

This is the crux of Lee's argument:

All the while he was "missing," La Salle kept notes and made sketches. On his death, these eventually passed to his niece, Madeleine Cavelier, who in 1756 wrote to the French government that in the second year of La Salle's "disappearance," he ventured down the Illinois to the Mississippi River.[1] This assertion was corroborated by the much criticized *relation* of Abbé Renaudot, the writer who interviewed La Salle during the latter's visits to Paris.

For his part, Lee believed that La Salle had good reason not to make a public claim. After all, the exploitation of the Mississippi was the centerpiece of his grand design, and he did not wish rival traders, nor the calculating Jesuits, to beat him to it. So what if Jolliet claimed to have gotten there first? Jolliet had done nothing to exploit the discovery, nor had he any intention of building forts, developing a waterway to the gulf, driving a wedge between the English and Spanish colonies, or leading a military attack on the Spanish settlements in Mexico. These were the ambitious, even wild aspirations, of La Salle, a visionary, not a trapper. No, Politsch believes that La Salle would have kept quiet about his discoveries until he was ready to move with all the resources necessary for a successful venture. Even Francis Parkman acknowledged, as do nearly all others, that La Salle was a man "not prone to vaunt his own exploits, who never proclaimed them in print."[2]

So if Lee Politsch could prove that La Salle carved the stone found in Cedar Creek, then La Salle, not Jolliet, should be credited with discovering the Upper Mississippi.

In the course of his research, Lee came upon an article I had written about searching for La Salle, and we had struck up a correspondence.

When he heard I was coming down the Illinois River, he urged me to visit.

I studied the charts for towns on the Illinois where we might leave *Pearl* and rent a car for the trip to Quincy. The two most likely were Beards-town and Meredosia, but they had neither docks nor rental agencies. The alternative was to continue on down the Illinois, then turn up the Missis-sippi and visit Quincy by boat. But it lay 140 miles upstream, and time did not permit such sidetracking; besides, with Steve in tow there was little chance Lee and I could fully discuss his theories.

When later we returned to Newport, there was a phone message from Lee. He was terribly disappointed that we hadn't met, and so I promised to make every effort to fly out the following spring.

The Beechcraft 1900 was dwarfed by the jets queuing for takeoff before and behind it. I looked out the window on that brisk and sunny day in March. I felt good that I was keeping my promise to Lee. When the Boe-ing 757 in front taxied into position, the twin-engine commuter shook and chattered in the blast. The flight departed Chicago O'Hare at 11:37, right on time. An altitude of seven thousand feet afforded a good view of the Illinois River, its northeast–southwest course cutting diagonally across the squares of farmland. This is the geometry of the contemporary land-scape that so shattered my pre-America. Its origins can be traced to the National Land Survey (Land Ordinance of 1785), when Thomas Jefferson devised a scheme for apportioning the unclaimed lands of the Great Plains into nearly innumerable mile-square parcels, each divided into 640 acres, so that squares inside of squares carved up pre-America from the Ohio River to the Pacific Ocean. Thus were formed our townships, our coun-ties, and, in some instances, our states. And the lines weren't always imagi-nary or known only to surveyors; roads were built along them.

Author and landscape historian John Brinckerhoff Jackson wrote:

> It was an ingenious, if unimaginative, way of creating a land-scape. . . . Still, by now, more than two centuries later, there are millions of Americans so thoroughly at home in the grid that they cannot conceive of any other way of organizing space. I have been in homes in Kansas where they refer to the southwest

(or northwest) burner on their stove. They tell you that the bathroom is upstairs, straight ahead south."[3]

The checkerboard fields were every shade of brown, mocha, chestnut, tan, beige, yellow, and mud. They were barren now and the flatness of the land was depressing, but not nearly so much as the industry of Greater Chicago we'd left behind. From the air, the works of man appeared as a blight on the earth—ugly buildings with tarred roofs, vents and fans, stacks blowing white smoke, all strung together with wires, and between them tracks and road strips that made me feel life would be better if the people lived in tepees and pole lodges—camouflaged, portable, biodegradable.

The flight to Quincy was a milk run, captained today by a female pilot whose long blond tresses hung across her shoulder, teasingly visible to the passengers. She touched down in Galesburg, taxiing up tightly to the terminal and spinning the plane on its front wheels. Four of the nine passengers disembarked. An American flag fluttered in the soft breeze. A sign: "Municipal Airport—Home of the National Stearman Fly-In." Beyond, cornfields stretched to the horizon, the stalks buckled and fallen. On the shady side of the furrows, ribbons of snow ran off in parallel lines to the vanishing point.

The middle-aged fellow who'd sat in front of me was met by two men, one about his age, also wearing a baseball cap, the other, a black leather motorcycle jacket. His hair was cut in a flat-top and I wondered if this was the passenger's son. He took the passenger's suitcase and placed it in the car trunk. Strange, I thought, that people *meet* people, how ordinary, how much the same. This act of adjoining another cries for the telling of a story—the purpose, the prearrangement, the duty, the favor, the relationship of the parties, all the linked elements behind the simple act.

In less than five minutes we were again airborne and I now thought of the man who was to meet me.

I called Lee Politsch from the Quincy Airport, then smoked a pipe waiting in the sun. He drove up in a Chevy Suburban, green with simulated wood panels as brown as the earth. Mounted on the tailgate was an apparatus to carry a scooter for the handicapped. In the backseat was an aluminum walker. Lee was tall, better than six feet, and had no trouble reaching across the front seat to open my door. His frame was thin though not frail and he wore a camouflage jacket, owing to his longtime interest in canoeing, fishing, and archery. Indeed, after his father retired, Lee closed the hardware store and next to it built an A-frame to sell outdoor gear. Lee's Sports was a southtown fixture for twelve years, a friendly gathering place for shooters and fishermen. But the polio worked against him. The smallest task, say, going to the bathroom, was a chore to be broken down into a dozen smaller tasks, each requiring planning and effort: standing, shuffling with the walker, positioning weight so that one hand could be freed to open the door, moving through, closing . . .

Of his patience and fortitude I would see more later. Now he wasted no time getting down to business.

Directly he asked, "Do you think La Salle was a martyr?"

"Not particularly," I answered. "No. Surely he was tired and frustrated, but I don't think he felt sorry for himself, if that's what you mean."

"The reclining cross," he said, "symbolizes the cross's angle as Jesus carried it to Calvary. At that moment, of course, *he* was a martyr. The cross on the bar of the *H* is a Jesuit and Franciscan symbol. La Salle had turned against the Jesuits. You've read of his many enemies. It occurred to me that he might have felt it necessary to carve the stone because he suspected his discoveries would be discredited. The Jesuits, you know, didn't like all this secular exploration."

When the material clues trail off, Lee spends a lot of time trying to get inside La Salle's head in a sort of psychohistory that might explain the stone. For Lee, all paths lead to the stone.

He drove into the countryside, away from the commercial strip, down two-lane roads that melded straight away into the farmland. Suddenly he stopped and pointed to a creek bed below.

"About two, three hundred yards down, that's where Cook found it. See up there to the right? That's where the Sauk and Fox Indian camp was. Now look behind you. The railroad was built right over Cedar Creek, but if you follow on the other side and bear to the east, eventually you come to Siloam Springs and McKee Creek, which connects to the Illinois River. I believe this was a shortcut the Indians used between the Mississippi and Illinois rivers. Across the Mississippi from here, and about fifty miles north, near St. Francisville, Missouri, are the remains of the big village of the Illinois Indians that Marquette and Jolliet visited in 1673. The farmers and locals called it to the attention of Roger Boyd, administrator of the nearby Battle of Athens State Park, who in turned called in

Larry Grantham, Missouri State archaeologist, to assist in protecting and studying the site. Now it is known that the Illinois spent some of their time along the Illinois River, at various locations at various times, but it is not known why they established a large village on the west side of the Mississippi River near the Des Moines River. Some sources believe the hunting was better; others believe it was fear of attacks by the Iroquois. It also is not known whether Marquette and Jolliet, on their descent of the Mississippi, already knew of the shortcut the Illinois River provided for their return north.

"At this point it is interesting to note that the Thevenot map, published with Jolliet's account of the journey, shows what is labeled *chemin du retour*, a 'return route' considerably north of the Quincy area, that some of the Illinois might have taken from the Des Moines to the Peoria–Starved Rock area to meet the Marquette-Jolliet expedition on its return.

"Now in the Quincy area, doesn't it make sense for the Indians, and early explorers, to use this shortcut rather than go all the way down the Mississippi to St. Louis, then back up? Cedar Creek and McKee Creek don't quite meet up, but after traveling all the way from the Great Lakes, a few miles' portage across the prairie wouldn't be an obstacle.

"See, La Salle always sought information from the Indians. It wasn't beneath him. They could have told him about this route. The site here that we're looking at was a perfect winter camp. The spring provided freshwater, and the hill a vantage of the Mississippi."

"There isn't enough water in the creek to float a stick," I interjected.

"Back then there was. Back then there were prairies and woodlands holding back the rainfall, releasing it gradually rather than in an immediate, eroding runoff. Things have changed. Ow-wee!" he trilled. (This high-pitched birdlike sound was repeated whenever a thought excited him.)

We drove on through town to Front Street, parallel to the river, where the stove foundries used to be, then to Clat Adams Park, which has beautified the waterfront, then to the Quincy Bay, where once stood sawmills, ice houses, fishermen's shacks, and a small stockyard. Turning from the water, Lee drove up the hill past the town square, past the memorial to the Lincoln-Douglas debate in this place on October 13, 1858, then into the old neighborhoods along tree-lined streets to the Quincy Museum. Lee tried to stuff two dollars into my hand and told me to go inside. I refused the money. "The stone," he said.

Here it now resided. The door was locked. A maintenance man came around the corner and recognized Lee. He showed me to the second floor, where at the head of the stairs the Ellington Stone was displayed. No plaque identified it as such. Just sitting there on a bed of dried leaves under thick acrylic. The maintenance man attached large suction-cup handles to either side of the cover, removed it, and set the box on the floor. I was mildly surprised that it looked just like its picture, the way I felt when I first saw the *Mona Lisa*—yes, that's it!—although the painting was much smaller than I had imagined.

Lee said some critics dismiss the stone as a hoax because it "looks new." But what is a "new" stone? Yet it did seem fresh and clean—recrystallized limestone from the Heightcreek member of the Burlington Formation—mixed with enough chert to make it relatively hard and firm. The stone had been preserved in clay and only lately freed; in the streambed its surface had been cleared of the clay, abraded by the friction of passing water.

*IHS. In hoc signo*, "in this sign," meaning Jesus Christ, savior of man.[4] 1671. The six was drawn with the loop open, typical of that period. La Salle's own handwriting made open sixes. I stared at it for several minutes, trying to see where the carpenter's screwdriver had gouged the mud from the letters, but could not.

I called to the maintenance man, who replaced the cover.

"You a friend of Lee's?" he asked.

"Yes."

"Pretty much everybody around here knows Lee. He's got a theory, eh? Who knows, he might be right."

"I'm not sure it matters," I said. "The hunt is half the fun."

"Right about that. Right for him."

I returned through the empty corridors of the museum to the exit. Lee reached across to open the door, pushing it ajar with his fingertips.

"Could it be a tombstone or an altar stone some priest carried with his portable altar?"

Lee shook his head.

"Too big, for one thing. My critics say, 'Well, if La Salle did discover the Father of Waters, why didn't he come back to Montreal and say so?' I believe he traveled in secrecy. He had competitors in the fur trade. Nor did he trust the Jesuits, who had their own dream of creating a sovereign religious state. No, he wanted to keep it quiet until he was ready. But in case others laid claim to the valley, he needed proof he'd been there first. So he carved this stone and buried it. He did the same thing at the mouth of the Mississippi, burying a lead plaque with writing scratched on it— *Ludovicus Magnus Regnat* [Great King Louis].

"People say, 'Why didn't he sign it?' Maybe he left his name some other way. The hole, probably made by a bow-drill, could have held a wooden peg. On the peg he might have rolled up a piece of paper with a note and stuck it in. Or he might have clamped his signet ring to it. Of course the peg is long gone, rotted, but a ring might be there in the creek bed. I'd like to look for it, but there's no way I could get down there. It'd probably be futile anyway. But you know, about a half mile north, on a neighboring farm, they found an old bronze or copper bowl with foreign writing on it. That was sixty years ago and nobody knows what happened to it. Too bad, because it might have been the key to the stone. At the delta, La Salle made a plate from a copper kettle. So you see, everything ties in."

Lee had theories about everything, and the need in him to share them was so strong that they erupted out of sequence in dribs and drabs of conversations, passages, orts of information from the cache in his brain.

I gathered we were nearing his house when he said, "My part of town is a little trashy. If I were looking for a place, I wouldn't consider it. But where I am is home."

Lee still owned the old hardware store, now closed and used for storage. On the door was a decal from Bear Archery: "Bow hunting spoken here." It was on Eighth Street, across from a supermarket loading dock. Next to it was the A-frame of the sporting goods store, it too closed. In between was a garage, which he opened with a remote control. Leaning out the half-open door, he watched for the lines painted on the concrete floor to show where to stop so there would be enough room for him to maneuver his walker. I hadn't expected the A-frame to be his residence. We entered through a sliding wooden door, into the wide overhead where once he'd held court with friends and customers, into Lee's World. There was a Bedford stone fireplace near the center, the chimney running past the high, hewn beams. On both side walls were blown-up eight-by-fourteen-foot photographs of the Minnesota Boundary Waters, where Lee used to canoe. That is where he wanted to be, on those rare summer respites from the heat of Quincy, among the granite and fir. In pre-America.

"Ever hear a loon call?"

The tall glass display cases that once had been used for shotguns, bows and arrows, traps, and fishing tackle, were now bookcases. A number of mismatched chairs were drawn in a large circle, and to one side was a sleeper sofa, made up for me with an army blanket and felt-covered pillow. The long, narrow room in the rear—the old store office—was Lee's all-in-one bedroom, kitchen, and office, the latter two areas accessible from a stool. Here he sat for the evening, bidding me to sit at his desk. On the wall above the door was a photo of Barbara Mandrell. There were several others of pretty young girls: the daughter of a friend, another who used to work for him. Never married, he said the girls of his day did not find him attractive, owing to the polio. The answer was too simple, and wrong.

There was also a picture of Bob Griep, his childhood chum who had died nine months before, in June 1995. Heart disease. Saw it coming but didn't care; told Lee he'd rather die than get cut. Though others call, and some cousins get him out for dinner once a month, Griep's passing left a void.

Before me on the desk was a thick album full of Lee's notes and clippings. Forty years of research. Records of phone conversations with historians and archaeologists. Carbon copies of letters painstakingly written on an old Underwood standard typewriter. (When I remarked about it, he rummaged in a drawer and produced the original sales receipt: $220.72, dated January 12, 1956, purchased direct from Underwood.) These were collated with letters received. Photographs. Logs. Pamphlets. And an index, which he had marked with a highlighter pen to save me time finding those items most relevant to the Ellington Stone.

"Don't need it," I said. "I'm going to read every page."

This pleased him. As I began he opened the freezer and showed me the frozen TV dinners from which I could select: Salisbury steak, carrots and apple sauce; chicken nuggets, mashed potatoes and peas; pizza. He popped two in the microwave.

When he spoke about his life, or of La Salle, I did not know where on the timeline he would begin . . . as if someone randomly placed the needle on a phonograph record.

"John Upton Terrell," he said, "places La Salle in the Illinois River valley in 1671. I called him on the phone eight or ten years ago. But he said his wife wasn't feeling well, nor was he.

"He told me, 'Yes, La Salle was on the Illinois that year; we proved that. But I wrote that book a long time ago. You're there, I'm here, and that's that.'

"Good book, more alive than most of the others. Maybe he took some dramatic license, but heck, I'm a canoeist, and if La Salle stopped to put his canoe up on the beach, turned it over, and slept underneath, telling you what La Salle thought about looking up at the ribs, I like hearing that."

There was a knock at the door, and it was then that Lee told me he'd invited the reporter Ed Husar of the *Quincy Herald-Whig* to visit with us. We talked for half an hour about the stone, La Salle, and my trip down the Illinois and Mississippi rivers. I thought perhaps that Ed was humoring Lee with his note taking, though he had written before about the stone, and slowly I realized that Quincy is a small place, sufficiently so that our meeting might actually qualify as local news.

After Ed politely bowed out, Lee played several tapes obtained from Quincy University (since Steck's time, the school had changed from a college to a university). An archivist found the tapes buried in a cabinet; Lee spent $200 converting the reels to cassettes. Stored on them were the conversations of Father Steck, author of *Marquette Legends*, and Stuart Streuver, the archaeologist who gained notoriety unveiling the "eleven horizons" (successive levels of occupation) of ancient Amerindian culture at the Koster dig near Kampsville, Illinois. Steck, the voice with the Irish accent, was now dead and Streuver was gone from the area, on to other digs. But for a time the Ellington Stone had captivated them.

The first tape recorded Steck and Streuver's effort to persuade Ed Cook to allow the stone to be scientifically examined at the Oriental Institute of Chicago. It went something like this:

> **Streuver:** "Tell us how the stone was found."
> **Cook** (who sounded like Edward G. Robinson): "Father lived on a farm four miles northeast of Quincy. Had a rainstorm the night before, see. My father had a habit of looking in the pasture for things, see. This stone was lyin' in the mud, see. He got my sister and washed off the mud, see. Put it in a bucket of water and scrubbed it clean, see. That was maybe fifty, sixty years ago, see. Then Mr. Politsch wanted to look at it, see."

**Father Steck:** "If it said sixteen seventy-five, we wouldn't be so concerned. The first white men on the river are thought to have come in 1673. If the stone is real, this is very important."

**Cook:** "Uh-huh."

**Streuver:** "We'd like to take the stone to Chicago for scientific analysis. Attempt to date it. There's no other way we can be sure."

**Cook:** "Is it going to cost me? I don't want to put any money in it . . . I don't got too much."

**Streuver:** "It won't cost you anything."

**Cook:** "What if they break it? I don't want nuthin' happenin' to it."

**Streuver:** "These are experts who will take very good care of the stone. They know how to handle such things. They'll take much better care of it than Lee Politsch, who keeps it in a wastebasket."

Lee smiled. "I put it in a fireproof safe after that." He turned the tape off and inserted another in which Streuver discussed the findings of the Oriental Institute.

Dr. Willard Schmidt, an epigrapher specializing in inscriptions from the Middle East, said the carving was done by an expert. "Whoever did it had to know something of history. He was not a dolt. The figures were made by an improved iron tool. Your best hope of learning the truth is to prove it a hoax."

Streuver concluded, "The man cannot tell us a great deal."

Schmidt examined the stone using infrared photography to identify the metallic traces left by the implement that made it. Unfortunately, he couldn't distinguish the original tool and the screwdriver or spike used by Cook's carpenter. There went the case. The answer, it seemed, if it could not be learned by the use of scientific instruments, instead would have to come through the search of forgotten pages of history.

Lee turned off the tape and looked at me. Undeterred.

"It would be a bombshell! I'd like to have the pleasure of whipping this. It's a duty. I feel I've been given this task.

"Bob Griep died last June, and suddenly all of this stuff pops: You decide to write a book. Tony Hunter [another La Salle freak] writes me from Texas. They link Marquette to this place in northern Missouri. I just got to ask: Is Bob working from the other side or what? Ow-wee!"

He pointed to an embroidered poem on the wall. "It's kind of my philosophy," he said. In essence, the poem said that life was worth living and that, Jesus willing, in the next life Lee Politsch would have good legs.

"My idea of heaven is that God clones bodies in their best year and infuses them with spirit. Heck, nobody would want to be in the second paradise with an old and broken body. But God doesn't tell us this because then everyone would be committing suicide. Ow-wee!"

Later Lee took me downstairs to the basement to play with his model railroad. Using handrails he was able to negotiate the stairs alone, though watching his one leg double backward at the knee, I was fearful he might fall. But like all the other routines of his life, this one was much practiced. When at last he turned on the light, there before me, on thirty-foot custom tables he'd built himself, were more than a hundred cars, twenty locomotives, handmade station houses, coal chutes, horse loaders, automatic switches, and light crossings. It took the two of us operating separate zones to circumnavigate the Amtrak and Santa Fe.

Back upstairs he showed me his autographed copies of Hal Foster's Prince Valiant books and the correspondence the two kept for many years, mostly concerning their mutual interest in canoes and archery.

The end of Lee's well-organized program was a video-cassette viewing of the Canadian film *Black Robe*, in which a Jesuit priest is sent into the Great Lakes region to learn what has happened to a mission that has fallen silent. "It's the most accurate depiction of the era with which we're concerned," Lee said. Unfortunately, something had gone awry during taping and the story was truncated by a baseball game played the previous summer.

The phone rang. It was John Helm, a local salesman and model railroad hobbyist, which accounted for their meeting some years earlier at a convention.

"Bob Griep's gone, but John checks in most every night."

As they talked, I checked out, slipping out the front door. I lit a pipe and walked uphill, into the neighborhood. The air was chilly and the stars crisply winking.

What difference would it make to anybody if La Salle indeed had beaten Jolliet to the upper river? Under the night sky, the question was easy to answer: not much. History texts would require slight revisions. Yet to Lee Politsch it would mean everything. A page of history still is a page of history, but more, he would have succeeded in solving the mystery of La Salle's early years, a mystery that Parkman, Delanglez, and many other famous historians could not crack. His hunch would be proved, the skeptics vanquished. Perhaps more important, the search gave meaning to his life. Where other men might have wasted away in self-pity, Lee's life was full and vibrant.

I pictured La Salle sitting on the knoll above Cedar Creek, a small limestone tablet clamped between his knees. The firelight flickers over its surface. Behind him a crude lean-to of sticks and animal skins breaks the wind. Farther out, at the edge of the circle of light, an Indian sits and watches the thin chisel scraping on stone. He smokes grass in a clay pipe, a robe of beaver wrapped around his shoulders. Neither speaks. In the distance a wolf howls. On the prairie, this is the way it has been for twenty thousand years, since the first people crossed the Bering Strait land bridge and scattered into the vast northern and southern continents. Perhaps the Indian believed it would always be so. The white man knew otherwise, though at this moment, in this abiding peace and darkness, he might have wished to stay the advance, to lie back and breathe slowly the moment now.

Lee's critics were of a number equal to his supporters. Richard Ahlborn of the National Museum of American History in Washington, D.C., wrote that the Ellington Stone might possibly be an altar stone, though on the large size. "I think the question of La Salle is hardly worth pursuing; it smacks of the 'great man' approach to history." He also wrote that there was a " 'newness' about the stone. . . . the form of the 's' and the 'ones' in the date are not typical of the period."

A historian at the archives of the Company of Jesus in Quebec wrote, "That it is a fake, is my first impression. The stone appears to be much too well sculpted, and by someone too crafty for the circumstances. Perhaps it was someone whose design was to indicate the entrance of the brook where the stone was found, as to be the entrance of the portage leading to the river, via a shortcut? The probability that La Salle might have come that way in 1671 seems to be nil." In a postscript, he added, "No known Jesuit traveled thither before Marquette (1673). The stonecutter must have worked on it at a later date, without really knowing the dates of Marquette's travels."

Lee long ago dismissed all suggestions that the stone is a hoax. But he seized on the statement "No known Jesuit traveled thither before Marquette." If not a priest, then who? Certainly not an illiterate voyageur or coureur de bois. Which could leave only La Salle, an intelligent man who had trained as a Jesuit and knew the symbols, who was deeply religious, and possessed the drafting skills to effect such an artwork.

Where Parkman and others discredited Abbé Renaudot's interviews with La Salle, chiefly because of geographical inaccuracies, Lee agrees with John Upton Terrell, who fastened on Renaudot's description of the Mississippi, that it bends from northwest to the southeast where it meets the Illinois. "Only someone who had been there could have known the river changes to such a course at that place," he said triumphantly.

Never mind that the historians Jean Delanglez and Father Steck believed Renaudot's description of the Mississippi was derived from Abbé Bernou, who obtained Gallinée's *Relation* and passed it along to Renaudot, meshing Jolliet's diary with his own fantasy.

The arguments were captivating but ultimately inconclusive.

"What we need," I said, "is for someone to discover Madeleine Cavelier's letters and maps. Perhaps they exist still, in someone's attic."

Lee nodded somberly.

My eyes weary, I excused myself to the old showroom of Lee's Sports, closed the accordion slider, and extinguished the array of fluorescent lights high on the ceiling of the A-frame. I pulled the army blanket to my chin and slept soundly among the ghostly memories of Charlie Politsch, Mr. Schild, and Prince Valiant.

In the morning, before first light, I was gone. The cab came at 4 A.M. and Lee hardly had time to say good-bye, waving a long thin arm from the bed as I hurried through the bedroom-kitchen-office to the bath. But just as I was pushing through my bags to the street, there he was behind me, clomping forward on his walker. He paused and stretched out his hand.

"Thank you," he said, "for coming."

"Thank you," I said. "I wouldn't have missed the stone, or you, for anything."

The sun was just rising over the horizon when the Beechcraft 1900 rattled down the runway and lifted into the misty morning air. There the Mississippi, there Quincy Bay, there the furrow of Cedar Creek and the knoll where I might lay me down and let the earth come over me. The silence of centuries. The silence of rocks.

*stone: "stone"*

# CHAPTER 10

# *The Great River*

*Question: What has four eyes and cannot see?*
*Answer: The Mississippi.*
*Comment: Any person who has traveled the river knows this to be false.*
*The river cannot be anthropomorphized. It "sees" by feeling the banks and*
*bottom, the megalithic concrete dams that try to stop it, the puny stone wing*
*dams intended to deflect its course, of which none entirely succeed. For a time*
*it seems they do . . . until the big rains come and the river floods. Then the*
*Mississippi overwhelms all in its way, not blindly, but according to the*
*physics of its nature.*

I want to go back to the beginning. Back 500 million years to the warm and shallow Ordovician sea that laid down the sedimentary river bluffs. Back 2 million years to the Pleistocene, the Ice Age, whose four major glacial advances, each named for the state of its most southerly advance— Nebraskan, Kansan, Illinoian, and Wisconsin—helped scour the Mississippi River valley. Back 20,000 years, when the Bering Strait land bridge still connected Asia and the Americas. Back just 10,000 years to the Wisconsin glacier, to the extinction of mastodons and woolly mammoths hunted by Paleo Indians, back to the ancient delta, back to the Woodland tradition and the effigy mound builders. Back before the first Europeans, so that I might imagine my home as it was before highways, smokestacks, and the spread of structures that transformed our perception of the land so radically that we cannot know it in any uncivilized way. Back to pre-America.

The mouth of the Mississippi was charted more than three hundred years before the headwaters. The Admiral's Map, imperfectly linked to

Christopher Columbus as its author, is a crude drawing showing a three-pronged delta purportedly on the north shore of the Gulf of Mexico. It was engraved in 1507 and published in 1513. Columbus set sail on his fourth voyage in 1502, voyaging to the Caribbean Sea and westward to Central America. It is not known whether he followed the Gulf Coast; if he did, that might account for the river on the map. Or perhaps he obtained reports of it from Spanish adventurers at Jamaica.[1] No one knows.

Amerigo Vespucci is another possible author of the map, made during a 1497 voyage to the gulf. But many historians, including Samuel Eliot Morison, believe that he invented the 1497 voyage to support his claim that he, not Columbus, discovered the South American mainland.

Alonso Alvarez de Pineda reported finding a large bay (Bahía del Espíritu Santo) on the Gulf Coast, which was probably Mobile Bay, not the mouth of the Mississippi. The butcher Pánfilo de Narváez might have seen the river's mouth had he not disappeared while looking for treasure along the Gulf Coast. Survivors of his expedition, straggling toward Mexico in makeshift barges, told of a strong current that pushed their boats out to sea.

Some give to Hernán Cortés the distinction of making the first reasonably accurate chart of the Mississippi's mouth; according to the historian Julius Chambers, he called the river the Arrestiosos.

Slowly, the Europeans developed an awareness of the Mississippi, first merely as a strong current that was detectable miles out at sea. Only when Hernando de Soto crossed the river at Lundell, Arkansas, in 1541 did a white come to gauge its breadth, come to understand its nature, come to make over pre-America.

Still, its course was a mystery. In 1684, the mapmaker Jean-Baptiste-Louis Franquelin got the basic outline down, but he incorrectly located the mouth much too far to the west, almost in Mexico. Not until the eighteenth century were the errors amended and the river charted from the Great Lakes nearly due south to the gulf.

Historians continue to debate who first charted the Mississippi, but the Texas historian Robert Weddle, whose research has shed new light on La Salle's triumphs and tragedies (based to a large degree on examination of Spanish documents compiled during a search for La Salle's lost colony), says most knowledgeable authorities agree on the following:

Columbus never entered the Gulf of Mexico or even knew that it existed.

The Vespuccian claim has been largely discredited—although his supposed discoveries have many advocates.

The credited discovery of the gulf was by Sebastián de Ocampo, who circumnavigated Cuba in 1508–9, although Juan Díaz de Solís and Vicente Yáñex Pinzón are said to have found the Yucatán Channel in 1508, but sailed on south without entering the gulf.

The mouth of the Mississippi remained uncharted and virtually unknown (excepting only the meager account of it by Soto's men) until La Salle's time.

Pineda, giving no representation on his map of either a bay that could be taken for Mobile Bay or the Mississippi delta, probably saw neither. He encountered the current from the Mississippi and recognized that it came from a mighty river. He named it Río del Espíritu Santo. He placed the name on his map sketch beside a rather small bay, which subsequent mapmakers enlarged many times.

The so-called Cortés map assuredly was not drawn by Cortés, but it was the first to enlarge Alvarez de Pineda's bay and suggest a course for the river flowing into it. The name was the same as Pineda's, Río del Espíritu Santo. Later mapmakers enlarged the mythical bay even further and named it Bahía del Espíritu Santo. Such a bay was purely hypothetical, representing what navigators supposed to be the mouth of an unseen river (the Mississippi), rather than Mobile Bay.

At the time of Narváez's disappearance at sea, he had long since given up his quest for gold and was merely trying to survive by reaching the settlement of Pánuco on the Mexican coast. His crude wilderness-contrived boats were swept seaward by the Mississippi's current.

Franquelin's 1684 map was drawn to interpret La Salle's exploration of the Mississippi in 1682. Franquelin had been assigned in France to La Salle as his draftsman. The record indicates that nothing had been learned of the Mississippi between Soto's *entrada* [first expedition and conquest] in 1541 and La Salle's 1682 expedition.

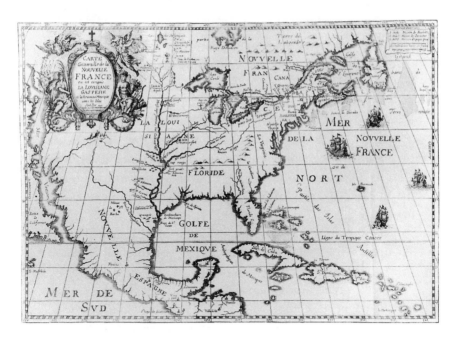

*Rouillard's 1692 map shows some improvements over Franquelin's 1684 map but still exemplifies the French conception of America in the latter half of the seventeenth century, especially as it shows the Mississippi entering the Gulf of Mexico far to the west of its actual mouth. From Chrétien LeClerq,* Premier établissement de la foi dans Nouvelle France, *2 vols. (Paris: Amable Auroy, 1691).* (UNIVERSITY OF TEXAS ARCHIVES)

The first delineation of the Mississippi's mouth, the so-called birdfoot delta, was by the Spanish voyage captained by Rivas and Iriarte, in 1686, while looking for La Salle. The chief pilot and diarist, Juan Enríquez Barroto, mapped the entire Gulf Coast. Up to that time there had been no accurate concept of the delta and its multiple river mouths; La Salle certainly had none.

Less controversial is the work at the other end: The headwaters of the Mississippi, Lake Itasca in northern Minnesota, were sketched by their discoverer, Henry Schoolcraft, in 1832.

The name and spelling of the Mississippi did not come simply or directly. Cortes's map called it Espíritu Santo, linking it erroneously to Pineda's bay. La Salle named the river the Colbert, after the minister of France. Native Americans had different names for different parts of the river, but the most commonly known, Messipi, means "big water" or "big river" (" 'Father of waters,' " wrote author Willard Price, was an "imaginative" translation by the French, but "a falsehood not only about a single name, but about Indians in general—for such a figure of speech would hardly have been used for a river."[3])

J. V. Brower compiled the following appellations:[4]

*Meche Sebe,* Algonquian

*Chucagua,* Indian, from Soto

*Tamaliseu,* Indian, from Soto

*Tapatu,* Indian, from Soto

*Mico,* Indian, from Soto

*Rio Grande,* Spanish, from Soto

*"The River,"* Spanish, from Soto

*Palisada,* Spanish, from floating trees seen near its mouth, giving the appearance of a palisade

*Escondido,* Spanish, meaning "hidden"

*St. Louis,* French

*Conception,* French, from Marquette

*Buade,* French, from Jolliet, after the family name of the Comte de Frontenac

*Colbert,* French, from La Salle, named for Jean-Baptiste Colbert

*Mischipi,* from Nicolás Freytas's visit to the Quivira tribes, 1661

*Messipi,* from Father Allouez in his *Relation* of 1667

*Meschasipi,* from Louis Hennepin

*Michi Sepe,* from Labal

*Misisipi,* from Labatt

*Missisipi,* from Marquette

*Mississipi,* French spelling of Indian name

*Mississippi,* the American spelling of the French version, adopted in the nineteenth century

We came upon the great river unaware of its imminence. Water levels had dropped sufficiently during late summer that the channels shown on the chart at the junction of the Illinois and Mississippi, between Island No.

525, Mason's Island, and Island No. 526 were dried up. Where in spring-time the muddy water had flowed, the bottoms of the shallow channels had become land, and already vegetation grew. The grasses and weeds blurred the demarcation of islands so that, viewed from the *Pearl*'s cockpit, they appeared as a single land mass, a peninsula of the mainland.

The houses of Grafton dotted the bank to our port side, as the chart indicated they should, but where to starboard was the Mississippi?

Slowly, from the haze we could see a line of cliffs appear before us, stretching down the same left bank as far as the eye could see. They were ragged and tall, nearly two hundred feet, topped unevenly with trees that here and there tilted over the edge like a slipped toupée. On the pock-marked face of the limestone cliffs were hollows and caves, and if we had been able to ascend the cliffs, we might have seen the Ordovician fossils of algae and benthic invertebrates, and the faint stains of pictographs drawn by the Indians who once lived along the shore. Or seen markings of the piasa bird, a painting so large and real that Indians in the north would not pass it for fear of losing their lives. "They are," according to the Thevenot account of Jolliet's 1673 journey, "as large as a calf; they have horns on their heads like a deer, a terrifying look, red eyes, a tiger's beard, a face somewhat like that of a man, the body covered with scales, a tail so long that it goes all around the body, passes over the head and turns back between the legs, ending in the tail of a fish."[5] The colors of it were green, red, and black, and the quality of the painting so good that the writer said artists in France could not have done as well.

Before us a number of small runabouts were beached in the lee of a sandy spit separated from the mainland by a channel of fast-moving water. It was Saturday and the river was spotted with teenagers, splashing like spawning carp.

Suddenly it dawned on me that we were no longer looking down the Illinois, but down the Mississippi, that here the lesser river merged with the greater body and was eclipsed. When I was able to see over the spit to the north, sure enough, there was the wide-bodied Mississippi bearing down on us, sucking us into its center. In La Salle's canoe, the force must have been easily perceptible if not dramatic. His feelings that day in 1680 were surely bittersweet. After fourteen years of searching, he'd finally sighted the river of possibilities. But alas, he could not proceed: There was no word of the *Griffon*, Fort Crèvecœur was destroyed, and on Tonti's whereabouts he could only speculate. Forced to retreat, his descent was postponed two years more. The rock he'd pushed to the summit fell back on him and he was fated to follow it . . . once again, overland to Fort Frontenac and thence to Montreal. But for an instant, there where the Mississippi revealed itself, he must have felt his spirits buoyed, as were mine.

Looking back at the Illinois, it seemed to me dainty and lethargic, a meandering trace feeding the hunger of the larger river. Where the two converged the water rolled over itself in a long line of froth, until the weaker current was consumed and the surface flattened. And it was brown, as promised, though never still, always turning on itself, twisting into bubble-rimmed circles that spun off like comets, sometimes vanishing, other times reappearing yards downstream. Too thick to drink, too thin to plow.

The effect of the current was not apparent until I glanced at the shore and saw that we were being set sideways at a rapid rate. I goosed the engine to move more quickly into the river. We watched and waited, testing the boat in this new environment to see if it would hold together. But there was nothing really to worry about, for upstream and down small boats flew past: water-skiers hanging on to their bridles, their legs and torsos inclined against the tow rope; families waving soda cans; and larger cruisers pressing upstream, the curl of brown water sneering around their bows. St. Louis was just a few miles below us, and the marinas that service the metropolis were within sight, across the river.

It was midmorning, and as we had until the next day to meet my daughter, Adria, there seemed no point in berthing now. We crossed to the west bank, ducking below Elsah Bar, where we ran the bow into the sand of a small, unnamed island. Several boaters were picnicking on shore. Steve tossed the anchor off the stern and made the line fast to a cleat with his proprietary knot. I jumped into the water, which pulled at me, sucking the muck and sand from under my feet. Before 1968, when the city of St. Louis finally built a sewage treatment plant, jumping into the water would have been a fool thing. Until that time, all of the city's waste was dumped directly into the river—300 million gallons a day.

I drew the bowline taut and tied it to a small log.

An elderly couple, walking the perimeter of the island, stopped near me.

Casually the man pointed at *Pearl*.

"She's getting away," he said.

So intent was I on Steve, careful that he not be carried off, I had been oblivious. The log "anchor" floated in the water. *Pearl* was slipping into deep water when I grabbed the rail and walked her back in. The man helped me roll a larger log down to the shore, to which we retied. He was, he said, a professor at a local college who found relaxation on the water, though it was difficult imagining this a soothing place, what with all the speedboats ripping around. As if to punctuate the thought, a couple on jet skis, he swarthy and she a bleached blonde, whizzed up onto the bank next to us, dumping their vehicles at the waterline. Each wore a designer wet suit, the graphics, colored bolts of lightning. They neither spoke nor nodded as they strutted off to rendezvous with friends sitting in the cockpit of a beached boat, rinsing beer in the shade of an overhanging tree.

Later, the professor and his wife returned and gave Steve a handful of tiny freshwater mussel shells. He whispered a thank-you, and they could tell by the way he clutched them, fingers over his palm, that he was appreciative. A good sign, I thought. Later, he sealed them in an envelope and tucked it in a hammock in the cabin. Weeks later he would find them reduced to dust, crushed by the ravel of fallen gear.

Late in the afternoon we left the picnic island. Hunting along the mainland shore, we found among the private clubs a marina that would accept transients. We filled the fuel tank and were assigned a covered slip. I did not mind cooking simple meals on the river, but it seemed pathetic in the marina: hunched over in the messy cockpit, heating noodles, cleaning pans and utensils in the muddy water.

Fortunately, there was on the grounds of My River Home Marina a small restaurant, the Lost Dog Saloon. The owner's daughter, Missy, a pretty, short-haired girl of about ten, drove us on her golf cart to a flight of steps that led to the restaurant's door. "You're welcome," she said with the faint haughtiness that comes to children who know they are privileged.

The Lost Dog was built on stilts, portending the ferocity of spring floods. There we ate our supper and later played billiards and Steve, video games. I was too tired to counsel against them; in fact, I welcomed his finding his own entertainment. Fatigue, after all, is the fatal failing of single parents.

That night it began to rain on the tin roof protecting the boats, and lightning burst in the west. I would have slept well were it not for the cacophony of raindrops on tin, loud and unnatural, and I wished we were camped on the riverbank, in the open, beyond the loom of the Philips 66 sign marking the marina entrance.

We hired a taxi to drive us the thirty miles to the St. Louis airport. Perhaps I was suckered into an age-old scam, but I did not protest the driver's circuitous route, which he defended on account of the spring floods and a number of roads still washed out. And in the lowlands we did see standing water, the cornfields ruined, collapsed and matted. The floods of '95 weren't as bad as those of '94, the driver said, but you wouldn't say that to the owner of these lands. He meant "extensive" rather than "bad." Which is just the way we speak, less specific than we might be, oblique and colloquial, but others know what we mean. Not as many farmers were ruined this year as last, but if yours is underwater, you're done.

We arrived at the airport just as Adria passed through concourse security, a bounce in her gait, dressed in one-piece overall shorts with snap straps, a beret, and an orange T-shirt. If that didn't turn your head, her smile would.

On the way back to the marina I had the driver stop at Grampa's department store. There I bought a large supply of granola bars, vacuum-packed noodle dishes, and a half dozen five-gallon polyethylene gas cans. These thirty gallons would extend our cruising range by 75 miles. Added to the 120 miles in the main tank, they meant that *Pearl* could theoretically make 195 miles between fuel stops. This, however, gave us a safety margin of just 7 miles between Memphis, Tennessee, and Greenville, Mississippi, the longest run. If we ran dry, I'd have to empty the six-gallon tank dedicated to the small outboard.

Back aboard, we wasted no time leaving My River Home. Soon we passed through the Alton lock and breasted the current where the Missouri River joins the Mississippi. On the VHF radio a tug captain advised the lockkeeper that the Missouri was moving ninety thousand cubic feet of water per second into the Mississippi. (During the Ice Age, it did not even flow this way, but north into Hudson Bay.)

A writer for the *Sioux City Register-Report* once wrote, "Of all the variables in creation, there is nothing so uncertain as the action of a jury, the mind of a woman and the condition of the Mississippi River."

Both Jolliet and La Salle were pummeled by the violence of the joining waters. Whole trees were thrown into the mix. After all, at 2,683 miles the Missouri is longer than the Mississippi, if one measures the latter from this point to its Minnesota headwaters. *Quimby's* says succinctly, "Missouri is very hazardous to all boaters, swift currents, thousands of dikes." It is the route Lewis and Clark took to the Continental Divide in 1804, still searching for a Northwest Passage. And there is no particular reason why it should be considered a tributary rather than the upper extension of the Mississippi . . . except that the whites came from the east.

A few miles down, the navigable course directs one into the Chain of Rocks Canal, which runs parallel to the river for several miles, separated from it by Chouteau Island. At the end of the canal was another dam, the Mel Price, the last we would see on the Mississippi. Gone was the relative calm of the "pools" between locks on the Upper Mississippi. From here to the Gulf of Mexico, the water would drop 422 feet and the current would increase from two to five miles per hour.

Nearing St. Louis, we found heavy commercial traffic, the barges loading and offloading at shoreside tanks and warehouses. Cheaper than rail, cheaper than trucks. Apex Oil, Illinois Sand, Union Electric, Drew Foods, ADM Growmark, Granite City Steel, Union Carbide. Their cargo was diverse: sand, grain, cement, oil, coal, fertilizer, soybeans, cottonseeds, salt, gravel, bulk liquids, construction equipment, and all classes of commodities. Four hundred seventy-five million tons of it each year. Food for the masses, materials for taming the wilderness, borne by the antlike tows up and down the arterial network of riverways. Handing off from one to another in a massive bucket brigade of barges. The commerce of the heartlands, making possible the opening up and building of America. The diesels and whistles and cranes, everywhere movement and bustle. What made America great.

Difficult as it was for us to believe, traffic was a far cry from what it was 150 years ago, before the railroads, before the first bridge that in 1856 connected Rock Island, Illinois, to Davenport, Iowa, before the span bringing freight over land and over water directly into St. Louis, and before the Civil War, when the steamboat was king. But like the wilderness, the golden age of steamboat travel was now but a memory.

Soon we saw the Freedom Arch, which we passed under leaden skies. During the Flood of '93, thirty of the sixty-three steps leading to the arch from the river were underwater. On August 1 of that year, the river crested at 49.58 feet. The levees were knocked aside as easily as an anthill kicked by a boot heel. The natural tendency to deconstruct and return to pre-America.

On entering the Mississippi we entered a new mileage system, one that begins at mile 868 near Coon Rapids, Minnesota, and counts down to mile 0 at the junction with the Ohio River. The Illinois River joins the Mississippi at mile 218. Clear of St. Louis, we sped on, stopping for the night at Hoppie's Marina at mile 158.5. This was not a marina in the conventional sense, but a cement barge that had been tied to the bank. An iron plaque identifier: "Missouri Valley Steel Co., Leavenworth, Kansas. 1949."

A dozen boats called this square of steel home—houseboats, runabouts, and an old wood cabin cruiser whose middle-aged owner was about to take a lady friend for an evening cruise. He stopped his preparations long enough to help us tie up, then cast off his own lines and gunned the engines to unpark his vessel. The swift current made such maneuvers difficult, especially as boats were tied tightly bow to stern. He was berthed in the narrow space between the barge and the shore, and with insufficient room to leave the dock in forward, he had to back out, careful not to be set down on the boat behind him, which would have driven his neighbor's anchor squarely into his barbecue grill. Two engines gave him better control than a single screw, however, and it was apparent that he was skilled at finding an equilibrium of current and throttle. It requires the same deft touch as a motorcyclist doing wheelies.

In the center of the barge was a makeshift lounge—several chairs losing their stuffing, a coffee table littered with beer cans and a full ashtray, all covered by a canvas awning. An elderly woman in flowered blouse and blue shorts walked down the steep grade from her house above the bank, then across the gangplank to the barge. She introduced herself as "Hoppie's wife, Fern." She collected her fee and directed me in the filling of our tanks.

"You're not from around here."

"No."

She studied *Pearl*'s registration numbers. "Where's RI?"

"Rhode Island."

"You didn't come by water?"

"No. We trailered to Chicago and came down the Illinois."

"How far you going?"

"New Orleans."

Though she had lived beside the river for many years and seen much, my remark seemed to startle her. "What's your range?"

"A hundred twenty in the main tank, seventy-five in the jugs."

When I had finished pumping and paid at the antique till set on a crude table in the "lounge," Fern opened her worn copy of *Quimby's* guide and proceeded to tell me which listed services were still in business, which had disappeared with the floods of the preceding years, and which had simply withered away. It seemed that selling fuel on the river was not very profitable, and that when men and women grew tired and had had enough of it, their retirement left a conspicuous gap in the chain of depots. Occasionally a son or daughter would assume the family business, not for money, just to be on the river. And if there were no interested offspring or inspired dreamers like Floyd Tucker, the recreational boater was severely inconvenienced. Up shit creek.

Fern spent some time with me, making calculations in the margin of the guide. At last she tired of it, concluding that we probably wouldn't make it.

All the while Steve tugged at my shirt, begging for permission to swim. Fern said it was safe at the foot of the sandy bank, just above the barge and inside a derelict crane moored adjacent to it. Said she allowed her grandchildren to play there, but not to go out past the crane as the current was swift and would surely transport him all the way to New Orleans.

For a time Adria and I floated in the shallows, watching Steve run down the bank to do belly flops into the silt-laden water. Between "Dad, watch this!" and cannonballs in our faces, we had fleeting moments to catch up.

Now twenty-four, she was graduated from art school, and until this summer had been employed at a large college bookstore in Ann Arbor. She'd quit in June to hike the Pacific Crest Trail with her former roommate. Her thought was to find new directions, guides, and spirits to point the way. Though she'd had much time alone, plodding the path in zen-like repetitions, nothing profound had come to her, only a strengthening of her commitment to art and a desire to learn the trade of fine bookmaking. Once the river trip was finished, her plan was to spend a week with an aunt and uncle in Alabama so that she might investigate a graduate program in Tuscaloosa.

When I was her age, I'd already been married six years, worked in the personnel office of a large teaching hospital, attended night school to earn my bachelor's degree, and fathered one child—her, Adria, my firstborn. I loved her like few things on this earth. Though her life was a bit at loose ends, I was happy that she was largely free to choose a career, unencumbered by the responsibilities of family or the need to make set wages. I envied her that.

At the moment there were no prominent boyfriends in her life, the last having moved away while she spent a year of study in Rome.

Watching her lying there in the river, Steve piling sand on her belly, I thought it strange how we live the lives of our children, feeling each pain and joy, wanting to pass on what we have learned, only to discover that we cannot. Each must learn the lessons anew. It is the great failing of man that his accumulated wisdom goes the way of his last breath, remembered, perhaps, but seldom built upon.

For me, too, there was the guilt of having left her years before, when she was eight, Peter four. Though the two had spent summers with me—and those were fine times—we all had missed much by my absence. I believed I was forgiven, but several times over the years, in discussion she would suddenly blurt, "But you left!" And I was wounded to the quick, struck in the heart.

Later, perhaps sensing my pain, she would acknowledge the influences I had had upon her—daring to change, to travel and seek adventure, to read and write and learn—and I would feel better. Still, there remained the question of how to make amends, and the sorrow of knowing that those years were lost and irrecoverable.

This day, while Steve climbed and flung himself from the bank and crane, releasing the energy saved sitting all day in the boat, Adria and I talked next about my lament for pre-America, that is, the death of wilderness. It was the sort of abstract discussion that interested her, and she was never without opinion.

Your grandfather, I said, was a conservationist, as opposed to a preservationist like John Muir. As a professional forester, his job was to make trees grow as fast, tall, and healthy as possible. Maximum sustained yield. A committee he chaired for President Richard Nixon was charged with determining what percentage of the nation's energy needs could be met by renewable resources. If industry was pushed, 30 percent, he said. Coal and petroleum still were essential. In the next millennium he saw atomic energy absorbing more of the load.

In a way, it could be said that his silviculture played a small part in the death of pre-America. He followed in the footsteps of his father, who in the 1890s got for himself a last piece of the mystery while mapping wilderness in Alaska.

He also followed in the footsteps of Gifford Pinchot, the first chief of the U.S Forest Service. In the 1890s, Pinchot actively promoted scientific management of the nation's timberlands. Lumbermen should not be allowed to log indiscriminately but should be encouraged, with the help of professional foresters. Only this approach could ensure the country a continuing supply of wood. Initially Muir and Pinchot were in agreement. Then, in 1896, Secretary of the Interior Hoke Smith appointed a commission to recommend specific policies for the management of the federal reserves. Muir wanted some parcels designated free of commercial use, while Pinchot thought the purpose of the committee was to get the nation ready for "practical forestry." Their break became final when Pinchot approved sheep grazing in the reserves. Muir termed sheep "hoofed locusts" and confronted Pinchot in a Seattle hotel lobby. When Pinchot affirmed his decision, Muir exclaimed, "Then . . . I don't want anything more to do with you. When we were in the Cascades last summer, you yourself stated that sheep did a great deal of harm."[6]

I related this story to Adria as a prelude to the questions I wished to ask regarding the possibility today of wilderness, for part of my quest was to learn whether the river was wild. Indeed, from the beginning, my search for La Salle hinged on the idea of my pre-America, the way it was before the whites. In its natural state. Parts of Georgian Bay, where Harrison John MacLean believed he had found remains of the *Griffon*, remain essentially wilderness. (By map I once figured the distance from the nearest road to myself, standing on a rock at Fox Island, to be fifty miles.) Though now surmounted by bridges, the Huron River, where La Salle built an elm-bark canoe, could be at least imagined as unchanged in any discernible way. On the other hand, Cayuga Creek, where the *Griffon* was built, was transformed into a depressing intersection of man and nature, the latter losing to pollution and poor taste.

It was to me ironic that what I saw there on the Little Niagara River was the "civilization" our forebears worked so hard to achieve. For the Puritan, his Christian view of the world taught that light was good and dark, evil, therefore the clearing was holy and the forest, ungodly, the place of devils and temptation. Not until the Romantic period did poets and artists and young men of means (who did not have to build their own houses) see in the unblemished wilderness the possibility of beauty and spiritual renewal, see that the mountains might actually be the handiwork of God.

The question I posed to Adria was this: Must all land be managed? A Japanese acquaintance once told me that every square inch of his country was managed, even the tiny portions that mimic wilderness, and that owing to the population density, this must be so. Was the same true of the United States?

You must define your terms, she said. Was the land on top of a mountain managed, just because it is contained within a reserve under the ostensible control of a government agency? Were these lands not as virgin as they were before the Forest Reserve Act of 1891? To lose the designation of wilderness, must the trees, game, and land actually be manipulated by man in some way as to change them? After all, the definition of wilderness has nothing to do with the law—rather it is simply a tract or region uncultivated and uninhabited by human beings.

Perhaps this is true, I said, but if the surrounding environment of this tract is altered, how can we be certain that the supposed wilderness above it has not been affected? A dam, for instance, might eliminate fish from the streams that feed the reservoir. Industrial emissions might cause seemingly insignificant species of vegetation to mutate on the mountaintop.

She then shifted to the idea of landscape. The changes to the land must be intelligently conceived, she said, and done so artistically that it might be pleasing to all those who live there or in some other way behold it.

That is the artist in you speaking, I said, not the philosopher. So you, too, are a conservationist, just like your grandfather! Even as John Brinckerhoff Jackson, founder of *Landscape* magazine, chronicled the distribution of land and the making of roads and gardens, some very beautiful, he lamented man's alienation from wilderness, from his origins.

Steve suddenly fell into the water between us, trying to pull my trunks down, laughing at the whiteness of my "butt."

"You farted!"

La Salle Descends the Illinois on the Ice, January 1682, *by George Catlin, painted in 1847–48.* (PAUL MELLON COLLECTION, © 1997 BOARD OF TRUSTEES, NATIONAL GALLERY OF ART, WASHINGTON, D.C.)

"No, I didn't."

Adria: "C'mon, guy."

Most of our river conversations ended like that.

By the time La Salle at last returned to the Mississippi for his historic run all the way down, it was December 1681, and this time he was ready for it. With him was the indefatigable Henri de Tonti, and the Recollet friar Zénobe Membré—in all, there were twenty-three Frenchmen in his party as well as about twenty-five Indians, some from New England, they having fled from the defeat in Rhode Island of the Mohegan chief, King Philip. The warriors hunted and the squaws cooked, strapping their babies to planks and hanging them in trees to free their own hands for work.[7]

The Illinois River was frozen and it was necessary to drag the canoes like sleds. When they came to the Mississippi, they found it also iced over and were forced to wait. They built fires on the bank and watched the eagles dive futilely to catch fish caught between layers of ice. Then, one morning, a rumbling awoke them, and they rose to see the ice crack, the fragments shift; soon thereafter the sun melted the ice and the river opened.

If La Salle's spirits were lifted, as I supposed, he apparently remained unimpressed. Of the five firsthand accounts written about the descent,[8] none made much fuss about the Mississippi. The historian Anka Muhlstein wrote: "It is as though the Saint Lawrence had dulled their capacity for surprise and enthusiasm toward any other river: the 'Father of Waters' drew not a single exclamation of astonishment from them."[9]

It could not have helped that here the party's one compass was accidentally broken, a misfortune that in the days ahead would spin an ever more intricate web of errors. And although La Salle had acquired a descriptive account of Soto's discovery of a large southern river—called in various Indian tongues the Chucagoa, the Tapatu, and other names—it, too, served only to confound him. During the 141 years separating Soto and La Salle, things had changed, presumably so much so that what the latter saw did not jibe with the observations of the former.

Traveling in Indian canoes, the large party quickly moved downstream. Where the Missouri enters, at a less oblique angle than the smaller Illinois, the spring torrent carried with it chunks of earth, trees, and other flotsam. Tossed by the turbulent meeting of waters, several of the canoes were nearly swamped.

On the western prairies thousands of buffalo grazed. In some places the animals were drinking from the river, so thick that the canoes could not find passage between them. The Indians among the party hunted the buffalo. However, La Salle, afraid of injuries, forbade his men from engaging the animals that writer François René de Chateaubriand (for whom the large, sauce-covered steak was named) described as having "the mane of a lion, the hump of a camel, the hide and hindquarters of a rhinoceros or hippopotamus, and the horns and legs of a bull."[10] The squaws cooked. They collected macopin, a root with an onionlike flavor. La Salle wrote that the squaws made "a hole in the ground and into it put a layer of stones that are red from the fire, then a layer of leaves, then one of macopins, another of reddened stones, and so on to the top, which they cover with earth and let the roots sweat inside. It is quite a good dish, as long as the roots are well cooked."[11]

On this stretch of the river all seemed well. The Frenchmen ate plentiful portions of buffalo, deer, turkeys, swans, and bustards, and the Indians were not afraid of their tribal enemies. No attacks came from either side, and the river was manageable. As the journey and the calendar progressed, the weather warmed. The river was lined with walnut, oak, elm, and plums, and everywhere the grass was the height of a man. But good fortune was not to last.

Adria slept on the deck of Hoppie's cement barge, making her bed with a sleeping bag and covering her head with a mosquito net that she had worn during her summer hiking. Steve and I slept in the cabin, tormented by insects of every imaginable species, large and small, crawling and flying, all swarming to the light by which I read. Huck Finn had just escaped his pa, faking his own murder by smearing pig's blood about the cabin. Then he took to the river, where he hid in a canoe, much as I had done one day when I was fifteen. My father had sent me to yet another psychiatrist. (His logic: If you have legal problems, call a lawyer. If you're sick, call the doctor. If you can't control your child's behavior, send him to a psychiatrist.) On returning home, I protested my displeasure by lighting out the back door. Down the ravine I scrambled below the house, following the frozen creek to the lake where we kept an aluminum Grumman canoe. I paddled out to a reedy marsh in the middle of the lake, in the midst of which was a small patch of dry ground. There, on a previous visit, I had concealed a few supplies for just such an emergency—a can of Spam and a can of sardines—which I ate, more to authenticate my mastery of nature than out of hunger. I overturned the canoe and pushed it far from the reeds in the hope that its discovery would not lead to my hideaway. But as the day waned I grew cold. Perhaps I forgot why I was even there. Half wading and half swimming, I came ashore on the far bank, walked the lake shore to the nearest bridge, and shuffled home. I snuck in the backdoor and drew a bath, deceiving myself that I might never have been missed. Until a sheriff's deputy, tall and solid, the butt of his revolver conspicuous in its holstered orientation, stood in the doorway and inquired of my welfare. I nodded. Then my parents stuck their heads in. "I'm fine," I said, as if nothing had happened.

"We found the canoe upside down on the lake," Father said.

"We thought you'd drowned," Mother cried.

"As you can see," I answered in the same snotty tone Huck might have used with the Widow Douglas, "I'm fine."

. . .

Steve turned on the light to swat a mosquito buzzing in his ear. Purely in the interest of science, I told him that only gravid females suck the blood of mammals, and do so to feed their young. Steve turned off the light and said, "Dad, if a nice animal like a snake has to bite me to feed its babies, I'd let it bite. I wouldn't kill it."

"That's nice," I said. "Just be sure it isn't poisonous."

There was a moment of silence and I wondered if he was asleep or still thinking.

Then he said, "If it is, cut the X on me with your pocket knife and suck out the poison. Okay, Dad?"

"Yes, I will suck it out."

Yes, I thought, I will die for you, too. And for Adria. I'd have died for Pete if that would have saved him. If I had been there, I would have tried. But I wasn't. That is my eternal shame. And so I silently promised Steve that for as many years as possible I would stay with him, knowing, as Margaret had known of Peter, that I could not forever shield him.

# CHAPTER 11

# To the River
# Calmer Than Air

*In my beginning is my end.*

—T. S. Eliot, *Four Quartets*

Come the dawn. Come the sun. The oblique rays shone on *Pearl's* topsides as she lay against Hoppie's cement barge. The air in the cabin warmed. With my eyes closed, it was the first clue that the day had begun. As I looked out the window, the orange orb was visible, shining through the trees on the opposite bank. Several mosquitoes clung to the overhead above my feet, beyond reach.

As always, I awoke before Steve. Partly because he is insensitive to those who still slumber, clamoring in the ear and tussling covers, but mostly because I feared his falling overboard. His habit was to leave a fishing line out overnight, and on waking his impulse was to kick off the sheet, launch himself into the cockpit, and jerk the line. This he would do standing on the aft seat, balancing himself against the rocking of the hull. I reached to touch him; yes, he was still there. Sleeping, his face was angelic, and as white. His blond hair was ruffled by the pillow, his lips slightly parted. Then a muscle in his jaw twitched; even in sleep he was busy—fishing, swimming, chasing snakes. . . .

Adria still lay on the dock, one leg showing through the unzipped side of her sleeping bag. She wore full-length nylon hiking pants, which I thought peculiar as they must have made her hot. Mosquito headgear covered her face. I lit the camp stove, filled the tea kettle with bottled water, then scrounged through the canvas bags for tea. In the cooler I found a bottle of cold juice. The ice was nearly melted. Nowhere had we been able to find block ice, and in the summer swelter twenty pounds of cubes lasted but a day. I sat down on one of the two swivel seats, propped my feet on the other, and peeled the wrapper from a honey granola bar.

The river was awake. Always pulling and pushing at the hull, it does not sleep as a lake or ocean sometimes does. The mooring lines quivered. A tow had passed as I was waking, but now the river was empty. The dark-green leaves above me were motionless . . . before the breeze filled in. The pastel colors of the predawn—violet, pink, and peach—were gone from the eastern sky, burned out by the sun. This day, like all the others, would be hot. No rain was forecast, no respite for the ataractic crew. I gave up listening to the VHF weather channel.

The St. Louis stretch had been thick with commercial shipping and though the barges and tugs broke the monotony of the earthen levees, I was glad to have the traffic behind us. In two days we'd come to the confluence of the Ohio and the beginning of the Lower Mississippi, what I now anticipated as the virgin river—untamed, prettier, but how wild?

Of equal concern was the big Evinrude outboard, which at least once each day bogged and kicked. It had been clear to me, ever since Henry, Illinois, that there was little hope of finding an OMC mechanic or anyone else qualified to examine it, and the odds would diminish as we moved south. There was little choice but to press on. At the worst, I would unpack the spare-parts kit and replace all that I could. I had a manual and a few tools, but no easy place to work—a dropped part would be lost forever, tumbling through the upper strata of clay, silt, and mud.

From a zippered compartment in my briefcase I drew out Peter's funeral card. For a moment I studied the picture of him. He sat smiling at the helm of a big catamaran, his arms and legs so thin it did not seem possible that he could have handled the helm. But he had begun to grow taller and in time would have filled out. Muscle strength, given the cerebral palsy, was less certain.

From the back of the card I reread the passage from *Siddhartha* in which the ferryman, Vasudeva, leaves the river for the woods. Margaret had selected it, and on every reading of the words I sought understanding not only of Peter's death, but also of his mother, clues to the thoughts that helped heal her.

"I have waited for this hour, my friend. Now that it has arrived, let me go."

As if Peter had expected his death. Twelve was too dear an age to be so burdened. But his cerebral palsy made him aware of certain things. He held my hand crossing streets, because he knew his legs could not be trusted. He held my hand on docks, because he could not swim. Once, at a Boy's Club camp, he was standing in a line of children. As they began to move forward, a boy behind pushed him down. Those that followed stepped on him. One spat on him. That night, when he told me, I was furious. The next day I met with the counselors—who loved him but were helpless to monitor everyone at all times. I pulled him from camp. "Pete," I said, "I'm so sorry." He looked at me with big, mournful eyes, as if he knew.

But why did Vasudeva go to die among the trees? Is not the river life *and* death? Once, when I was a child, my best friend's dog disappeared. We asked the advice of our neighbor Julie. "Look to the river," she said. "Dogs go there to die." And so we searched the banks of the Huron, and among the snags we saw at the surface his black matted hair, the body thinner than we remembered. Was not the river then the natural conveyance of life to death? Siddhartha "saw that the water continually flowed and flowed and yet it was always there; it was always the same and yet every moment it was new." Time, he concluded, does not exist. All things are transitory. Everything is necessary.

If the river is life, then death is a necessary way point. But the journey does not end there, no more than the river ends at a dam. On Peter's death I had tried to console myself with the idea that everything existing always has existed and always will exist. Forms change: Mass becomes energy but does not stop being. Nothing disappears or ceases to exist. That is why I continued to spread Peter's ashes, always thinking of the union organizer Joe Hill's requiem: "Perhaps some dying flower then, will come to life and bloom again." A few particles of mineral matter go up the stalk. That, to me, was the very real root of the Buddhist idea of reincarnation. And nothing more. If a cow eats the flower, Pete has not been reborn as a cow.

I don't buy the idea of spirits being distinct from bodies. Christians think God has a trunk full of spirits and infuses one in each new embryo. One of man's most important spiritual tasks, then, is to come to know the mission God has imprinted on his soul. On death, the spirit separates and survives, beatified or tortured, depending on how the person lived his life. But is this not a trick to beat death and nothingness? And is not nothingness precisely what the Buddhist seeks, the end of suffering, which is caused by cognition? How strange that the Buddhist desires what the Christian fears! (Which is not to say there is no such thing as spirituality, the immaterial intelligence of a creature!) Here the supposed commonality of world religions seems to break down.

And what of the Native American belief that all life forms are imbued with spirit—buffalo, wolves, trees, flowers, and man with two spirits, one of the body, which on death dies or becomes a ghost, and a free spirit that travels to the afterworld? But again I did not understand how the *orenda*, or spirit, of, say, a fallen warrior passes to the one who slew him, even if the slayer ate the warrior's heart with his hands.

No, for me the "life spark" is simply electricity, measured in microvolts, that winks and blinks like a firefly, and on the precipice of death shines for an instant more brightly (as does a lightbulb) before being extinguished. That is all.

Afterlife is the memory of the living. And if immortality is having a turnpike service area named for you in the dead zone of New Jersey (Grover Cleveland, Walt Whitman, et al.), let me go.

Steve seemed to be reborn each morning. Each day with more energy than the last. While I sat eating my granola bar, he pushed through the hatch screen, scrambling on hands and knees into the cockpit as if kicked from behind. He picked himself up and checked the rod. This morning there was a small catfish. He lowered the fish into a bucket, where it flapped for its life. Seeing that it was too small to eat, I added some water.

"Adria!" he yelled.

"Ssh!" I said. "Let her sleep. I think she had a rough night."

Ignoring my plea, he crawled from the rail to the dock and tugged at her bag.

"Wake up! Adria! Come see my fish!"

She sat up as if awakened from the dead, removed the net from her head, and asked for the time.

"Seven," I said.

She fell back as if terribly disappointed.

Her night had been broken by the sound of passing trains, which ran behind the ridge, and the searchlights of the tows playing across the water. And of course there were mosquitoes, many of them, which accounted for her putting on the nylon pants. Then, at first light, while Steve and I slept soundly below, a man had come along the dock to ask why she was sleeping there. Apparently he thought she was a vagrant, perhaps a runaway. She told him she belonged to *Pearl*, which he accepted grudgingly before returning to his houseboat moored several lengths above us.

Soon Steve was in the water, the "safe" area between the shore and barge and crane. Despite his entreaties, Adria and I declined to join him, whereupon he grew annoyed with us and refused to come out. I told him he could swim until the cockpit was cleaned. Afterward, he still refused. Patiently, I gave him until ice was bought and emptied into the coolers. When he persisted, I stalked into the water and lifted him kicking. Sat him down in the cockpit and told him to stay put. When Adria stood to handle a mooring line, he stole her seat. And I'd thought we were making progress.

I advanced the throttle just enough to keep us from being swept backward into the boat behind. The bowline was let go first and the bow pushed from the dock. Quickly we untied the stern line and I gunned the engine to jolt us away from the barge. By the time I executed a slow turn, the current had carried us well downstream. Once *Pearl* was up on plane and I thought to look over my shoulder, Hoppie's barge was gone.

In the first hour we covered twenty-five miles. Steering down the empty river, banking into the gentle turns, was like driving a race car in a video arcade game. The trees on the banks sped by. The air was cool on my face. My shirt flapped. When the sun slanted under the Bimini, I wore a baseball cap to shade my forehead, but if I raised my head the wind would catch under the brim and blow it off. A boat hook was kept at the ready for fetching. Putting it back wet on my head felt good.

At mile 122.5 we turned toward a narrow side channel on the west bank. Slowing, *Pearl* squatted in her own wake, nearly drifting past the entrance. Pointing the bow upstream, I pushed the throttle hard and we squirted free of the current, settling in the still backwater of Gabouri Creek. The change in motion awoke Steve and Adria, both of whom had fallen asleep, he on the seat beside me, she on the beanbag between the chairs.

The nap had done little to reverse Steve's dark disposition. When he awoke he refused to come ashore at the Marina de Gabouri. I could not leave him, and so lifted his thin frame onto my shoulders and carried him up the steep hill, past the fuel tanks to the crest. Below us to the west stretched the floodplain, green where wet, brown where dry. Overlooking the river was a cinder-block building, at one end a restaurant, at the other a tackle shop and chandlery. We took a table. Steve refused to eat. He demanded change to play video games in the back. I refused. So he stood staring at the lights generated by the automatic preview, pushing the inactive buttons.

"What's his problem?" Adria whispered.

I shrugged. "Maybe it's because we wouldn't swim with him. Maybe he woke up cranky. He hates it when he can't have his way. I'm working on it, hoping this trip might turn him around."

Knowing I couldn't feed him under way, I ordered an extra hamburger and French fries. I carried him from the video machine to the booth, ignoring the reproachful eyes of the other patrons. After much argument, he picked at the meat. The bun he tossed onto my plate, backhanded like a Frisbee.

When *Pearl* was refueled we darted from the creek, running another hour to the mouth of the Kaskaskia River. Opposite, on the west bank, was a town of the same name, plumb in the middle of Kaskaskia Island, which isn't an island at all, though it used to be, before the Mississippi bulled its way across a stretch of land into the Kaskaskia River and abandoned itself. Slithered out of the west channel like a snake leaving its skin.

The origins of the town reach back to the site of Starved Rock Marina, where we'd launched the *Pearl*. There, across from the flat-topped bluff fortified by La Salle, was the first of six Kaskaskia villages. This succession is a logbook of those transitional years that mark the beginning of the end of pre-America.

In 1673, Father Claude Allouez, a Jesuit, journeyed down from his Green Bay mission to indoctrinate the Indians of the Illinois River valley, the Peoria, Miami, and Kaskaskia tribes. In the waning years of pre-America, news traveled faster than one might suppose. Some Peoria Indians who had been camped on the Mississippi and had met Jolliet during his descent of the river arrived in Kaskaskia to inform Allouez that the Jolliet party intended to return to the Great Lakes not by the route they'd come down, but by ascending instead the Illinois. Perhaps because Jolliet's enterprise was a government-sponsored expedition, Allouez had no interest in it, timing his return to Green Bay so that they did not even meet. But four years later, at the behest of his superiors, Allouez returned to minister to the Indians during the years that La Salle and Tonti erected Fort St. Louis atop the rock (1682–83).

After La Salle's death, the Indians informed Tonti of their intention to move "because fire-wood was remote and because it was so difficult to get water upon the Rock if they were attacked."[1] With Tonti's cooperation, the village relocated fifty miles downstream to the tribe's winter hunting grounds at Peoria Lake. Another fort was built there, completed in 1692. From the journal of Tonti's cousin, Pierre Delliette, who lived at Fort Pimitoui, comes this description of the missionaries, who made daily rounds tending to the sick, often bleeding them:

> After which they have it cried through the village that they are about to say Mass. Then they teach the catechism or they preach sermons. In the afternoon, after having applied themselves to the language, they return to the village to teach the catechism, which always takes two hours. The pieces of wood, husks of Indian corn, and even stones which are thrown at them do not dismay them; they continue their cries, contenting themselves with saying that it is the Master of life who orders them to do what they are doing.[2]

Pierre Le Moyne, Sieur d'Iberville, who succeeded in doing what fate took from La Salle—colonizing the delta—in 1699 commanded two hundred soldiers and settlers in Louisiana. At the same time, the Kaskaskia Indians were feeling threatened by the Fox and Iroquois. In September of 1700, accompanied by Father Gravier and Father Marest, they broke camp and, led by Chief Rouensa, headed south to solicit the protection of Iberville. At the confluence of the Des Peres and Mississippi rivers, just south of St. Louis, Father Marest fell ill and the plan was abandoned. Chief Rouensa's 1,200 people joined with others there of the Tamaroa, Metchigamia, and Cahokia tribes, as well as some French traders.

Afraid of a Sioux attack, in 1703 the Kaskaskia chief moved yet another sixty miles downstream, where the people established themselves about four miles up the Kaskaskia River. Thus the fourth Kaskaskia.

The fifth arose when in 1718 the French commandant of the Illinois country, Pierre Boisbriant, established a fort in the fourth, and Chief Rouensa, feeling crowded by too many whites, moved his tribe five miles farther upstream. For Chief Rouensa, pre-America was a memory.

The sixth occurred because of the Mississippi, which during the flood of April 1881 broke through into the Kaskaskia. The townspeople endured for several years, finding themselves treading water in times of flood. Finally, in 1894, they moved the settlement across the river to its present site on Kaskaskia Island. Though situated on the Missouri side of the river, Kaskaskia belongs to Illinois, one of several towns that over the years has flip-flopped with the river.

A few miles downstream we hoped to find dockage at the town of Chester, Illinois. A single-track railroad ran along the waterfront. Below the highway bridge a coal barge was being loaded. As we were coming to expect, there was no marina, no fuel dock, and here was not even a launch ramp where we could run the bow ashore. Thus there was no opportunity to explore the town, in particular the six-foot statue of Popeye, created in 1929 by Chester-born Elzie Crisler Segar. It is said that he modeled his cartoon characters—Olive Oyl, Wimpy, and Bluto—on local residents. More succinct than Herman Hesse, Segar once observed, "They ain't no myskery to life. Ya gits borned and that's all they is to it."[3]

South of Chester, just below the Southern Illinois Sand Pier Light, we turned in to inspect the mouth of the St. Mary's River, where La Salle and his party had camped during the frigid winter-spring of 1682. Now, a railroad bridge crossed the stream, preventing us from proceeding more than a few feet up it. Begrudgingly I idled *Pearl* down along the bank until we came to another small stream with an island at its mouth. Behind it we dropped the anchor. The island was not made of the mud we were used to, but sand. This was a pleasing change, as we did not lose our sandals in the muck or track globs back on the deck and into the cockpit, which generally required constant cleaning. The footing was firm, and we swam without filtering silt through our trunks.

Looking back toward the mouth of the St. Mary's, I thought not only of La Salle but of Reid Lewis, the Elgin, Illinois, French teacher who in 1976 reenacted La Salle's descent of the Mississippi.

Reid, like Lee Politsch, was fixated on La Salle, harboring a long and abiding interest in the explorer. Reid named his journey "La Salle: Expedition II." His aim was to replicate the event with as much authenticity as possible: handmade Algonquian-style birch-bark canoes, moose-hide moccasins, and a diet of boiled peas and cornmeal. To accompany him, Lewis hand-picked twenty-three other voyageurs—a Franciscan priest, a playwright, five teachers and seventeen high school students. "I wanted young people because most of the original voyageurs were young people. In those days, a man of thirty-five was over the hill," Lewis said. "I had another reason. During the past few years, I've watched my students get more and more cynical about the possibility of individual accomplishment in this society. And I've watched my own generation get more and more contemptuous of youth's ability to respond to challenge. The reenactment was a chance to show both groups that the independent spirit of the voyageur was still alive in America. Our main purpose was educational. Besides reenacting the voyage, we were also interpreting it to the communities along our route, and using it to dramatize our concern with historical and environmental preservation."[4]

Lewis's group began its 3,300-mile trip in Montreal and paddled down the St. Lawrence River to Lake Ontario, which they traversed as far as Toronto. In La Salle's day, the portage between Lake Ontario and Lake Simcoe was known as the Toronto Carrying Place, then a thirty-five-mile dirt path through forest. La Salle had chosen it over the easier Lake Erie–Detroit River route because hostile Iroquois had banded on the Lake Erie shore. Lewis chose it because this was the way of La Salle, and he was obliged to follow. It took Lewis about as long—twelve days—and required two and a half round trips to move the supplies through downtown Toronto and north to Lake Simcoe. The men stuffed grass in their moccasins to cool their burning feet.

By design, Lewis's timing coincided with La Salle's, and he found himself crossing Georgian Bay and thence Lake Michigan in wintertime. Fires were started with flint and steel, courses plotted with a quadrant, shelter from the rain was found under overturned canoes, and distances measured by the hourly break for smoking pipes. Clothing was handmade and included knitted stocking caps called *toques*; knee breeches or *haut-de-chausses*; linen shirts with ruffled collars called *chemises*; scarves, or *foulards*; a leather jerkin called *paletot en cuir*, leg ties, or *jarretières*, and leggings, called *mitasses*; headbands called *bandeaux*; and loincloths, or *pagnes*. At night they slept under canvas tarpaulins stretched between canoes and supported by paddles. When the lakes and rivers froze, they built sleds of saplings and pulled their supplies behind them. The men had trained for such hardships, directed by a physical conditioning expert who noted that "the original voyageurs didn't need to train. Their way of life had already conditioned them for the work. They would have found the idea of voluntary exercise mystifying." Indeed, La Salle's trek between Lake Michigan and the St. Lawrence River had become an almost annual ordeal. Rowing, the men maintained a pace of fifty to sixty strokes per minute for up to fourteen hours per day.

The expedition member Ken Lewis said of his brother, Reid, that "for two and a half months, he [came] as close to actually *being* La Salle as anyone is likely to come."

While I was preparing *Pearl* for the Mississippi, more than one friend said that I ought to do this in a raft, like Huckleberry Finn and Tom Sawyer. And I would reply, no, I ought to be doing it in a canoe, like La Salle. But it took La Salle and Lewis two months to paddle from Chicago to the gulf. At an average of twenty miles per hour, *Pearl* covered the same distance in sixteen days. Leisurely. Yes, I would have liked to slow it down—not on *Pearl* but maybe on a canoe or raft whose speed was tied to the current. But not as slow as Harlan and Anna Hubbard, a couple who in the late 1940s spent three and a half years drifting from Ohio to New Orleans in a home-built shantyboat. I guess it is a necessity of modern living to speed things up: In 1814, the steamboat *Orleans* made the 268-mile run from New Orleans to Natchez in six days, six hours, and forty minutes. Another steamboat, the *Robert E. Lee*, in 1870, did the trip in seventeen hours and eleven minutes. In the same time period, the passage from New Orleans to Louisville shrank from twenty-five days to four. Compared to the round-the-clock boiler feeding of the general's namesake, our cruise was a honeymoon of short days and long nights.

No, I did not regret the constraints that forced me to rely on a motorboat. I understood Lewis's motivation—but I wasn't trying to be La Salle. I had the inclination, but neither the time nor money (Lewis spent $500,000). And the farther we traveled down the river, the more I realized that while deeds might transform a man, he cannot become another. Everything is transitory. Even the river. Especially a man.

. . .

During the afternoon we made a good run of forty-six miles to Devil's Island, just above Cape Girardeau, Missouri. Since leaving St. Louis, the river had flowed southerly and mostly straight. But here, suddenly, it swung westward and we were blinded by the falling sun, which flecked the water silver and gold so that it sparkled like sequins.

We beached *Pearl* just below a wing dam, a wall of rocks conceived by potamologists and laid by the Corps of Engineers to center the current and so keep the midstream channel scoured and deep. The dam provided some protection from wakes, and in the countercurrent that swirled in its lee many fish jumped. As Steve unbuckled his tackle box, he was hopeful. He'd come around sometime during the past few hours, returning to his usual silly self—leaping, pouncing, chattering. I wished he could explain his changes, but I believed he did not know himself. He is what he is when he is—"no myskery."

Adria and Steve built a campfire in the sand. She fanned the tiny flame

*Adria and Steve built a campfire on the white sand of a towhead, an alluvial island or sandbar.*

leaping up from paper and twigs. Steve added driftwood found along the beach. Though it was surface-dry, much of it did not completely burn. We had neither hot dogs nor marshmallows, so we heated noodle packs on the camp stove. Steve would not leave the fire, eating ashore sitting on his haunches. In a dream state I watched, seeing an Indian child picking flesh from the spine of a fish, sucking the fat from his fingers, the firelight making shadows dance on his brown skin.

When the mosquitoes came I emptied the cabin of our duffels and stuffed the beanbag in the well between the berths. The sleeping bags were laid out three abreast. We lay shoulder to shoulder. Before reading from *Huckleberry Finn*, we had to kill the insects drawn by the cabin light. Steve suggested I read by his penlight—an excellent idea. Huck and Jim had stumbled across each other on a midstream island, the boy having escaped from his drunken father, the slave from his owner. Together they had taken off down the river on a raft, Jim hiding by day in the tepee. They caught a large catfish, a discussion of which terminated my reading. How long? How heavy? What bait did they use? Did they use pliers to skin it, like you, Dad?

Before dawn we heard the purr of an outboard motor. A solitary man sat at the stern of an open skiff, directing the boat into the channel behind Devil's Island. In the faint light, the figure of man and boat were black and silhouetted against the lighter water. As we watched, he shut off the motor and moved forward, then bent over and pulled to the surface a series of hoop nets. The fish leaped and flapped, their bodies silver, bellies white. The fisherman emptied each net into the boat, then returned it empty to the bottom.

Steve stood on the bank.

"Three in that one, Dad!"

He cast his own rod as he counted.

"Just one fish in this one, Dad!"

His casting was rhythmic and reflexive, the repetition sublimating his excitement. He wouldn't have noticed if he'd hooked one himself. But as many fish as there were in the water, none took Steve's lure, and when the fisherman started his motor and left the channel, Steve returned to *Pearl*. Failure did not disturb him, as I had expected it might. He understood that that is the nature of fishing. In time he would come to understand that it also is the nature of life.

After breakfast and a swim, we ran two miles downstream to Cape

*At Honker's Boat Club on the outskirts of Cape Girardeau, Missouri, Steve made friends with the fisherman who brought in this thirty-pound catfish. This fish, for Steve, was the river god.*

Girardeau. The chart showed a small boat dock, which we found on the outskirts of town. A sign said "Honker's Boat Club—Private." A small cabin cruiser followed us in, a large catfish gasping in the cockpit. The mate held him up for Steve.

"Now that, son, is a catfish."

"How much does he weigh?"

"Thirty pounds."

This, to Steve, was the river god. While he studied the fish—peering into its mouth, running his hand over the smooth and slimy skin—I walked up the hill to a trailer where sat a man in coveralls.

"Fern Hoppie says there's fuel here."

"Used to be," the man said. He pointed up the drive toward the state road and an empty filling station. "See that mud line 'bout eight feet up, that's the flood of '93. There's another station toward town. How many jugs you got?"

"Six."

"Most folks doin' like you pay me to take 'em in the pickup."

"How much?"

"Fifteen."

"Sounds like a deal to me. But the sign said 'private'; I wasn't sure we could come in."

He shrugged, as if that hadn't stopped anybody before.

Adria and I fetched the jugs. Steve and Adria climbed in back. I sat in the cab.

The driver said his name was Tom Woolsey, but did not offer his hand.

"It's hot," I said.

" 'Bout what you expect."

We turned off the drive onto the paved road, pausing long enough to take further note of the mud line on the station wall.

"Come up pretty high last spring, but nuthin' like '93. Put him right out of business."

Folks older than Woolsey still talked about the flood of '27: 26,000 square miles inundated; every bridge between Cairo and the delta swept away, save one; 650,000 people homeless; maybe 500 dead. Nobody knows for sure.

No sooner had we started down the road than I saw the next gas station. Though it was not visible from Woolsey's trailer, this second station was no more than a few hundred feet from the first—I'd been snookered!

Tom watched as we filled the jugs. When the attendant tallied the bill, the total seemed low.

"Should be more," I said.

"You want, I can charge you more."

"The gallons are low."

Adria stooped to look. "Dad," she said, "you bought two-and-a-half-gallon jugs. Not five."

She was right. How stupid! In my rush back at Grampa's department store, I'd grabbed the wrong size. While they were easier to handle, we weren't carrying as much fuel as I had thought. Our range was about thirty-five to forty miles short.

The station had no jugs for sale, so we returned to the boat, paid

Woolsey, and poured what we had into the tank. When the two fisher-men prepared to leave, I asked for a ride to town, citing the urgency of our situation. The skipper allowed as how we could sit in the back of his Jeep with the catfish, which suited Steve fine.

We walked the streets of Cape Girardeau, which like so many Ameri-can cities had been abandoned for the malls. A jeweler said we weren't likely to find gas jugs anywhere short of the Napa store out by the free-way. At the grocery I asked about wine and was told the same. Having succeeded in obtaining fuel for neither the boat nor myself, we began walking back to Honker's Boat Club. A young man with a bag of bread passed us on the sidewalk.

"You're looking for wine?"

I nodded.

"I can sell you some at the restaurant. Follow me."

He led us to Griffin's, a pleasant corner tavern with dark wood walls and heavy chairs. We ate the loaf of bread and left with two bottles of Fet-zer Chardonnay and a bottle of Walnut Crest Merlot.

Fifty-two miles south of Cape Girardeau we saw to port the town of Cairo, Illinois. Behind us were two wide river bends, Dogtooth and Greenleaf, together making an S-curve so that the boat's compass had moved from south to northwest to west to south to southeast, then to east, to south, to west, and to south again. The Ohio snuck in behind us, much like the Mississippi when we left the Illinois. But here there was a remark-able clue to its sudden appearance: The water from the Ohio was green—"opaque," Parkman called it. "More transparent than crystal, calmer than air," wrote Chateaubriand. Indeed, its Indian name means "beautiful river." The Mississippi was a diarrhetic brown; the line between the two rivers was sharply defined, and this line remained quite distinct for a mile, when the two waters mixed, though thereafter the river was never quite as dark and muddy as the Upper Mississippi.

Huck and Jim had planned to turn up the Ohio and make their way to the free states. But they passed it in a fog: "When it was daylight, here was the clear Ohio water inshore, sure enough, and outside was the old regular Muddy! So it was all up with Cairo."

Some say that here the Ohio joins the Mississippi; others say the Missis-sippi joins the Ohio, for both are long, wide, and formidable.

．．．

In 1669 La Salle had explored the Ohio at least as far as the rapids at Louisville, but during his 1682 descent he began to suspect that the Mississippi was actually the river mentioned in accounts of the Soto *entrada*: the Chucagoa, of which the Ohio, he conjectured, was merely a tributary. Robert Weddle, the Texas-based historian and La Salle authority, says that La Salle believed that the Chucagoa formed a separate river system parallel to the Río del Espíritu Santo, which had been shown on maps since 1527 (that of Diogo Ribeiro).[5] But the Chucagoa did not exist; the misconception (because the river he was on, the Mississippi, did not seem to match the details of the charts he had) only reinforced the other errors of his navigation. The effect was momentous, rippling through his subsequent decisions.

It is easy to find fault with La Salle. The man was confused. But not only was he trying to decipher the wilderness, he was trying to reconcile his observations with descriptions of the river he'd found in accounts of Soto's *entrada*. If, in 1669, his critics might ask, he had descended the Ohio to the Mississippi, as Abbé Renaudot asserted, why did he not now recognize the green-brown junction? Because Renaudot's narrative was fiction? Could La Salle have recognized the juxtaposition of colors yet said nothing to his men? Or if he had, could the diarists in his party have omitted or altered certain facts? Maybe he was going crazy, all the rivers becoming like serpents from a hole in the ground, each nearly the same as another.[6]

Ah, but these are his "missing years," Lee Politsch's years, pages of history blown from their binding.

Along the banks were moored fleets of barges extending downriver as far as one could see. Tugs moved in and out among them, mooring and rafting, the roar of their diesels carrying across the water.

Two miles below the junction we anchored off the main channel, between sandbars in shallow water. Below us a tree trunk was caught on the bottom. I wanted to get in closer to the bank but could see no path, which made me appreciate all the more the skill of the steamboat pilots. Churning upstream and swept down, they picked their course by the way the water ruffled, and some remembered knowledge imparted by another pilot in another state. Navigation on the unimproved river was a tricky business, despite the help of snag boats, which captured the tree trunks between their catamaran bows. With hooks rigged to blocks and tackle hung on gin poles, the crew lifted the trunks to the deck, where they cut them into little pieces. Beginning in 1833, the crew of Henry Shreve's *Heliopolis* spent five years removing the notorious 150-mile-long "Red River Raft," an enormous pile-up of tree trunks and other detritus. Still, there were the abundant sandbars, a menace until the advent of the dredger.

For a time we waded around *Pearl*, inclining our bodies against the current. When the sun passed over we dried ourselves in the cockpit, then retrieved the anchor, here at the beginning of the Lower Mississippi and yet another mileage system. In midstream, just below the point of land at Cairo, the chart showed mile 0 of the Upper Mississippi, mile 980 of the Ohio, and mile 953 of the Lower Mississippi. It seemed we kept starting over, fooled by arbitrary conventions into thinking that the river may be subdivided when we knew that in reality it is a circle with neither beginning nor end, flowing everywhere at once.

# CHAPTER 12

# Surrendering to the Stream

*"What is the shape of Walnut Bend?"*

*He might as well have asked me my grandmother's opinion of protoplasm.*

*"Boy, you've got to know the shape of the river perfectly. It is all there is left to steer by on a very dark night. But mind you, it hasn't the same shape in the night that it has in the daytime."*

*"How on earth am I ever going to learn it, then?"*

*"How do you follow a hall at home in the dark? Because you know the shape of it. You can't see it."*

*"Do you mean to say that I've got to know all the million trifling variations of shape in the banks of this interminable river as well as I know the shape of the front hall at home?"*

*"On my honor, you've got to know them better than any man ever did know the shapes of the halls in his own house."*

*"I wish I was dead!"*

—Mark Twain, *Life on the Mississippi*

Hickman, Kentucky, population 5,566, does not border the river proper; rather it is concealed behind an earthen levee a mile up Obion Creek. The town had no dock, just a dirt drive terminating at the water's edge. Abruptly it ceased, like a trail that disappears after rains fill an arroyo. But this in all its simplicity was the town landing, a place of congregation and importance. Down by the river. Here is where we mean. The place where fishermen launch their lightweight fiberglass and aluminum boats, parking their pickups and trailers sideways on the steep slope. The place where people sit to think, wait to be mesmerized by the slow-moving water. To meditate and to learn what the river teaches, like Siddhartha.

Last spring, the hillside had been underwater; now it was tufted here and there with a few weeds and grasses sprung from the drying muck. Still oozing, opalescent where seeping oil refracted in the light. Unreliable quick muck. Walk it at your risk.

In the dying light of day the water of the creek grew dark and the tangled growth along the shore, blacker and more sinister. A bird call announced the setting of the sun . . . or perhaps it sounded a warning: hawk, heron, snake, bobcat, man. . . . Everywhere the fish jumped, gulping insects on the surface, their tails slapping so loudly that Steve was raised to a state of severe agitation. He too jumped about as if he were about to wet his pants, banging the rod on the gunwale and making a strange clucking sound that emanated from the back of his throat. Unfortunately, the bass were so gainfully occupied that none was interested in his heat-seared worms, nor in the bait cast by a solitary man drifting near shore in an olive-green johnboat. Both cast, both reeled, neither landed dinner.

We anchored in the middle of the creek, thinking it unwise to make ourselves vulnerable to those on shore who might later, when the bars closed, come down to finish the night.

The moon rose. An owl hooted. Fish tails slapped. *Pearl* rode still in the airless night.


Storytelling time.

Not long after the sinking of the Chinese junk, John and Jim returned to Smith's Ledge. They brought rented scuba gear with the aim of finding the sunken vessel. Again they anchored the lobster boat near the buoy. This day there was no fog and the metronomic clang of the bell blew away in the breeze.

They donned wet suits, flippers, tanks, and face masks. Sitting on the boat's rail, they fell backward into the cold Maine water. Together they swam toward the bottom. At the base of the reef they saw the wreck, canted on its keel, a hole in its bow.

John, always the braver of the two, swam through the main hatch and pulled himself forward down the ladder to the cabin where earlier they had confronted the Chinaman. Jim followed nervously, pulling at John's shoulder in the hope he would give up this mad quest.

"Who cares about the pearls. What about the dragon?"

"Drowned," said John.

The door to the inner cabin was stuck, and John had to kick it free of the frame. As they entered, the door closed behind them. The blackness was illuminated only by two red spots. As their eyes adjusted, they made out the form of the dragon and Chinaman, who sat in the corner as before, legs akimbo. Even underwater they heard his words clearly.

The boys did not know what they had expected, but certainly not this—the Chinaman alive and speaking. They began to shake.

"Your accomplishments, no matter how great, will not be remembered. Worry not what your neighbors think of you. Seek satisfaction and happiness in the now. There is no tomorrow, only an endless series of 'nows' with remembrances of past 'nows' and anticipation of future 'nows.' What is fifty, a hundred, even five thousand years in the face of eternity? Ancient storytellers greater than Shakespeare have been lost in the dust.

"Our bodies are reducible to basic elements, parts inside of others like Chinese boxes. Elements that always were and always will be. You seek immortality of consciousness, but you cannot possess it. Devote yourself to this truth: Earth is simply a cell of the universe. The laws that govern it are fewer and simpler than you suppose, the applications more manifold than you suspect. Do not worship what you do not understand. In time, the sense of all that you see and suspect will be revealed.

"Therefore, let us raise this ship. Sail with me to my home. I will show you fantastic things—mountains, jewels, colors, girls dancing . . . yourselves."

Then the eyes of the dragon grew brighter and brighter until they blazed. Its tail swung out, striking John's mask and tearing it from his face. He struggled to refit the mouthpiece. Jim pulled him backward through the ragged opening in the hull. They floated down to the sandy bottom. John finally got his face mask back on and exhaled the water so that he could again see. Things went from bad to worse: Jim stepped on a giant tridacna clam, which closed on his foot. Neither of the boys could make the jaws open. Their air supply was running dangerously low.

Then the Chinaman appeared at their side, and with an old ceremonial sword, he forced open the serrated lips of the clam. The two halves parted and Jim's foot came free. John and Jim swam to the surface, breaking into the upper world just as their air supply ran out. They gasped and spit seawater.

Steve, lying next to me in the darkness, asked, "What is immortality?"

"Live forever," Adria answered.

"That's stupid."

"Why?"

"Who'd want to be so old you couldn't fish or play? Like, who'd want to be a hundred?"

"The person who's ninety-nine."


My father always said he'd live to be eighty. When I asked how he could know, he said that he'd simply decided. And that's all there was to it. As if the will could overcome death.

He nearly had me convinced. But the seed of his death had already been sewn. Years before. Before he learned how wrong he was, that the obstinacy that carried him to a university presidency wasn't enough to carry a weak heart.

In 1963 he held three jobs at the University of Michigan—dean of the School of Natural Resources and vice president and dean of the Rackham School of Graduate Studies. From one of twenty analects found among his papers: "For the next year, I held three full-time administrative positions (but unfortunately only one salary). I would start out at the Graduate School at 8:00, walk to the School of Natural Resources at 9:30, leave there for the Administration Building around 11:00, and retrace my steps in the afternoon. It was exhilarating and, I think, useful."

Useful? No wonder that ten years later the cardiologist would blame his atherosclerosis on stress. Social situations made him uneasy. Encounters with powerful persons probably more so. He knew that worry hardened the arteries and choked the fuel supplying his life. Surrounded by learned men, he was too informed to be fooled. He tried to release tension through jogging and swimming, but if it worked at all, the purging only delayed the fate scripted in his genes. And if he was wrong about the efficacy of willpower, he had fatalism to fall back on.

And the university wasn't the half of his professional life—he was also a trustee of the Educational Testing Service (responsible for the dreaded SAT), trustee of the Carnegie Foundation for the Advancement of Teaching, a governor of the Nature Conservancy (which among other activities buys up wetlands along the flyway between Canada and Mexico), a member of the Yale University Council, the president of the Michigan Academy of Arts and Sciences, the chairman of the Graduate Records Examination Board (more mechanisms to screen the chaff from the wheat), a member of the Harvard Board of Overseers, of the American Philosophical Society, the Sierra Club, the Cosmos Club, the Druids, Les Voyageurs (campfire clubs for people who like to sing in the woods), et cetera, et cetera.

My accomplishments measured up poorly to those of this *Übermensch* with the big balding forehead, he who had founded scientific periodicals, served the president of the United States on environmental committees, and won for his university million-dollar grants from industry. Realizing that I had few rounds of his intellectual firepower, he accorded me one advantage, and that was the ability to get along with people. It was the confession of an antisocialite, oddly bequeathed to a loner. Like a river, he tried to be everywhere at once. Like La Salle, he could hardly talk about it.

Nor did he talk of his desire to write. Probably he inherited the urge from his father, the geologist, who in retirement wrote love poems to his wife. That she found them sufficiently charming to copy and bind for family members did not elevate his verse beyond the turgid. The thought of having them shared would have made him aghast. Better reading were my grandfather's books, *Through the Yukon Gold Diggings* and *Log of the Kuskokwim*. Perhaps that is why my father was circumspect about his adaptation of *The Iliad* to the theater. I remember him, between writing forestry textbooks, emerging Sunday afternoons from his study, revealing only that in his dramatization the mortals occupied a lower stage, while above, on a second stage, the gods acted out their own drama, occasionally meddling with the mortal heroes, as gods are wont to do. It seemed to me brilliant, but I never read a word of the screenplay.

The cooler ice was melted, the milk, suspect. For breakfast we ate granola bars, cookies, and dry cereal. We brought up the anchor and drove the bow into the reddish ooze of the bank. *Quimby's* guide listed a fuel service in town that would bring gas to the landing. With the book in hand, Adria disappeared over the levee and through the gate in the wall that surrounded the town of Hickman. A medieval castle was no better protected than the houses below, but here the enemy was not rampaging Visigoths but the river.

Adria returned shortly with the disheartening news that the company required a minimum purchase of two hundred gallons. The good news was that a service station and convenience mart lay just over the levee.

I carried three empty jugs in each hand. The crest of the levee ran like a train track in either direction. In two trips I had all the jugs down the other side at the pump. I bought ice and pieces of fried chicken. A woman in a pickup drove me back over the levee.

Adria was cleaning the cockpit. Down the shore, Steve sat on an overturned milk crate plopped in ankle-deep water. A pole's length to his right sat an old, white-haired black man, reclined in a broken, aluminum-framed porch chair. He wore overalls with brown suspenders and a plaid shirt that seemed too warm for the weather. Both were fishing, but at this distance I could not tell if they were together or if Steve had sidled into his power field, hoping to catch some of his karma and then his fish.

"What's up with Steve?"

"Made a friend," she said. "He went down there to ask what was running, then came back for his pole and tackle box. After a while he wanted the milk crate. Pretty funny, huh?"

One by one I lifted the jugs to her. She opened the deck-fill cap and, using the funnel, began pouring gas into the main tank. Once it was full, I'd have to carry the jugs back to the station to fill them again.

I walked along the bank toward Steve, once losing a sandal in the mud. "Catch anything?"

Steve showed me a small catfish swimming in his bucket.

"Too small to eat," I said, saying the words he hated to hear.

"Keep him for bait," he said.

"You know the deal."

I turned to his companion.

"He bothering you?"

"Oh, no sir. Jus' fine. Jus' fine. We havin' a nice talk. Catching some fish, too."

There were a dozen or so fish in his bucket, most so small I immediately regretted disparaging Steve's fish, which compared well. The man's "tackle," if you could call it that, was kept at his side in a small cardboard box.

"Don't you worry 'bout your son. I like to see a boy fish. He's a good one. I been tellin' him a few things and he listens right up."

Steve cast, paying me no mind, probably thinking I'd butted into his business, inserted myself unnecessarily between him and his fishing friend. And somehow I could see that as unlikely a pair as they were, they'd come to a common understanding. And that understanding was fish. What Huck and Jim had. Black and white. Old and young. Everything must balance. Everything *does* balance. When it rains, the river must rise.

And so I left them sitting there in the mud. From the vantage point of *Pearl*'s cockpit I watched the two discreetly while I worked. The old man would say something and point to the water. Steve would nod and say something in return, but would not look, too intent on his own line or perhaps just keeping his distance. After a while, after Adria and I had finished filling all the jugs a second time and cleaned and secured the cockpit, Steve came walking down the bank holding his rod and milk crate. I took them from him. He raised his arms and I lifted him, dragging his muddy feet through the water before landing him on the deck.

"All done?"

He nodded.

I started the engine and, after letting it warm, untied the bowline and backed into Obion Creek. Steve sat in the chair next to me. The old man waved. Steve raised his hand, staring as we moved away.

Sometimes people come in and out of your life on the same day. Sometimes you just know that when they leave it is forever. The idea can set you back, back where the feeling of safety is broken by the loneliness of the now.

Midday. The sun high and hot. The rows of willows appeared as flumes stuck in the sand, blown upward by blasts of air. Swallows flew among the branches. Slowly and almost imperceptibly the look of the river changed. Dirt became sand. When we stopped and climbed over the banks we saw that instead of corn there now were fields of cotton, rice, and soybeans. The oak and elm had given way to a predominance of willow. In the last century willows were woven to make mats for covering the levees, to prevent erosion. Now these "mats" are made of concrete squares four feet

wide, twenty-five feet long, and three inches thick, lifted from supply
barges by gantry cranes and laid on the bank. It is an annual rite of the U.S.
Army Corps of Engineers, beginning each August when the river is
low. Five hundred laborers work in shifts round the clock, eating and
sleeping on quarter boats that look like cheap Pocono hotels. Clerks, deck-
hands, drag-line operators, electricians, gantry-crane operators, mechanics,
stewards, surveyors, 'dozer drivers, winchmen, pneumatic-mat-tying-tool
operators. Constant is the relentless river and the sky, the same cloudless
blue. The entire west bank from Cairo to the delta is fortified by a levee.
Eventually, one presumes, the entire Mississippi will course between concrete walls and the river will be nothing but a giant culvert.

The course became more and more diverse, curling back on itself like the
bulbous twist of an intestine. No wonder La Salle was confused! One
minute we were heading west, the next north, and never enough south to
think we'd ever reach the Gulf of Mexico. At places we could see across the
narrow neck of land to the river on the other side, only to discover that the
shape of the river took us twenty miles in a great circle before we found
ourselves at the spot we'd glimpsed.

Mark Twain noted that occasionally some scoundrel plantation owner
would in the moonlight dig a ditch across the neck to bring the water to
his doorstep. At stake were property values, waterfront real estate was then
and always will be valuable. At "needful times," watches were kept of the
necks, "and if a man happens to be caught cutting a ditch across them, the
chances are all against his ever having another opportunity to cut a ditch."[1]

For these reasons and others, the river from time to time dramatically
shortens itself. When La Salle descended, the distance of the lower river
between Cairo and New Orleans was on the order of 1,215 miles. In
Twain's day, after cutoffs at Hurricane Island and the now deserted towns
of Napoleon, Walnut, Council, and American Bends, it was 973 miles. In
mine, 851.

At the head of Groom Towhead, the town of New Madrid sits on the
Missouri side. The so-called "double loop" here is twenty-six miles long
and the neck one thousand feet wide at the base. The Corps of Engineers
refuses to cut through because the river drops ten feet from one side to

the next. The rapids would be hell to steam through. In time, Nature will do it herself, like a woman straightening and arranging the pleats in her skirt.

I began to realize that the Mississippi we traversed was not the same river La Salle paddled three hundred years before. Then, there were no levees and the river spread itself into the flatlands. Indeed, during the Pliocene this section of the valley was flooded with saltwater, an arm of the gulf extending as far north as Cairo.

More recently, on the morning of December 6, 1811, a thunderous earthquake struck New Madrid. It was estimated to be as strong as the 1933 Japanese earthquake that registered 8.9 on the Richter scale, and the river was altered beyond recognition. Shock waves were felt as far away as New Orleans, Colorado, and Canada. Thomas Jefferson was awakened in his home at Monticello. In the nation's capital, church bells rang as if by the hands of ghosts. Godfrey Lesieur, a local who witnessed the quake, wrote, "The earth began to shake and totter to such a degree that no persons were able to stand or walk. This lasted perhaps for one minute, and at this juncture the earth was observed to be as it were rolling in waves of a few feet in height, with visible depressions between."[2] The fissures came up from two to three thousand feet beneath the riverbed. Large areas of earth collapsed and the river poured in. Islands disappeared and new ones formed as if from nowhere. When it was over, the original townsite of New Madrid was on the opposite bank, in Kentucky.

Up and down the Lower Mississippi, citizens have from time to time involuntarily changed sides of the river. And though it is generally thought that the river is the boundary between those adjoining southern states, a close look at a large-scale map informs that at some double loops the boundary marks an old line of the river, not its present position. The governors and their legislatures can't stop the river, but they can keep taxpayers on the same rolls.

We stopped for lunch at the Cherokee Dikes, at Little Cypress Bend, sixty miles below Hickman. Tennessee to port, the boot heel of Missouri to starboard. Adria warmed clam chowder on the stove and made peanut butter sandwiches. Afterward we floated in the warm water, hanging on to the beanbag tethered to *Pearl*.

*For lunch and at night, we tethered* Pearl, *a 1978 Proline cuddy-cabin model, to a stake driven into the sand. A stern anchor was set to keep the current from pushing the boat ashore.*

When Steve returned to the boat for more fishing, Adria rested on the beanbag and I floated on my back, holding myself to the tether with my toes. I said, "Hemingway was a nihilist; he viewed the world as a malevolent place. Not only did God not exist, but the universe was configured against man to ensure his misery. At the end of *A Farewell to Arms*, as his lover lies dying in childbirth, Lieutenant Frederic Henry recalls once watching ants on a campfire log, running to the cool end, until 'there were enough of them and they fell off into the fire.' He thought to save them by pouring water onto the log, but only steamed them. A metaphor signifying the futility and senselessness of man's existence. We are consumed not by hellfire, but nevertheless tortured. For Hemingway, at this point in his life, the only potential solace was in self-sacrificial love. But he, and love, are impotent to save not only the lives of mother and baby, but his own soul. He walks home to his hotel in the rain. At best, love is a temporary palliative. Do you agree?"

There are different kinds of love, she said. First, romantic love—what one person feels for another, often with sexual undertones. Which is different from, say, love for humanity or a photograph of an orphan, or the sadness you feel reading about the death of someone you didn't even know.

I said that the second kind seemed more like empathy, to which she replied that empathy is part of that kind of love, more spiritual. Whereas love for a specific person often gets hung up in sensuality.

"Then again," she asked, "what is love?"

"Affection? Adoration? Attachment?"

"What about commitment? Responsibility?"

"I didn't mean for you to define love. Rather, is love a sufficient reason to make life meaningful?"

"You're assuming I don't believe in a god," she answered.

"When you were six, I took you for the weekend to Lake Michigan. It was a few days after Thanksgiving and the air was cold. We slept on our old sailboat, which sat in the yard on its cradle. We slept opposite each other on the settees. During the night a nylon jacket fell on the alcohol heater. The cabin filled with smoke and I awoke dreaming of fire. I couldn't see. I couldn't breathe. I flung open the hatch and threw you into the snow-filled cockpit. I followed, holding you on my lap. Below I saw the embers of the smoking jacket. I took a deep breath, climbed below, and threw the jacket out, stamping it in the snow. We almost died, but I did not tell you that. Maybe you already knew.

"The next day, driving home, you asked who made me. I said my parents. You asked who made grandma and grandpa. I said your great-grandparents. You asked who made the first man. I said some people call it God. You said, 'But if everything was made by something, then something must have made God. Who made God?' "

"And what did you say?"

"I said, 'Nothing.' Beyond that, I did not know."

"Well, neither do I." Then she took hold of the tether and pulled herself back to *Pearl*. I lost my toehold on the line and drifted, watching her recede, watching the sandy shore go by, and I did not stop until my heels raked the end of the spit. If I did not get out here I would be swept away. Strange to think that such a small non-act could lead to death. Where would my body be found—lodged on a wing dam? Snagged by the branch of a fallen tree? Washed up on the sandy spit of a towhead? It would have been very easy to succumb to the inertia of floating, to keep the spell a little longer, surrendering to the stream.

. . .

We came upon the Caruthersville (Missouri) Shipyards. Alongside the company's railway floated a newly launched barge. We had passed hundreds of barges on the river, all old, dented, paint-bare, rusted. I had been curious about their origins. Now we saw the maker of barges, and I wondered if finding origins was simply a matter of looking long enough.

Beyond was an elevator filling the hold of an old barge, which squatted one end down. When all the compartments were filled equally, it would sit on its lines. A tug would then lash it to its fleet. Another would come and move the lot of them upstream or down and the cargo would be offloaded. Transferred perhaps to a train, then . . . what? The old Teamsters slogan: "If you've got it, it came by truck."

The shore was rocky and again there were no docks where we could safely tie up. But our main tank was nearly empty and I decided we ought to investigate the town. Already we'd passed mile 852, where *Quimby's* said Bruner's Fuel & Lubricants Service would deliver to the riverbank. Truck it up from Portageville. Yet we had seen no facilities, no phone booth, not even a ramp, just an old pickup in the trees.

Below the shipyard the casino steamboat *Aztar* was moored, a horrifying representation of what some designer thought riverboats ought to look like: fake stacks, rainbow-colored trim, white gingerbread, a decorative paddlewheel. Nearer I spotted the crumbling concrete ramp of the town landing. Next to it was an area of mud that appeared relatively free of the suitcase-size rocks dumped on the revetment. Steve tossed the anchor off the stern as we glided in. Adria jumped ashore with a line, which she made fast to a rock. A passing tow sent a wake to the shore, picking *Pearl* up and dropping her keel on a submerged rock. The thud sent a shudder through her parts.

We'd have to hurry.

Adria watched the boat while Steve and I carried the jugs to the top of the overlooking bluff. He brought along his wallet, tucking carefully in its pockets his pipe tool knife and Grandmother's fifty-dollar bill.

Under the trees, an old man in a pickup sat and watched the river. I walked over to ask the distance and direction to the nearest gas station. He told me to throw the jugs in back; the distance, he said, was several miles and he couldn't see the boy making it that far. Nor me, I'd wanted to add, when all those jugs were laden. His name was Alexander and he'd driven a truck all his adult life. Saw most of the country at one time or another, but never Rhode Island, which he said was easy to miss unless you had a reason. And he hadn't.

That's okay, I said. We like it like that. Which seemed rude, and I hoped he wouldn't take it the wrong way. But he seemed to understand people who keep to themselves, being, I supposed, like that himself.

When he returned us to the riverbank, I offered to pay.

"Never asked for anything, won't take anything."

At that he helped us unload the jugs, moving stiffly. Then he got back in the cab and backed up under the tree to the exact place we'd found him. He watched as Steve ran down the hill waving his candy and wallet. Adria pulled him aboard. Behind, I lugged two jugs per trip.

When I was done I called for Steve. Adria mouthed words I could not make out. At last Steve walked to the bow and held out his wallet, his face pained.

"I lost my knife," he moaned.

Three times I climbed up the rocks, and three times down, resisting the urge to say that knives ought to be kept in pants pockets, not in wallets.

"I think I went around this one," he said. "Then here. I remember this bottle." His memory seemed to change with each trip, and we could not find it.

"Will you buy me another?" he asked as soon as we'd gotten under way.

"Someday, probably."

We climbed aboard *Pearl*, pushed off and left the knife there. Ahead a tow came round the bend, pushing barges rafted seven across and seven down. I moved across his bow to take him on the inside of the curve where we might slip past the edge of his wake.

Suddenly Steve burst into tears. "I lost the fifty dollars, too!"

"What?!" I jammed the shift into neutral, stopping the boat.

"I had it on the rocks, but it must have fallen out while we were looking for the knife. Dad, I *had* it!"

Adria asked if we should go back and look, but I said it was hopeless. I put the throttle down.

"I'm sure you're more upset about this than I am, and I'm pretty upset."

We ran another thirty-one miles, stopping late in the day at Tamm Bend, where there was protected water behind a large sandy island. Shaped like a kidney, it curled around the bend a distance of six miles on its outer perimeter and was a mile across. The southern end was barren while the northern end was forested. As the day closed, the river was all blue, sparkling in the backlight of the setting sun. Strangely, a few miles back the river had become smooth as glass, broken only by the occasional ripple of pooling current. Where now were the effects of the corkscrewing current, turning down the cavity like a revolving Slinky? Had the river god been appeased? Did he sleep? Or had the bottom fallen out, dropped into the subterranean chasm of the quake?

As was becoming our custom on the lower river, we collected drift-wood and lit a fire. On saplings cut from the edge of the forest we cooked hot dogs and roasted marshmallows. Steve announced he would sleep in the cockpit, his way of making penance, I presumed. I let him, but out of worry did not sleep well. Further disturbance came from the searchlights of passing tows, periodic and unceasing, waking me instantly each time.

The sun came up as red as it had set. We hiked across the beach toward the trees. In some areas, the glacial sand was a pointillist rendering, the grains standing up in tiny dimples where the rain had hit. The striations and patterns of the sand and clay were infinite in their texture and design. Along the shore the receding water had left succeeding elevations of con-tours, and in the middle of the island were hundreds of small pools. Where some had dried the clay had cracked into a mosaic of brown shards. Deer tracks cut from the forest and returned. Everywhere along the bank were the three-fingered marks of the heron. Closer to the trees were the pad prints of a large feline, which we supposed must be a bobcat. Steve walked with his sharp eyes tuned for life. In one of the pools he found a foot-long snapping turtle, catching it with his hands. In another there were min-nows, which he snared with a net.

We followed the cat prints along a shallow channel across the island through the trees, climbing over a large, silvery fallen log. Frogs and spi-ders hopped and crawled in the shade. It was the insects that drove us out.


Little Egypt, springtime 1682. The river swelled, overflowing its banks. Willows near the bank were engulfed and stayed submerged so long that they sprouted tendrils from their trunks. Visibility through the water was two inches. Locals have long liked to say it is thick enough to cut with a knife. Later, when the water had subsided, the thin roots hung like dried hair. After days of fasting, the Indian hunters killed two deer and two bears.

La Salle was content to face no obstacle greater than the river. He could deal with it far more easily than with the machinations of his political enemies back in Montreal. Tonti and Father Zénobe Membré were good company.

The bad news was that they were hopelessly lost. Not only was the compass broken, but the seven-inch astrolabe La Salle had bought in Montreal also was faulty. All during the expedition it gave erroneous positions, but worse, he had no way of knowing it. As far back as the mouth of the Illinois, when it had given him a reading of 37 degrees north latitude instead of their actual location at 39 degrees, the astrolabe had deceived him to the tune of about a hundred miles. And when the sun was obscured by clouds, as it often was, the instrument was completely useless.

Even if he had suspected the erroneous readings of the astrolabe, there were, of course, no known landmarks against which he could check the accuracy of his sightings. All he had to go on was the sketchy information gleaned from accounts of Hernando de Soto's *entrada*.[3] Garcilaso de la Vega, the son of a Spanish conquistador and Chimpa Ocllo, a niece of the Inca emperor Huáscar Capac, was raised as a Christian in Spain and became a prolific writer. His book, *La Florida del Inca,* was based on oral testimony given by survivors of Soto's expedition. In it he relates that the largest river the Spaniards encountered was called by the natives Chucagoa, that it was well populated with tribes whose names La Salle did not recognize; that the river was much wider than La Salle found; and that Soto had ridden horseback along its banks, which to La Salle seemed impossible, owing to the thickness of the canebrakes. These reasons and more suggested to him that his river and Soto's were not one and the same.

With nothing to do but to do it, on February 24, just above present-day Memphis, they landed on what then were snake-infested shores. On the hills were mulberry, walnut, laurel, and oak trees. Then as now, herons stepped cautiously through the shallows. They do not wade, but lift each foot high out of the water as if they don't like getting their feet wet. Pelicans watched for small fry. Beyond the canebrake the men saw buffalo. Food was a constant need—get it while you can. The company's armorer, Prudhomme, unskilled at stalking game, insisted on trying his hand at hunting. The Indian and French hunters scattered, all returning by nightfall. Prudhomme did not. For six days La Salle and his men searched the marsh and reeds. Local Chickasaw Indians made themselves evident, but did not come forth, concealing themselves among the grasses. Believing that the Chickasaws had captured and were holding Prudhomme, La Salle sent presents to their chief. Meanwhile, anticipating the possibility of attack, the party constructed a small stockade on the Third Chickasaw Bluff, with an excellent vantage of the river.

Though he was loath to leave the gunsmith, La Salle ordered the expedition to proceed downriver. Providentially, they soon rounded a bend and saw Prudhomme riding a log, haggard, half dead, and evidencing signs of delirium. He told La Salle that he had become lost in the reeds and had had only roots to eat between his departure and discovery. In an act at odds with the assessment of his character by critics of both his own day and ours, La Salle sympathetically christened the stockade Fort Prudhomme. More, he left Prudhomme there in charge of it, with a few men under his command.

We drove down the river between the bordering banks of willows and kudzu vines. Steve sat below listening to Ziggy Marley on the portable tape player.

> *Tomorrow people,*
> *Don't know the past, don't know the future.*

When we stopped to swim I propped the boom box in the cockpit and tuned the radio to a local country station.

> *That's my girl, my whole world,*
> *But that ain't my truck in her drive.*

The flies drove us crazy, drove us back onto the river. At a distance, the Chickasaw Bluffs hung over the river valley, prickly and steep, foretelling the imminence of Memphis. And we ran, ran until we made the city late in the afternoon. Found the first and last dock for hundreds of miles in either direction at the Memphis Yacht Club, hidden behind Mud Island, 1,500 feet up the Wolf River. It wasn't a real yacht club but a small marina catering solely to powerboats. Here, unlike in St. Louis where we'd seen a few sailboats getting set downriver as fast as they moved across, the residents seemed to understand the futility of sail power.

At the fuel dock I bought three more jugs from a fellow who'd just returned from a week's trip up the Mississippi and Ohio to the Tennessee River. His jugs, like mine, were brand-new, confirming that there were no secret ways of finding fuel on the river. Like a bedouin, you carry what you need. Combined with our existing inventory of red plastic jugs, these would give us enough fuel to make the 188-mile run to Greenville, Mississippi, uninterrupted. Stops at Helena, Arkansas, or Friar's Point, Mississippi, could be considered optional—I hoped.

Remembering how much I'd disliked sleeping aboard *Pearl* at My River Home Marina, I made reservations across the channel at the Comfort Inn. Salve the bites, rinse the scum, sleep in air-conditioned splendor. We rode the tramway across the Wolf River into the heart of the city. Men in suits, women wearing heels. Financial institutions with revolving doors. Ate dinner at a basement rib joint called Rendezvous, which sold take-home bottles of its "famous" sauce. On the walls were signed photographs of celebrity patrons. Ice cream at Scoops. How strange it all seemed, how loud and frenzied compared to the river.

That evening I called Andra. She said a rabid skunk had been found in the backyard. The animal control officer came and shot it. She was worried about Tango because someone had told her that standard vaccines don't work on wolf hybrids. She wanted to know whether she should have her put away—"You get it, you die." Our discussion occupied an hour and left me depressed, despite her agreeing to seek the counsel of a veterinarian.

Adria slept in one bed, Steve and I in the other. Lights out.

"Dad," he whispered. "You know that guy on the river?"

"Which guy?"

"The old fisherman."

"The one you fished with back at Hickman?"

"Yeah."

"What about him?"

"He makes his own hooks."

"Really?"

"He knows a lot about fishing, Dad."

CHAPTER 13

# Death of the Pilot's Mother

*Ships that pass in the night, and speak each other in passing,*
*Only a signal shown and a distant voice in the darkness;*
*So on the ocean of life we pass and speak one another,*
*Only a look and a voice; then darkness again and a silence.*

—Henry Wadsworth Longfellow, "The Theologian's Tale"

There was nothing Steve loved half so much as fishing, and so long as he had a rod in his hand or was rummaging in his tackle box, he was happy. But he could not do this when we were running. This forced him to plead the virtues of trolling. So I'd slow down and he'd switch from a hook to a lure. If it worked on the ocean, it did not on the Mississippi. Probably because it was so bloody hot that all the catfish were hunkered down in holes on the river bottom. There are 240 species of fish in the Mississippi— including paddle fish, dogfish, sheepshead, and shorthead redhorse—but all we caught were two, catfish and buffalo fish. Once, back in La Salle's time, there were giant pike and sturgeon that might have hit a lure, but not now, not our lure, not on the lower river.

We'd read about the practice of "noodling" catfish by cornering one in a beaver dam or other obstruction, then driving your hand into its mouth and pulling it out by the lip. It is done entirely by feel. With a little dumb luck, you might withdraw instead with a muskrat bite, poisonous-snake bite or a boned forearm. You might not come up at all. A big catfish, it is said, can hold a man down. It helps to have two friends on the bank, one to pull the noodler out by the legs, another to club the fish with a baseball bat to make it let go. An Oklahoma expert named John Pidcock says, "There's nothing more gratifying than getting bit by a big catfish."[1] It's illegal in some states, but why? Because it's too easy? More cruel than a hook? Even if noodling is a lost art of the Indians, a tradition that preserves a small part of pre-America, I was not tempted.

Between fishing and fussing with his tackle, Steve sat below listening to a reggae tape. Sometimes he read. Still there were protracted periods when dread boredom formed about him like a cloud, overwhelming my efforts to direct his attention toward bird sightings or word games. But there was one notable sign of progress: He no longer turned to the Game Boy, sparing me the idiotic repetitions of its electronic audio.

He did not reveal much of himself, other than accidentally. When he sulked, he would not say why. When he was angry, he would not explain himself. At his tender age, it was not surprising that he lacked the vocabulary of emotions. Or perhaps this was just his nature, that he simply chose to keep his own counsel, like his grandfather, who wrote: "I remain without confidants, even my alter ego. I do not feel that this is wrong or that I should seek psychiatric help. This is the way that I am and also the way that I like to be."

La Salle, too, was self-contained: "With little vivacity or gayety or love of pleasure, he was a sealed book to those about him."[2] Accompanying this introversion was a devotion to an almost unattainable standard of moral behavior—the priest in him. In a 1680 letter to a creditor, he suggested that an agent be sent to oversee their mutual trade interests:

> He need not be very savant, but he must be faithful, patient of labor, and fond neither of gambling, women, nor good cheer; for he will find none of these with me.[3]

La Salle thought it repugnant to make excuses for the loss of the *Griffon*, the desertion of his men, and their theft of goods. Honor and integrity were paramount. One time, a political enemy plotting to discredit him hid in a closet while his wife attempted to seduce the reticent guest. She took La Salle's hand and placed it on her breast, whereupon La Salle rushed from the house.

To achieve his grand design—the opening and civilizing of the Illinois and Mississippi river valleys for France, which he no doubt intended to govern—he depended almost entirely on his own resources. Though Governor Frontenac and King Louis XIV made him various grants to explore and establish forts, they offered no funding. He had little recourse other than to engage in trading furs. Unlike his father, Robert was no merchant and usually delegated the administration of his affairs to others, mostly with disappointing results. He lost considerable sums, and he found himself defending his actions to creditors and political enemies on many counts: explaining the losses and his strict treatment of the men under him, even to his brother Jean, a Sulpician priest.

Jean worried that Robert might, of all things, marry. Though Robert intimated to his brother that he reserved the right to betroth himself, there is little indication that he had time for either love or family. His constant trekking precluded any furtherance of his relationship with Madeleine de Roybon d'Allonne, toward whom he apparently showed some affection during his time at Fort Frontenac. She did, however, lend him money—2,141 livres—which he needed more than love. Were it not for his seemingly helter-skelter rushings to satisfy creditors and politicians and to complete his explorations, things might have turned out differently for the two, but we will never know.

Regarding his alleged mistreatment of some hired help, he defended himself to a correspondent:

> The facility I am said to want is out of place with this sort of people, who are libertines, for the most part; and to indulge them means to tolerate blasphemy, drunkenness, lewdness, and a license incompatible with any kind of order. It will not be found that I have in any case whatever treated any man harshly, except for blasphemies and other such crimes, openly committed. These I cannot tolerate.[4]

Of his social shortcomings and preference for a life in the wilderness, he wrote:

> If I am wanting in expansiveness and show of feeling towards those with whom I associate, it is only through a timidity which is natural to me, and which has made me leave various employments, where, without it, I could have succeeded. But, as I judged myself

ill-fitted for them on account of this defect, I have chosen a life more suited to my solitary disposition; which, nevertheless, does not make me harsh to my people, though, joined to a life among savages, it makes me, perhaps, less polished and complaisant than the atmosphere of Paris requires. I well believe that there is self-love in this; and that, knowing how little I am accustomed to a more polite life, the fear of making mistakes makes me more reserved than I like to be. So I rarely expose myself to conversation with those in whose company I am afraid of making blunders, and can hardly help making them. . . . It is much the same with letters, which I never write except when pushed to it, and for the same reason. It is a defect of which I shall never rid myself as long as I live, often as it spites me against myself, and often as I quarrel with myself about it.[5]

He was far more effective in his dealings with the Indians than with his own kind. Even when he was confronted with hostile tribes, rare was the occasion that arms were required to resolve the matter. In one confrontation after another, with words alone La Salle managed to stall and dissuade his aggressors. Indeed, the Indians had come to respect the white who wore a plumed hat and dressed in his ceremonial coat with scarlet mantle bordered in gold, who spoke in stentorian tones of the father in France who would vanquish all enemies, protect his children, and ensure their prosperity.

Though admittedly better suited to a solitary life in the wilderness than the "polite life" of court, he rose to the critical occasions with at least a show of confidence and ability.

Such was the case when his party departed from Fort Prudhomme on the Chickasaw Bluffs, and resumed their descent of the Mississippi.

Parkman described the scene thus:

The mystery of this vast New World was more and more unveiled. More and more they entered the realms of spring. The hazy sunlight, the warm and drowsy air, the tender foliage, the opening flowers, betokened the reviving life of Nature. For several days more they followed the writhings of the great river, on its tortuous course through wastes of swamp and canebrake, till on the thirteenth of March they found themselves wrapped in a thick fog.[6]

From shore came the sounds of war drums, whoops, and cries. La Salle gave the order to land the canoes and throw together a "rude fort of felled trees." When the fog cleared, the Frenchmen and Indians viewed each other from opposite banks. Several Indians paddled across in a wooden canoe. La Salle showed the calumet (peace pipe) and a meeting was arranged.

The Indians were the Kappa band of the Arkansas, after which the nearby river was named. The French were well received. Everyone in the village came to meet them except the women, who had run into the woods. Father Membré described them as

> . . . gay, civil, and free-hearted. The young men, though the most alert and spirited we had seen, are nevertheless so modest that not one of them would take the liberty to enter our hut, but all stood quietly at the door. They are so well formed that we were in admiration at their beauty. We did not lose the value of a pin while we were among them.[7]

Membré, who had lamented the lack of privacy on the journey, was sufficiently impressed with the Arkansas Indians' discretion and respect for their guests that he did not even employ his usual method of scaring away overly curious guests from the tepee: showing them his clock, and telling them that the spirit inside was about to ring.

A three-day feast followed, with much dancing and ceremony. The French watched solemnly, which, wrote Parkman, "their hosts would have liked less, if they had understood it better." For at its conclusion, a cross was planted showing King Louis XIV's coat of arms and a notary donned his black hat and with a goose-quill pen, wrote a document attesting La Salle's taking of the land. The Indians touched the post, then rubbed their bodies on it, as if it conferred some magic or good luck. Three musket rounds were fired. Membré chanted and sang hymns. The men shouted, "Vive le roi!" La Salle made his declaration in the king's name. Afterward, Father Membré attempted to explain to the Indians the mysteries of the faith, and La Salle, to extract some acknowledgment of subservience to the king.

And so it was here, at the confluence of the Arkansas and Mississippi rivers, that France took formal possession of the Mississippi River and all the land drained by its tributaries.

Yet La Salle continued to be uncertain of exactly which river he was on. Here, it wound in such a serpentine course that without a compass, it was difficult to know in which direction progress was being made, the loops taking one to every point of the compass.

We set out from Memphis toward the Arkansas on the twenty-fifth of August. We ran three hours to the mouth of the St. Francis River, anchoring a hundred yards upstream. Ashore, beyond the levees, the land was depressed below water level, as in the Netherlands. Here, the cause of the great depressions was the New Madrid earthquake of 1811, on whose epicenter we now floated idly in the noonday heat.

Adria remarked that it looked like alligator country, but this did not deter us from swimming in the warm and muddy water. We had no other means of relief from the heat save a water bottle that Steve had rigged in a sling under the Bimini. He had poked holes in the cap and suspended the bottle in such a manner that by pulling a string the bottle inverted itself, dribbling spring water over the operator's head.

On the nearby bank an elderly couple fished. They sat in lawn chairs slowly sinking in the mud. Perhaps because we had disturbed the tranquillity of their scene, they soon departed, by what means we could not discern, for no houses, cars, or roads were visible. Steve and Adria chased butterflies among the trees, deepening into the woods until the insects repelled them from the shade back into the light.

Now the river charts took on a new look, showing as they did signs of the river's historical journey down the continent. Within the time of an old man's memory, double loops and oxbows had been cut and isolated, excised from the river like tumors by the hand of a surgeon. They now appeared as inland water bodies, crescent-shaped lakes in various arcs of their original 345-degree circumference. The mapmaker had colored these waters blue.

Farther from these lakes was depicted an earlier generation of drying lakes colored black and white, hatched with grass marks that the map legend identified as swamp.

Beyond these calcifying bogs the cartographer had drawn the elevation contours that, like a fossil, showed the course of the river thousands of years ago. Viewed in terms of its evolution, it was clear that the river has struggled to find the path of least resistance, shortening its run from head-water to mouth, ridding itself of all obstacles, natural or man-made. The east-west undulations were growing more and more compressed, narrow-ing from a breadth of perhaps fifty miles to about half that today. Slowly, the river was straightening itself.

*Quimby's* did not list any fuel sources between Memphis, Tennessee, at mile 725, and Greensville, Mississippi, at mile 537—the formidable 188-mile run of which Dale Nouse had warned me weeks ago. We were pre-pared for it, laden with jugs filled in Memphis. But at mile 663, more out of curiosity and boredom than necessity, we stopped to investigate the town of Helena, Arkansas. The landing, here just a slope on the levee, was located, as at all the other towns, up a backwater.

For insurance, Adria set off into town with an empty gas jug under each arm. I watched her climb, impressed with her confidence and not a little doubtful of the wisdom of my letting her go.

As I engaged in my constant tidying of the cabin and cockpit, Steve spotted a man fishing on the bank. He grabbed his rod and tackle box and soon was at the man's side. As before, at Hickman, he said nothing as he "baited up" and made his first cast. After a time I walked over to see how he was doing, offering a beer to his companion. The man wore rubber galoshes cut at the ankle and a red Chevron shirt. He was grateful for the beer, addressing me as sir.

His name, he said, was Anthony, and in his bucket were a number of small fry, crappies and river bream. His rod was bamboo, "the best kind." The line was string and the hooks homemade. The worms he'd dug that morning, in the woods miles away. With a practiced motion he swung the hook and worm toward several rotten pilings, dropping the bait in their shadows. "Fish like it there," he told Steve. "Put it in tight."

Steve tried, but his technique was too eager, lacking deftness.

Some time past, Anthony said two black boys had killed a family on a boat, "right where yours is, yessir. This town ain't been the same since. You keep your gun ready and enjoy yourself." Which made me worry all the more about Adria.

I returned to the boat for a while, then brought Anthony another beer, which he said he would save for supper. Married at the age of fourteen, to a girl thirteen, now he had two sixteen-year-olds, one still at home, and four younger ones, plus a seventeen-year-old son who'd left home and was himself a father.

"My wife don't like it, but I gotta come," he said. "I love it here on the river. Cleans out my mind. Don't mess with trouble. Tonight I'll take these fish, fix some rice, biscuits, that's good eating, yessir!"

All the time he kept a constant chatter with Steve, remonstrating with him on his technique, pointing where to aim the cast. But despite the coaching, Steve could not land one fish.

"See that barge down there? They fillin' it with cornmeal. Catfish love cornmeal; rice, too. You go down there, I guarantee you catch somethin' big. I have. But they don't like people hangin' round, so unless it's dark, bes' be up here."

Suddenly Anthony's rod bent over on itself. A dorsal fin broke the surface. He reached out to grab the string line and brought it in hand over hand, jerking a three-pound catfish onto the bank. Kneeling, he extracted the hook, then looked up at me. "You want dis fish, Sir?"

The fish was larger than the rest of his catch combined. Thinking of all the mouths he had to feed, I could not accept.

"That's really nice of you, but you should keep it. After all, you caught it."

He turned. "Steve! Do *you* want this fish?"

Steve looked at me for a sign.

"I'm not talkin' to your father, Steve, I'm ax-king you. You want this fish?!"

Steve nodded timidly.

Anthony laid it forcefully in Steve's outstretched arms.

Just then I saw Adria walking down the bank. My relief was followed by a moment of panic. Beside her walked a tall man wearing tight jeans and an oil company hat. He smoked a thin cigar. Trouble, I thought: Parking without a permit, transporting gasoline on sidewalks, consorting with blacks . . . what? I walked over.

"Dad, this man gave me a ride. The station was a couple of miles."

"Name's Pete Summerhill." He saw that I was sinking in the mud. "This is called gumbo. The only mud in the world that don't leave tracks . . . 'cause you take your tracks with you! Hell, you can patch a boat with it. I took some on my thumb once and plugged a hole in an aluminum canoe. It'll last half an hour, long enough to get home!"

We talked for a few minutes. When we were ready to leave, Summerhill said, "Come back for the Sonny Boy Williamson King Biscuit concert. Lots of good food and music. Have a safe trip, don't listen to the niggers, and watch out for the wing dams."

Robert Dudlow Taylor sang the "Old Helena Blues":

> *I'm goin', goin' to old Helena,*
> *I'm goin' to walk down Cherry Street.*

When Summerhill had driven off in his pickup, I got Steve aboard, started the engine, and backed from the bank. I kept thinking about the murder.

Anthony called out, "Steve! You stay sweet!"

We drove in silence down the river, back between the lines of willows, the river bending this way and that, passing the tows. Always the tows, whose huge engines threw up a froth of muddy water. If we were caught too close to shore and had to buck the wake, the steepness of the waves slammed so violently into *Pearl* that it seemed she would break. Better to guess which was the wide side, though it wasn't always easy. Coming round the bend, the raft of barges seemed skewed across the river, heading for the opposite bank until the captain advanced one throttle beyond the other, with twin engines pivoting the fleet of barges about its axis. Until they straightened course, it was hard to know which way they'd end up. Pete had had the same problem when he first saw the train round the bend, trying to figure on which set of tracks it ran. The three boys jumped back and forth between the two, never noticing that one was polished, the other rusty. The conductor thought they were playing chicken. Pete's two pals jumped. Pete tripped. Trying to wave off the onrushing locomotive was his last chance. Steve asked why he didn't jump. Because he was afraid of the water, afraid of the train, I said. Panicked. Frozen. He didn't know about trains and how long they take to stop. I honestly think he believed in the efficacy of waving.

I was reluctant to hug the shore too closely, for fear of hitting the wing dams, which were everywhere submerged, a line of roiling current the only clue to their presence.

The tug names were clues, too, not to the river but to the men and women who worked them: *Randy Eckstein, Floyd Goodman, Bobby Jones, Cindy L., David McAllister, James G. Hines, Butch Barras, Inez Andreas,* pilots, brothers, wives, and mothers, all memorialized in paint; and *Stone Power, Cooperative Spirit, Cooperative Mariner, Seminole Chief,* and *Seminole Brave,* derived from ideas and memories, other origins.

Out of the blue Steve asked, "Dad, what would happen if you had surgery on your penis?"

"Depends what was wrong with it?"

"I mean, if they cut it off you couldn't pee."

"They'd have to put a tube into your bladder. It would be embarrassing, horrible."

We stopped for the night at Jackson Cutoff, mile 628, tucked behind a tombolo. We fried Anthony's catfish. Steve tried to make a campfire ashore but the breeze was too strong and the wood too wet.

After reading another chapter of *Huckleberry Finn,* I turned off the penlight. Steve said, "I don't like to close my eyes. I just like it to take me."

I felt his hand on my nipples. He said, "It's like a mosquito bite with a pimple on top."

Then I heard him ask Adria, "What's this?"

"My hand."

"What's this?"

"My arm."

"What's this?"

"My shoulder."

"What's this?"

"Keep your hands to yourself, buddy!"

No, we hadn't yet discussed the birds and bees, but that was coming. Neither of us was ready, not for a few more years. Time still to be a boy. If he'd let himself. If the world would. Here on the river we were if not in the wilderness at least remote among the willows. No houses, no lights, just the fish and the birds. Late at night even the tows disappeared, parked like tractor trailers with engines running, the noses of the lead barges run into the soft bank. In the morning the captain would back off, then throw the engines into forward, and the whole structure would shudder until it achieved an equilibrium of thrust and momentum.

Near midnight, Adria and I were awakened by the searchlights of two approaching tows. I turned on the VHF radio to listen to the pilots' conversation. Perhaps, I thought, they'd mention sighting us.

One pilot spoke to the other about memories of Dennis Landing, a grain terminal sixteen miles below.

"I had a few days off, and meant to go see my momma," he said slowly, measuring his words. "But I got busy and didn't make it. I thought, well, I'll go see her soon as I get back. You know how it gets when you're off; you get busy with the wife and kids. And you know I've always been active with the Masons."

The other said, "You know what they call a Shriner?"

"Yeah."

"A drunk Mason."

"Uh-huh. Pretty much true. I wouldn't make a very good Shriner. I've known some and don't mean to pass judgment. But as I was saying, I left town without seein' Momma. I felt bad but kept telling myself just a couple of days."

He went on for the longest time, sounding miserable and tired. It did not seem that navigation was keeping him very busy; moving the searchlight and wheel must have been reflexive, done absentmindedly.

Then he said, "So we come up on Dennis Landing at night. A feller come down and hollers out, 'You gotta call the office. You gotta get off.' "

"I says to myself, 'Now what could be so important this time of night?' "

"Soze I call the office and the man says, 'Your mother has passed away.' "

This was years ago, and still he felt terrible, it gnawed at him every time he passed Dennis Landing. He mumbled and burbled, wracked with self-recrimination, and I thought he might break down in tears.

The other pilot murmured uncomfortably, not knowing what to say beyond offering condolences. "Know how you feel," he said. "My step-father died not long ago. I remember when he and my mother were married, up on Mud Island in Memphis, under an arbor. I was seven; remember it like yesterday. The flowers. White dresses. When they said 'I do,' I went up and hugged his leg and called him Daddy."

I lay back and closed my eyes. I was aging and my father was gone. Like the pilot, I'd been absent. Maybe our dead had planned it that way.

Then I was consumed with regrets dating from my childhood. What a jerk I'd been my fifteenth year, overturning the canoe on Barton Pond. Would I have been a different son if he had been a different father, relenting on those early curfews, not weeding out those of my friends he didn't like, not demanding better grades?

Not until he became president of the University of Texas at Austin did he finally ease up. At least in his relations with me. Though busier than ever, and constantly battling with one or more of the regents, he no longer seemed to feel the same pressure to *make it*; he *had* made it (the way La Salle would have felt as governor of Louisiana). There was no higher job to which he aspired, not even deputy cabinet level posts in Washington for which he occasionally was mentioned.

These were the years 1970–73: Lyndon Johnson had retired to his ranch outside Austin; Darrel Royal's Longhorn football team beat Notre Dame for the national championship (behind quarterback James Street, wide receiver Cotton Spreyer, and field-goal kicker Happy Feller); Chicano and black students campaigned for minority quotas; and the UT alumna Farrah Fawcett married Lee Majors, both stars of their own television shows, *Charlie's Angels* and *The Bionic Man*. James Michener successfully negotiated with my father the construction of a new wing on the art museum to house his considerable collection of modern American paintings and sculptures—Thomas Hart Benton, Franz Kline, Mark Rothko, Helen Frankenthaler, Richard Anuskiewicz, Larry Rivers, Alexander Archipenko . . . At the 1973 Cotton Bowl I sat behind my father and LBJ, Country Charley Pride to one side, Michener to the other.

Then my ninety-four-year-old Grandmother Orton passed away. She'd lived with my parents for nearly twenty years. The funeral was held in Morgantown, West Virginia. At the gravesite, Peter, then two, played in the dirt with a plastic car. My mother, flanked by her sister and brother, spoke, saying that the first person she wished to thank was her husband, who had brought her mother into his home so many years ago. It was the first time I saw her, always overshadowed by him, step into the light, step *away* from him and define herself as a separate entity. Perhaps that too unburdened him.

After the burial there was a reception at the home of a family friend, a faculty member at the University of West Virginia. Father and I sat in the living room conversing with a number of engineering professors who were clearly impressed to be rubbing elbows with a university president.

For what seemed an interminable time they told Father about their school and the innovative curriculum that was evolving.

Father was never good at small talk, and I could see his eyes glaze over. At last he decided he ought to say something.

"Have you heard about the new engineering program we're offering at UT?"

The professors set aside their coffee cups and leaned forward.

"No, Steve, tell us about it!"

"Well, it's essentially a survey of plumbing practices in the ancient world."

"You don't say!"

"Yes. It's called a Pharaoh Faucet Major."

Father's eyes squinted, his shoulders jumping, the laugh in his chest. The others stared at each other, wondering if they'd been made fools of. Father looked toward me, pleased with himself. We excused ourselves to the garden.

Later that year he was invited to give the commencement address to officers at Bergstrom Air Force Base. Military brass and local politicians spoke first, rambling on as speakers at such events are wont to do because they cannot help themselves. Father saw that the audience was growing restless. At last he was asked to step to the podium: "Dr. Spurr will now give his address!"

Father strode to the stage, surveyed the room, and said, "My address is 4231 Meadowbrook Drive, Austin, Texas. Thank you very much and good evening." He sat down.

The graduates jumped to their feet and gave him a rousing ovation.

Unfortunately, our conversations did not often go much deeper than the pun. In high school, I could not talk to him about the girl on the school bus I wanted to date, nor tell him why I could not say no when some friend suggested we drag-race his Mustang. Later, in my thirties, I tried to explain why my marriage had fallen apart, but he had little to say. Puritans don't tell about private lives. It seemed we couldn't talk any more frankly than Steve could talk to me.


I switched off the radio and sat up. By chance, the two tows were passing right in front of us, one silhouetted against the other, the hum of their giant diesels radiating through the water, through *Pearl*'s hull, the force rattling a bolt or a glass or tool stowed somewhere. And then the vibration lessened and the noise faded.

A Pawnee dream song:

> *In the great night my heart will go out,*
> *Toward me the darkness comes rattling,*
> *In the great night my heart will go out.*[8]

I looked once more and saw the two searchlights cleaving the night in opposite directions. One north, the other south, or maybe it was east and west.

CHAPTER 14

# The Fires of the Natchez

*By firelight, we talk about the snow leopard. Not only is it rare, so says
GS, but it is wary and elusive to a magical degree, and so well camouflaged
in the places it chooses to lie that one can stare straight at it from yards away
and fail to see it.*

—Peter Matthiessen, *The Snow Leopard*

We awoke to a beautiful blue sky stamped with gray clouds. The tows
had been rocking us since five o'clock, making the boat quiver as the bow
was set down on the steep bank. The first thunk was the hardest, but the
thunks gradually lessened as the waves diminished, until again the boat
sat still.

I sat on the rail dangling my feet in the water, watching the current
swirl around my ankles, bubbling at the toes. When I slipped over the side
my feet could not find the bottom. The dropoff was short and steep.
Hoisting myself back aboard, I walked to the bow and jumped. One foot
hit hard sand and the other sank in warm ooze. Flies flew up around my
calves.

Around eight a man in a mud-caked bass boat motored into the cutoff.
He slowed to an idle, then shifted into neutral while checking his nets
strung across the channel. There were a few fish, which he dropped on the
cockpit floor, out of Steve's sight, which frustrated his attempts at identifi-
cation . . . to know what was *running*. He was still expecting a thousand

bluefish to corner ten thousand pogies in a shallow cove, so thick you could jag them in the sides with a squid jig.

"Two bass and a buffalo," he guessed.

Overnight three mud turtles had become tangled in the net and drowned; these the fisherman tossed over the side. At home, on the Atlantic, the lobstermen do the same with crabs and skates—no time or use in caring about waste. The current carried the turtles down to us. Their pointed heads and tubular tails, which house their protuberant anuses, seemed of equal dimension and shape, making it difficult to determine which end was which. Steve swam out to grab one and inspect it more closely.

"Turtle soup!"

The man dropped two buffalo fish into a bucket.

"You folks from around here?"

"Rhode Island."

"You're a long way from home."

"Yes, we are."

A protracted silence.

Steve broke it. "Catching anything?" he asked.

"No."

Apparently the buffalo fish didn't count and the turtles were unworthy of mention, mere by-products of his commerce.

Steve caught a five-inch perch, which I made him throw back.

"Only keep what you eat."

Without a word, he threw it back. If he was disappointed, it was no wonder, considering the guppies Anthony fed his children. He disappeared below. Later I saw that he'd found the flare gun, which I made him put back in its cabinet. Next time I looked he was diddling with a plastic bag of brass cup hooks, which were still clutched in his hands after he fell asleep.

Looking down the river I could see Sunflower Cutoff a mile distant. This island in the stream at mile 624.8 marks the closure of Sunflower Bend, a loop in the river of six miles' diameter. Overgrown now, this stretch of water was the place where on May 8, 1541, Hernando de Soto came upon the Mississippi, the first white to cross above the mouth and behold the river's muddy breadth.

The most substantial account of Soto's *entrada* written by an expedition member was published anonymously. The author was known only as "a gentleman of Elvas." In his narrative he observed, "The stream was swift, and very deep; the water, always flowing turbidly, brought along from above many trees and much timber, driven onward by its forces."[1]

Over a period of several weeks, Soto's band constructed barges for the men and horses. They made the crossing despite a hail of arrows from hostile Indians stationed on the other side. The site was quite near to the small town of Lundell, Arkansas, though due to changes in the river's course, today the town is not quite so close to the water. Soto moved his troops north to a settlement called Pacaha, inhabited by the Casqui clan, who had connected their village to the big river by digging a channel that the Spaniards found filled with fish. A sort of early trout pond.

As usual, Soto helped himself to the Indians' food stores and the women. The men he pressed into service as guides and bearers. Except on the few occasions when he recognized that he was at a tactical disadvantage, he was merciless in his dealing with the Indians. A favorite tactic was siccing his dogs on any rebellious Indian, tearing him to pieces. Sooner than later, Soto would get his.


At midday we passed the mouth of the Arkansas. Unlike La Salle, who passed it in a dense fog, we saw the Arkansas under a blazing sun in a clear sky. Still, if we hadn't been looking, we would have missed the narrow river, its entrance camouflaged by what appeared to be an unbroken line of trees and further concealed by sandbars. The single feature that drew attention was a bluff of reddish-brown sand on the southern bank. It seemed a shy meeting for a river that begins in the Rocky Mountains of Colorado, tumbles down the eastern slope of the Continental Divide, and pushes through the Royal Gorge before meandering 1,450 miles through the Kansas wheatlands and the oil rigs of northern Oklahoma, draining 160,000 square miles of flatland as it goes.

In 1957, the Army Corps of Engineers began constructing between Gore, Oklahoma, and Dewitt, Arkansas, the McClellan-Kerr Arkansas River Navigation System of seventeen locks and a dredged channel where a minimum depth of nine feet is maintained. *Quimby's* said the waters are turbulent, with strong currents and hidden obstacles. There was a fuel stop twenty-two miles up, beyond two locks.

Nearer, thirteen miles away, was the Arkansas Post historical monument, built on the site that Tonti settled in 1686. Having been granted trading rights to the region, here he established the first settlement in the Lower Mississippi River basin. The site's being also the approximate spot, near the Indian village of Guachoya, where La Salle first took possession of the Mississippi watershed for France as well as the terminus of Jolliet's 1673 expedition, Mark Twain wrote in *Life on the Mississippi*, "Therefore, three out of the four memorable events connected with the discovery and exploration of the mighty river occurred, by accident, in one and the same place [the fourth event was of course Soto's crossing of the river a few miles to the north]. It is a most curious distinction, when one comes to look at it and think about it. France stole that vast country on that spot, the future [town of] Napoleon; and by and by Napoleon himself was to give the country back again! make restitution, not to the owners, but to their white American heirs."[2]

Alas, the river's course had changed so much in three hundred years that the site now lay miles from us, still on the Arkansas, but a long way from the Mississippi.

The Louisiana Purchase of 1803 was a perfunctory ending to La Salle's dramatic initiative 121 years earlier to gain French control of the Mississippi River valley. Besides La Salle, Tonti, Iberville, and a few others, the French it seems had little appetite for colonizing America. Unlike the Spanish and English, who dug in with their heels and fought tenaciously to protect their ground, the French developed little infrastructure to support their few settlements along the river system, and in the end they left quietly.

That morning, the Evinrude lapsed into such severe paroxysms of coughing and missing that I feared it would stop altogether. When it bogged, I eased the throttle, letting it idle as we drifted with the stream. After a time, I'd try again, and more often than not it responded. We limped into the Caulk Neck Cutoff for lunch. As Adria and Steve swam and chased butterflies ashore, I removed the cowling from the engine. Dumbly I stared at the perplexity of hoses and wires and carefully tooled chambers of the cylinders. The troubleshooting section of the manual suggested dozens of possible causes, but I soon closed it with a feeling of utter bewilderment. Limited as I was to a few spare parts and simple hand tools, most of the diagnostics were irrelevant. Start with the simple, I decided, which meant replacing the spark plugs. Unfortunately, I had forgotten to bring a spark-plug socket and so was forced to use a crescent wrench, which did not fit well. I succeeded in removing one plug. On examination, it did not seem excessively dirty, oily, or pitted. The other five were intractable. I replaced the cowling and gave up.

Thirty-seven miles to Greenville. I emptied the last jug into the main tank.

Rounding Miller Bend, seven miles upstream from the city, we were hailed by a down-on-their-luck family inching toward us in a metallic green bass boat. The enormous outboard was tilted out of the water. The father stood on the bow in a heroic stance, à la Washington crossing the Potomac, manipulating the remote controls of a small electric trolling motor.

"Engine quit," the man said.

"Need a tow?"

"Be obliged."

I made a bridle between *Pearl*'s two after corner cleats and tied a tow line from the middle. I threw him the bitter end, which he made fast to a bow eye. Then he sat down with a harrumph. His disgust at his broken engine was plain. His two boys stared at us. The mother did not look at anyone; no doubt she hadn't wanted to go fishing in the first place. "I told you so" was written all over her face.

We could make just five knots without upsetting the bass boat. *Pearl* strained and soon the engine began to miss again. Now I began to fear we were running on fumes. Still I kept at it, listening to the sickening cough, dreading the prospect of the outboard's failing altogether. The run to Greenville seemed interminable, our parlance with the family awkward. The man stood and pointed toward the narrow opening of Lake Ferguson, which was really all that was left of an old loop of the Mississippi, sanded over at the upper end. I turned beam to the river and felt *Pearl* slide sideways, skidding, as it were. As if aware of the circumstances, she accepted a little more throttle and freed herself of the current. There were yet some miles to go up Lake Ferguson, miles I hadn't figured on, and there was no fuel gauge to watch, no needle flickering over the big *E*.

With considerable relief, we set the family adrift a hundred feet from the town landing, the father revving the electric trolling motor to make the ramp. He seemed embarrassed, but composed himself sufficiently to offer buying us gas. Feeling very much like a stranger in a strange land, I waved him off, for which he seemed grateful. Probably the only good thing that had happened to him all day.

Next to the landing was the Las Vegas Casino boat, another of the horribly ostentatious fake paddlewheelers permanently moored to the land. Its saving grace was a gas pump mounted on a floating dock tied outboard of the ship. For the first time in a week we wouldn't have to carry jugs into town. And we had completed the longest run between fuel supplies, thanks to the two jugs filled at Helena.

I rang the service bell and after a few minutes the attendant looked out from the backdoor of the ship, then scrambled down a series of metal ladders and through wire gates, each of which required a key from the hoop he had slung on his wrist. *Pearl* took on nearly eighty gallons, for which I was asked to pay inside, at an office in the center of the clanging slot machines, whirring roulette wheels, and silent blackjack tables. The hall was dark and cool, a galaxy of flashing lights, noisy with the sound of falling money. All the patrons were dressed to the nines, the players pensive, those just entering aggressive and full of laughter. So surreal was the contrast with the kids and fishermen and raw white heat outdoors, the casino might as well have been a flying saucer landed among cotton pickers. Wearing flip-flops, shorts, and a loose-fitting tropical shirt my father had had sewn thirty-five years ago in Papeete, Tahiti (why did his clothes last so long?), I felt terribly out of place and left quickly, the *whup-whup* of my sandals following me to the backdoor.

Another thirty-one miles brought us to the Corrigidor Light at mile 507, where we anchored in four feet of water behind a beautiful white and sandy towhead on the Arkansas-Louisiana border. The levee was lined with willow oaks and in their limbs were turtle doves, woodpeckers, and female cardinals all atwitter. Beyond, sweetgum for making pallets, and pecan, popular for paneling and flooring. Everything had a use in the dismantling of pre-America.

That night, my reading took Huck and Jim into Arkansas to meet the "world renowned tragedians" and flim-flam artists.

Afterward, Steve asked for another John and Jim story, which he preferred. Twain, of whose writings Marquis Childs said, "There is above all else an onslaught against the dead and sterile forms of civilization that had been brought over the mountains," was, I think, too wordy for Steve, and the action sparse. In fact, I had had to edit the long discourses on manners and religion, which were entirely lost on him.

Quite by coincidence, a copy of *USA Today* I'd bought back in Greenville ran on the Op-Ed page an "Our View" and "Opposing View" on the fitness of *Huckleberry Finn* for modern readers. The critic claimed it to be "the most grotesque example of racist trash ever given our children to read."[3] The paper's editors rebutted: "The story transcends race. Huck and Jim build a relationship on respect and loyalty." The following January, *Harper's* magazine ran a piece of criticism by Jane Smiley, who challenged Huck's "real elevation into the pantheon . . . by Lionel Trilling, Leslie Fiedler, T. S. Eliot, Joseph Wood Krutch, and some lesser lights." She, too, objected that "neither Huck nor Twain takes Jim's desire for freedom at all seriously." She doesn't blame Huck, who is "just a boy trying to survive. The villain here is Mark Twain."[4]

Even before reading the controversy, in my reading to Steve I'd changed "nigger" to "black." Parental discretion implemented. If there had been more fishing, I'd have kept on. But pirates, fish, and gold, that's what widened Steve's eyes and in the darkness made him revert to sucking his thumb. I guess he didn't know how else to handle suspense.


One day John went fishing by himself in his father's lobster boat. In the middle of the ocean, where no land could be seen, he shut down the engine and let the vessel drift. He baited his deep-sea rod and before long caught his first fish. It was small, and he had no intention of keeping it, but as he was reeling it in, the fish was eaten by another, and that one by another, so that he had three fish on one hook. Before he could pull them into the boat, a mako shark came along and ate all three! Chomp!

John had never seen anything like it, nor had he ever heard his father or the other fishermen relate such a fantastic story. Thinking it a bad omen, he set down his rod and wondered what to do next.

Scanning the horizon, he sighted a tropical island. Where the island lay the chart showed only the vast, blue expanse of the sea. Deciding to investigate, he started the engine and motored toward it. There was a tall peak in the middle, which because of its conical shape appeared volcanic. But it must have been a long time since the last eruption because the slopes were green. He beached the lobster boat and stepped ashore among the palm trees, ferns, and sawgrass. He struck out inland until he came upon a beautiful meadow, where stood a snow-white unicorn. He approached it quietly and was about to pet the strange animal when a half-naked cannibal-giant yelled "Stop!" He was the size of the Cyclops that chased Odysseus from Sicily, and was covered with tattoos.

The cannibal rushed toward John, picked him up with one hand around his waist, and carried him up the mountain to his cave. Fortunately, John's hand *had* brushed the unicorn, which was good luck. He would need it.

The cannibal tied John's hands behind his back and bound his ankles with a sinewy fiber pulled from the vines that grew outside the cave. Then he built a fire under a big copper kettle. He licked his lips. Even his tongue was tattooed! But he'd forgotten something—vegetables! He ran down the mountain to his garden to pick some sweet potatoes, carrots, and onions.

John was about to despair of ever seeing his home when suddenly a mermaid wiggled into the cave propelled by her tail. Her face was as fair as a seashell, her hair as white as sand. Her nose turned up every so slightly, and her eyes were pointed at the corners, which, because there are few Asians in Maine, gave her an exotic look. She cut the ropes with the cannibal's knife, which he had carelessly left by the fire. She held her finger to her lips and motioned for John. He followed her out of the cave and down a path to a stream. There they dove in and were swept down the crystal current and over a waterfall. In the lake below, they swam to the center, to avoid being seen by the cannibal picking tomatoes in his plot along the shore. They dove straight down and swam through a tunnel that led to the ocean. Though she had no gills, the mermaid could of course breathe underwater. John could not, and was forced to hold his breath until she signaled him upward. He broke the surface gasping. Nearby was the lobster boat.

John thanked her for saving his life. She kissed him good-bye. The cannibal spotted the two and was very angry. He ran to the ocean shore. In the nick of time, John hopped into his boat, started the engine, and roared off. The cannibal threw vegetables after him, which landed all about the boat like cannonballs.

When he was safely out of range, John turned to wave good-bye to the mermaid, but she was not to be seen. He did not know where she had come from nor where she had gone, nor if he would ever see her again. She was his first kiss, and it felt tingly and strange.

Steve said, "I don't like kisses either."

"How come?" Adria asked.

"I don't know."

"Who said John didn't like it?" I asked.


A haze covered the orange sun. Steve awoke and leaped ashore to find two long sticks, between which he intended to stretch a homemade net. This, he had observed on several successive mornings, was how the local professionals caught fish. Most of the day he prodded Adria into cutting lengths of string from a ball and tying them into tiny squares. After a time, she'd had enough and turned to painting watercolors.

By midafternoon we reached Vicksburg. Beyond the gaudy fleet of casino boats—*Isle of Capri, Ameristar,* and *Rainbow*—moored by the I-20 bridge, there was not much to see from the big river. At flood stage (forty-three feet), water passes the bridge at 1.4 million cubic feet per second. As elsewhere, the town had walled itself in. Up the Yazoo Divertment Canal we stopped to take on fuel at the Quarterboat & Fuel Barge. Two days without lugging jugs! The office was inside a wooden shed set at one end of the barge. We were met at the door by a lad dressed in a brown uniform. His hair was cut very short and he had an impish smile, not so much in the mouth as in the cheeks. He was, it is fair to say, the slowest-talking person ever created. Yes, the owner had fuel, but not on the dock. He kept it in a tank in the back of his pickup. In an hour Dennis Schaefer would return with his river tour group and we could buy all the fuel he had, whatever amount that happened to be.

We sat and waited. The young man told us that we'd have had a different trip last spring, when the river flooded.

"Me and some friends went water-skiing over cottonfields four, five feet under."

After each sentence, he lapsed into an awkward silence, smiling at us until we made known our next interest.

Adria noted the stuffed bobcat on a bookshelf, frozen with one paw raised, fangs bared.

"Ah've a friend with a bobcat for a house pet," he said, grinning slyly. "Gits a little rowdy sometimes."

Steve bought a Coke from the machine; even in the air-conditioned room it soon turned tepid. Adria and I studied the used paperbacks stacked on a shelf with a sign that said, "Take one, leave one." On the opposite wall was a rack of tourist brochures. The lad sat as stilly as the works of taxidermy above his head. When I asked him a question he smiled and answered slowly and succinctly. Then shut up.

I stepped outside to smoke my pipe. The heat hit me like a hammer. Coming up the cutoff a red aluminum pontoon boat churned the backwater. The fringe of its canvas canopy curled back from the vessel's own breeze. The sign on the side panel said "Mississippi Adventure Charters."

The lad joined me on the dock and took its lines. When all the passengers, most of whom were Asian tourists heavily armed with cameras, had disembarked, he said to Schaefer, "Folks want some fuel."

Dennis Schaefer, a tall, heavy-set man and much more gregarious than the young man, flirted with the persona of the great white hunter—the canvas hat, the khaki shirt with epaulets, the easy movements. He shook my hand and told me to come inside. There he bought a soda and sat down. "We'll wait awhile," he said. "Hot. Mighty hot." So we sat and looked at one another and waited until he cooled down. I asked about groceries and bait. Schaefer nodded. By and by another man, old enough to be Schaefer's father, stepped in sideways through the door and joined us. "This is John Jack George," Schaefer said. "He can take your daughter to the store while we fuel your boat."

John Jack George was not a pretty face, the skin pitted with deep craters and his nose misshapen. A little reluctant to let Adria go with him, I chatted up the man with three first names. A character test. He was, he said, born in 1920. Worked for the Army Corps of Engineers as a diesel mechanic from 1938 until retirement in 1978. Witnessed the transition from steamboats to diesel.

"Machines taken the work of fourteen men," he lamented. "So now they're forced to steal. That's why there's so much crime and drugs. Machines to blame."

This seemed an odd conclusion for someone who'd spent his life fixing them, but I did not say so.

"Vicksburg used to be catfish row, but the farms have ruined the river fishermen. Pond catfish don't taste worth a damn anyway."

I got Adria off to the side and asked if she minded riding with John Jack George.

"Of course not, Dad. Why?"

"Just checking." Just a Dad thing.

Steve and I motored *Pearl* over to the town landing where Schaefer met us in his pickup and handed over the hose that led from the tank braced in the bed. Later, he drove us to the Klondike, a service station–breakfast eatery–bait shop. The backroom employed several men full time who tended large pools of minnows, cages of crickets, and goldfish for trot lines. We bought some crawlers and sinkers.

John Jack George was a long time returning, and I began to doubt my decision. When at last he and Adria entered the Quarterboat, he explained that they'd been stuck for twenty-eight minutes at a railroad crossing. Timed it, he said.

"Used to be a train up yon and every day it stopped soze to block the men getting off work at the grain terminal. They couldn't get home or the bar or nowheres. One day the workers locked the train's brakes; the engineer ain't stopped there since."

"Another machine gone bad," I said softly. To which he said, "Huh?" And I said, "Nothing."

Once the groceries were stowed, we took directions from Schaefer and ate dinner at the River Road Restaurant. It was early and there were no other customers. The waitress was sullen. She dropped a drink and shouted, "Shit!"

Recovering, she sallied up to the table and addressed Steve.

"Don't ever say that word, honey."

Schaefer had invited us to spend the night moored to the Quarterboat, but we were happier on the river. So we ran twenty-seven miles to a sandbar. That night there were few mosquitoes but an abundance of earwigs, which kept crawling under the screen until I pressed a piece of duct tape across the seam.

To keep cool, we swam until dark. The water was just a foot deep, the bottom grazing our chests. On shore a flock of pelicans stood weathercocked to the wind. I'd never seen them in a group, never in the Florida Keys, Texas Gulf Coast, or anywhere else in the subtropical world. Yet here they were, perhaps a hundred, sitting on the sand as evenly spaced as cadets on a parade field. Adria floating down on them, riding the beanbag, closing the shore like a commando. When she stood they spooked, ascending skyward, their long necks outstretched. In a V-formation, the two white bands of birds circled overhead, blew down with the breeze, and landed at the southern end of the island.

. . .

The sun rose red and already waves of hot air rippled across its face. The pelicans had returned and stood on a nearby point of sand. Each regarded us warily with one eye.

Adria was brewing tea when suddenly before us a bobcat waded into the channel. It startled me. How had it come across the sand unseen? Steve jumped to his feet. The cat was the size of a small dog, its fur piebald, its ears equilateral triangles. The water folded over its back and a small ripple followed as it began swimming across the channel toward the mainland. Its pointed ears were swept back nearly flat against its head. The rate of its progress was steady though not rapid, the current setting the animal downstream so that its course across was diagonal. As it distanced itself from us, we took up the binoculars. Several times the bobcat dove. And when it reappeared Adria said it was the primordial "snout" coming out of the water to live on land. Though we waited breathlessly to see it scamper up the far bank, eventually the fading shape was lost in the shadows of overhanging trees.

Later I reread Peter Matthiessen's *The Snow Leopard*. During his two-month search in Nepal with the zoologist George Schaller, he saw tracks and scat, signposts along the path to satori, for which the snow leopard might be taken as a metaphor. But Matthiessen did not succeed in making an actual sighting. Only after he had left the area did Schaller, working alone, happen one morning to see the rare animal.

I realized that truth and beauty are not compelled to reveal themselves simply because one is looking. Simply living in the now isn't enough. One must first learn to forget.

I had thought of the bobcat many days after we had followed the large, unidentified paw prints in the caked mud of the towheads, thought of the animal live when I saw the dead one stuffed on the shelf of Schaefer's Quarterboat; considered the likelihood of sighting my own bobcat when the fuel jockey told of the friend's pet. But it was not a quest. I'd forgotten. And then it came to me, startlingly close, crossing the bar.

Mile 406, the Grand Gulf Nuclear Station, the ominous white cylinder strangely juxtaposed against the green and yellow landscape. Another flock of pelicans floated with the current down the cut. Onshore, more bobcat tracks, the signs coming after the sighting, like seeing the tail of a comet. Remembrances rather than clues and warnings.

To the west, at mile 373, was the southern terminus of Lake St. John; below mile 373, Lake Concordia. More sealed oxbows where once the water flowed but was now still, no longer needed, made obsolete by the needs of the river always pressing to straighten itself.

It was in this vicinity that Hernando de Soto, after three years tramping back and forth across the southern states, became feverish and in three days died, so ending his grim and brutal march, a scourge that would be duplicated when William Tecumseh Sherman rode through with a torch 322 years later.

The Indians believed Soto was a demigod, and the surviving soldiers were fearful that if his death were made known, the Indians might lose their awe of the Spaniards and attack. So when curious Indians asked why they had not seen Soto, the Spaniards replied that he had ascended to heaven for consultations with the Father. Soon, they said, he would return. Soto's body was buried, but the Indians noticed the freshly turned soil and were suspicious. Fearing the body would be found, Luis de Moscoso, who had assumed leadership, ordered that it be disinterred, weighted with stones, and sunk in the river.

Edward Moran's fanciful painting of the scene is a spooky, surreal depiction of ghoul-like priests bending over the shrouded corpse, while in the rear armored men bear torches dimmed in a fog, faintly illuminating the swirling river moments before he was dumped.

Other accounts say he was concealed in a hollow log and set adrift, borne on his own River Styx.

Moscoso and the hidalgos (Spanish noblemen) managed to build new barges to carry the party downriver. They fought off numerous attacks from the Indians, who had learned from experience that the Spaniards were an evil upon their land. Eventually the party reached the mouth of the Mississippi and turned westward, toward New Spain. For six weeks they sailed the barren coast, until on September 10, 1543, they reached Pánuco, the Spanish settlement at the mouth of the Pánuco River, which empties into the gulf near Tampico, Mexico, about 250 miles south of Brownsville, Texas.

At Natchez we ran the bow onto the reddish-brown mud of the bank, in which were embedded large rocks that we used as stepping-stones to dry ground. Nearby was moored a small steel barge, and on its deck was a stack of traps made of wood and netting. I thought to tie to it, but did not wish to trespass.

A short walk up the concrete landing were several stores and restaurants. Andre Ferrish, proprietor of the Mark Twain Guest House, said he would take us to procure fuel after lunch. He suggested that we kill time by dining down the street at the Magnolia Grill. I remember the ice tea and the crunchy bean sprouts, the old ladies in a window seat, a young couple's stilted conversation, a few businessmen in suits, and, mostly, my bare knees, which felt so cold and good I wanted to start drinking and stay the day and night and damn the kids.

When we returned, Andre had grown busy in the bar he tended on the first floor of the inn. Not wanting to be pushy, we waited outside.

"You ready?" he called.

I nodded.

"I'll call my brother, Jeff."

Soon a small pickup truck pulled up in front of us. We were not hard to identify, standing as we were by our pile of red jugs.

"Take you over the bridge to Louisiana," he said. "Gas is cheaper there."

I happily paid fifteen dollars, feeling I'd gotten a lot more for my money than I had from Tom Woolsey at the Honker's Boat Club, especially as Jeff had left work to do us this favor. But locals care for river travelers. The Mississippi bonds all those who live near or upon it.

One of Andre's hangers-on helped carry the jugs down to *Pearl*.

"I'm an amateur archaeologist," said Skip Burnett. "See this mud where your bow is? This is the oldest junkyard in America. One day I came down here and saw some boys skipping coins, right there by the Tarzan rope."

He pointed down the bank toward a tree, from which hung a long rope, knotted at the end. Steve started toward it until Skip said he'd seen a water moccasin there just the other day.

"I sez to the boys, 'Let me see what you're throwing.' So he puts one in my hand and I knows it's gold. Because I've trained myself you see. I asked them where they found 'em, and they showed me how they'd come up out of the mud. I paid 'em five dollars for the lot!

"A few years ago I found Indian mounds. Ever hear of Moundville? Mine was like that, but smaller. The Natchez Indians came from Mexico you see, and their king was the deposed brother of the Aztec king. All along this shore here there was houses. And each house had a fire. They built earthen temples and made sacrifices. When the king died, they strangled his wives and servants and threw them into the grave with him, to keep him company in the next world. Just like the Aztecs. Yeah, I found one of their mounds. In the woods it was. The stuff we were bringing up was worth two hundred fifty thousand, but the state confiscated it. I'm in it for the money, but it's interesting. You have to understand some history to know how to look. I like digging the old Indian privies for bottles, *punnel*; the men, you see, drank *away* from their wives. At the outhouse. Strange, huh?"

He kicked at the rocks and mud by his feet. "I come down here every few days. Stuff keeps seeping up. Never know what you'll find. There," he pointed suddenly. "See that?" He picked up a small porcelain figurine. "This is at least a hundred years old. Worth maybe twenty dollars." He flashed it to Adria, then slipped it into his pocket.

While we transferred fuel from the jugs to *Pearl*'s tank, Skip filled our chest with ice from the Mark Twain Guest House. When we were ready he put a hand on the bow and shoved it from the bank, saying next time we ought to tie to the barge. "That's what it's there for. Used to be a bigger barge, but the old man died. His son don't mind."

It was difficult for me to contemplate "next times" on the river for I did not think I would come this way again. The idea of repeating seemed to detract from this experience, making it less valuable. No, this was it, here and now.

But Skip had been partly right about the Natchez Indians. There were influences among them of Mesoamerica—the mound building, the crafts, the political structures whereby one man was recognized as king and was carried around on a litter by servants who, along with the wives, were strangled and buried with their master. And the perpetual flame, tended by old men/priests who were at risk of death should the light fail. But there is no evidence that the Taensas were directly related to the Aztecs. Charles Hudson, author of the comprehensive work *The Southeastern Indians*, says that traders may have helped transfer customs from one land to another, not only to here, but as far north as west-central Illinois, where one finds

Monks Mound, the largest prehistoric earthen construction in pre-America—22 million cubic feet of dirt.

Parkman wrote that during La Salle's visit in 1682 neither he nor Tonti had ever seen anything like the village of the Taensas, which they found just above Natchez, on an old meander now called Lake St. Joseph:

> Large square dwellings, built of sun-baked mud mixed with straw, arched over with a dome-shaped roof of canes, [were] placed in regular order around an open area. Two of them were larger and better than the rest. One was the lodge of the chief; the other was the temple, or house of the sun. They entered the former, and found a single room, forty feet square, where, in the dim light,—for there was no opening but the door,—the chief sat awaiting them on a sort of bedstead, three of his wives at his side, while sixty old men, wrapped in white cloaks woven of mulberry-bark, formed his divan. When he spoke, his wives howled to do him honor, and the assembled councillors listened with the reverence due to a potentate for whom, at his death, a hundred victims were to be sacrificed. He received the visitors graciously, and joyfully accepted the gifts which Tonti laid before him. This interview over, the Frenchmen repaired to the temple, wherein were kept the bones of the departed chiefs. In construction, it was much like the royal dwelling. Over it were rude wooden figures, representing three eagles turned towards the east. A strong mud wall surrounded it, planted with stakes, on which were stuck the skulls of enemies sacrificed to the Sun; while before the door was a block of wood, on which lay a large shell surrounded with the braided hair of the victims.[5]

It was here that La Salle intended to establish his colony, sixty leagues from the gulf, probably because so much of the land farther downriver lay underwater.

Farther downriver, at Natchez, they found another village much the same as that of the Taensas; they held that their chief was brother of the great chief, the sun. Indeed, the entire privileged caste was descended from the sun. At the village of the Coroas, two leagues below, they learned something of the social structure:

As descent was through the female, the chief's son never succeeded him, but the son of one of his sisters; and as she, by the
usual totemic law, was forced to marry in another clan,—that is,
to marry a common mortal,—her husband, though the destined
father of a demigod, was treated by her as little better than a slave.
She might kill him, if he proved unfaithful; but he was forced to
submit to her infidelities in silence.[6]

After La Salle's visit, the Frenchmen who followed observed the Taensas and Natchez Indians in decline. By the time other Europeans passed
through, the five-hundred-year-old Mississippian culture of the Mound
Builders was virtually extinct. At some time there had been a massive
dying off, possibly caused by epidemic diseases introduced by Soto. The
coup de grace occurred in 1729, when angry Natchez Indians massacred
some French settlers; in revenge, the French drove the Indians from their
land. The few survivors joined the Creeks, but their peculiar customs were
lost forever.

Still lost was La Salle, whose calculated latitude of the Taensas village was a degree off. This gave him new doubts as to the identity of
his river. According to the Spanish maps, the Río del Espíritu Santo
entered a large bay that joined the ocean at 30 degrees north latitude;
La Salle's reading of 31 degrees suggested that he already should have
entered the bay. But of course there was no Bahía del Espíritu Santo,
a fact that confounded the French, Spanish, and English for years to
come. Not only does the Mississippi not flow into a bay, but it has no
readily discernible mouth; in fact, it dissipates into swamp and marsh,
its three main passes virtually indistinguishable from the dozens of
side channels. By some line of reasoning, La Salle now decided that
they were on the Abscondido, or Escondido, River, which Tonti said
he and La Salle later found to be correct. It was not, for the river
the Spanish called the Escondido enters the gulf far to the west, at the
bow in the shoreline where the river today called the Nueces meets
the city of Corpus Christi. That's where La Salle figured he was—at
the bow.

The course of the Mississippi made matters worse, and the men became
disoriented. Minet wrote that "in descending the river they almost always
saw the sun set in front of them."[7]

So did we, and were it not for the compass mounted on *Pearl*'s dashboard, at this point I too might have concluded that the sum of our bearings led more west than south. As in a fog at sea, one begins to imagine things, to think one is where one is not. It is an effect of wilderness, of pre-America, a place without signposts, and I was tempted to toss away the compass in order that I might enjoy the same feeling of fear.

# CHAPTER 15

# *Deliverance*

*And for a long time yet, led by some wondrous power, I am fated to jour-ney hand in hand with my strange heroes.*

—Nikolai Gogol, *Dead Souls*

In late afternoon we stopped at the Raccourci Cutoff, mile 298. Beyond a log dam was the land of the Louisiana State Penitentiary. Inmates worked a farm there. Against the setting sun cattle stood lowing in the shade of a solitary tree.

A few miles back, we could see up into Old River, an earlier course that connects the Mississippi to the Red and Atchafalaya rivers. There's a lock to keep the Mississippi where it is, keep it from choosing the Atchafalaya instead of its present channel. As recently as 700 B.C., that's the way it sent itself, swinging westward near Lafayette and south of Morgan City. If you used time-lapse photography from space over a period of just several thousand years, the main channels of the Lower Mississippi would look like a multipronged lightning strike "walking" east and west across the map.

Steve, who had given up making a net, contrived a makeshift trotline in three feet of water—two sticks set six feet apart, connected by a string from which we hung a half dozen monofilament lines with baited hooks. A small catfish took one.

Steve set it free.

I did not ask why.

In the gloaming he and Adria built a campfire on which we roasted hot dogs and marshmallows. Four hundred years ago, our fire might have been but one of the thousands lit by the Natchez in their wigwams lining the shore like luminaria bordering a long path. Today there were no other lights visible, no burning wood, no incandescent bulbs, and though we knew better, it almost seemed that the river was wilder now than then, man having been driven from its roiling banks, inland, away. Leaving only us, and the tows, the iron-hearted tows, always the constancy of the tows.

For reasons none of us could explain, we each awoke in the middle of the night. Steve wanted to fish. Adria wanted to watch the sun come up. Reaching my hand out the hatch into the moonlight, I saw from my watch that it was 1:40 A.M. We slept again until we grew restless in the heat of the risen sun. The prison farm, spare of trees, looked like the Serengeti; from a distance, the cows might have been taken for elephants or zebras, silhouetted as they were by the blazing orb.

Steve carried ashore his big fishing net with the long handle, looking for pools with turtles, amphibians, minnows—anything alive. A flock of swallows swarmed overhead teasing him. He chased them up and down the bank and in circles, sweeping wildly at the air. When they rose up over him, he threw the net into the sky. And it struck me how comfortable he was with the land and animals, as if this were his natural state, as if this were pre-America.

"He'll never catch them," Adria said, laughing.

"Never underestimate Steve's ability to catch any kind of critter," I said.

Soon he turned his attention to butterflies, and at this he was successful, snaring several for Adria's inspection. When Steve saw that she intended to keep them for a collection, he reproached her with the senselessness of the kill.

"We only keep what we eat," he said.

I did not say a word, unsure whether he had really adopted my ethic, or was simply mimicking my words. In any case, I regarded this as a victory, and was perfectly content to let him assume my role as the rule-maker, even if it meant his being a tad fresh with an elder.

The air began to smell different. I was not sure whether the new smell emanated from the rotting vegetation of neighboring bayous, a backed-up septic system, or the imminence of the ocean. The answer revealed itself at mile 227, when round a bend we saw the skyline of Baton Rouge. Smoke poured from the multitude of rising stacks. Everywhere ran the pipes and docks and Orwellian-looking structures of Kaiser Aluminum, Exxon, Gulf Oil and Mobil Oil, Formosa Plastics, making . . . what? The connection between raw materials and finished products—say, petroleum and the plastic case of your bedside clock radio—is difficult to make when looking at a factory the size of your hometown. And you might wonder whether you'd give up the product—say, now, sandwich Baggies—in exchange for getting rid of the factory.

Surrounding every building and stack was a sheet of concrete or asphalt, as if to seal the very earth. I looked at it and saw in my mind a *National Geographic* photograph of a World War II runway built by Seabees on a South Pacific atoll—maybe Truk or Palau. The jungle had burst up through it, splitting the asphalt into a thousand pieces, so that it, and the fighter planes parked there since 1945, were virtually hidden by the matrix of roots, vines, and leaves. The caption should have read "Hope." If you believe Friedrich Nietzsche, believe in the eternal recurrence of all things, then given infinite time and infinite space, all things will pass and come again. You just want to find yourself on the right side of the cycle.

Acting on the tip that they might sell a small quantity of fuel to a small craft such as ours, we steered *Pearl* to one of the innumerable fleeting services, Cargo Carriers.

The offices and workshops were located on a large steel barge anchored on the riverbank opposite the city. We tied up next to the gangway, against edges of rough-cut steel. Moving up and down the river were large, oceangoing freighters, some light, some laden, but all displacing enormous volumes of water, far more than the shallower-draft river tugs and barges whose wakes we'd jumped and dodged for a thousand miles, the way a skier runs a mountain of moguls. A big ship's wake, taken at the wrong angle, could easily swamp *Pearl* or crush her against the steel barge.

Up a short flight of stairs two black men wearing thick work aprons sat and joked while a third toiled with a torch and hammer, repairing a piece of bent metal. It was hotter than hell and as pleasant. They directed me toward the other end of the barge and up yet another flight of stairs to the offices, where I found several white men complaining of the heat. Their office was clean and air-conditioned. They wore slacks and clean shirts. One said it was too goddamn hot to go outside, so directed another to find me some gasoline. Reluctantly, the underling bid me follow him back to the metal shop, where he told the torchbearer to pump me some fuel. Whereupon the white man quickly returned to the cool of his office.

One by one we handed over our jugs for filling. The man recorded the number of gallons on a slip and told me to pay in the office. A secretary calculated the bill for my 52.9 gallons. I gave her a hundred-dollar bill, expecting enough change to buy lunch. She returned $1.60 and I felt I'd been had, though we both knew that in Baton Rouge I had no other recourse. That was most of the cash I had left and still we were more than a day's run from New Orleans.

There were no small-boat facilities in Baton Rouge, and we rushed from the place as from a fight. At Plaquemine we beached the boat long enough to make several telephone calls, one to Stanton Murray, the New Orleans yacht broker storing our car and trailer, to advise him of our impending arrival.

From here on the channel was narrow, the ships a menace. The Mississippi is unique in that the closer it gets to the sea, the deeper it works itself, thus making possible the deepwater port of Baton Rouge.

There was but one island left on the river and because it would have been suicide to anchor in the open, we had no choice but to spend our last night at Bayou Gaula Towhead, mile 196. The engine faltered as we glided into a pile of sticks obstructing the short expanse of beach. We tied the bow to a fallen tree and tossed out a stern anchor to hold us against the current and above the tangled branches. The wake from a passing ship rocked the boat deeply to port and starboard, but the hull did not hit anything solid.

Steve swam but Adria demurred, noting that it looked like snake water. Soon the boat was infested with strange, winged bugs with black bodies and red heads, moving in pairs, one lining up the hind end of another to copulate.

After a time, I climbed gingerly over the side, standing waist-deep in the current. Steve, now on the bank, beckoned me ashore, where on the beach we saw the tracks of bobcat, raccoon, and, sure enough, snakes. Thunderheads drew overhead but brought no rain; no such luck.

By morning the bugs were gone. Now we were anxious to be done with the river—gone were the willows and bleached sands of the tow-heads, the pelicans, falcons, and miles of silence. The engine faltered in successive episodes that were increasingly stressful. Each time we felt it necessary to anchor as near to the revetments as we dared and rest the machine. Ship traffic became intense, and as soon as the engine would start, we pushed forward.

By 2 P.M., the city of New Orleans, slowly sinking in the dried-out muck on which it was built, lay abeam. It seemed as though we'd made it. Just across the city was Lake Pontchartrain, Murray Yacht Sales, our car and trailer. I promised dinner at Robear's and showers at the nearest hotel. With great anticipation we passed the line of tourist paddlewheelers lining the waterfront and turned into the Industrial Canal, which connects the river to the lake. One lock, several bascule bridges, and we'd be home free.

I keyed the radio mike: "Industrial Canal Lock, Industrial Canal Lock, this is *Pearl*. Requesting permission to lock through."

There was no answer. I called again, expecting to see the shape of a man moving in the tower.

At last a voice: "Lock's closed."

"What do you mean, 'closed'?"

"Closed to Friday."

"How else can we get into Lake Pontchartrain."

"Go down to Venice and come in through the gulf entrance."

I backed *Pearl* away from the lock and grabbed the chart. Eighty-three miles down the Mississippi to Venice, another hundred across the gulf to the channel into the lake, then another thirty or so back to West End. More than two hundred miles! We couldn't make it in one day. Nor did we even have enough fuel to make it to the marina at Venice. What we needed, I concluded, was a ramp where we could leave the boat long enough to fetch the car and trailer. Take a taxi if necessary, call Stanton, whatever it would take.

Nearby was a Coast Guard station. We tied up and hailed the guardsman installing electronic instruments on the bridge. He had no clue about ramps along the Mississippi.

"Plenty on the lake," he offered.

"I know," I replied. "But our boat's on this side."

"Oh."

Anxiously I studied the chart. No ramps anywhere. A mile down I saw that there was a state park not far from the water. Perhaps the rangers would know.

As near to the park as we could get, we ran *Pearl*'s bow into a narrow expanse of mud that had accumulated around a culvert. Adria, armed with my telephone card and address book, jumped into the water, sinking to her knees. The sandals suctioned off her feet. At last she extricated herself and with mud still clinging to her legs, she scampered up the bank, waved, and was gone. Steve and I waited. He fished off the stern. I watched the river for ships. One passed. I sat dully watching the wake bear down on us, deceived of its size until it was almost too late. At the last second, I grabbed Steve and pulled him down into the cockpit. The wave curled over *Pearl*'s transom and crashed over, filling the boat. The water in the cockpit was waist-deep. The cabin filled. Everything wet and ruined. All my notes, books, charts, sleeping bags, food.

Steve and I were laboring with buckets when Adria returned. There were, she said, no ramps on the Mississippi; the nearest would be on the Barataria Waterway. To reach it, we had to go down the river a few miles more, pass through a lock to the west, then motor an indeterminate number of miles to Rosethorn Park. Just as she was completing her report, her eyes widened and we turned to see yet another wave sweeping toward us. Again, *Pearl* was filled to the gunwales. Much of the water washed out of its own accord, over the sides and transom. After it abated, we set to bailing, but we could not get the transom high enough to keep more water from coming in. So we turned the boat around, bow to the waves, and with Steve and I standing on the bow, managed to raise the stern just high enough so that Adria, standing in the mud behind the stern, could bail out the water and so float *Pearl*. We used buckets for the next hour, turning to a pump for the little left in the bilge. With the water came the mud, which could not be bailed. We scooped out what we could and left.


In the spring, La Salle made his final rush to the sea. The river was contained only by natural levees formed by alluvial deposits carried downstream. On the other side of these deposits, the land was flooded, yet lower. All that showed of the paludal plain were the tops of grass stalks and reeds. Palms became more regular, and the other species of trees able to survive the climate were much smaller than in the north.

After leaving the Taensas and Natchez, the party passed the mouth of the Red River and the village of the Oumas, obscured by a fog that seemed to come each morning. Unlike Huck and Tom, who in similar circumstances had unknowingly been swept past the Ohio, La Salle noticed the clarity of the Red River's water and did not miss the mouth. Several miles farther downstream, they came upon Indians fishing from wooden canoes, who fled at the sight of the strange white men. As always, La Salle made a great effort to communicate with the Indians. But when he sent several men into the marshy sidewaters they were greeted by a hail of arrows from beyond the canebrake and were forced to retreat.

Moving on, they investigated an empty Tangibao village situated on the eastern bank, only to find it pillaged and strewn with corpses.

The hungry men killed cormorants. In the reeds they found a canoe. Inside were smoked caimans and human ribs, which they ate, noting that the human flesh tasted better than that of the small reptile. At night they piled up cane to form dry beds.

Now the party had progressed to a point south of the present city of New Orleans, well into the delta. On April 6, they came to the Head of Passes, mile 0, where the Mississippi divides itself like a pitchfork into three distinct channels. La Salle tasted the water and pronounced it somewhat briny. Several of his men disagreed, whereupon he grew angry with them. On second thought, the men said, "You will pardon us, monsieur. We find it salty."[1]

Jean Bourdon d'Autray was instructed to follow the eastern passage, now called Pass a Loutre, and Tonti the middle one, or South Pass. For himself, La Salle chose the western passage, or Southwest Pass.[2]

Parkman wrote,

> As he drifted down the turbid current, between the low and marshy shores, the brackish water changed to brine, and the breeze grew fresh with the salt breath of the sea. Then the broad bosom of the great Gulf opened on his sight, tossing its restless billows, limitless, voiceless, lonely as when born of chaos, without a sail, without a sign of life.

After a brief investigation that included taking soundings and bearings, the three met back upstream at a point probably near the town of Venice. Here, on high ground, La Salle again claimed the watershed of the

Mississippi for his king and country. A column was made from a tree trunk and squared. It was then engraved with the arms of France and the words *"Louis Le Grand, Roy de France et de Navarre, Règne; Le Neuvième Avril, 1682."* A cross was planted, and buried near it was a copper plate made from a kettle bottom, engraved with the names of La Salle, Tonti, and Father Membré, and the words *Ludovicus Magnus Regnat*.

Parkman wrote:

> The Frenchmen were mustered under arms; and, while the New England Indians and their squaws looked on in wondering silence, they chanted the Te Deum, the Exaudiat, and the Domine salvum fac Regem. Then, amid volleys of musketry and shouts of Vive le Roi, La Salle planted the column in its place, and, standing near it, proclaimed in a loud voice,—
>
> "In the name of the most high, mighty, invincible, and victorious Prince, Louis the Great, by the grace of God King of France and of Navarre, Fourteenth of that name, I, this ninth day of April, one thousand six hundred and eighty-two, in virtue of the commission of his Majesty, which I hold in my hand, and which may be seen by all whom it may concern, have taken, and do now take, in the name of his Majesty and of his successors to the crown, possession of this country of Louisiana, the seas, harbors, ports, bays, adjacent straits, and all the nations, peoples, provinces, cities, towns, villages, mines, minerals, fisheries, streams, and rivers, within the extent of the said Louisiana, from the mouth of the great river St. Louis, otherwise called the Ohio, . . . as also along the river Colbert, or Mississippi, and the rivers which discharge themselves thereinto, from its source beyond the country of the Nadouessioux . . . as far as its mouth at the sea, or Gulf of Mexico, and also the mouth of the River of Palms, upon the assurance we have had from the natives of these countries, that we are the first Europeans who have descended or ascended the said river Colbert; hereby protesting against all who may hereafter undertake to invade any or all of these aforesaid countries, peoples, or lands, to the prejudice of the rights of his Majesty, acquired by the consent of the nations dwelling herein. Of which, and of all else that is needful, I hereby take to witness those who hear me, and demand an act of the notary here present."

A lead plate with the words Ludovicus Magnus Regnat, was buried and the travelers sang the hymn Vexilla Regis: "The banners of heaven's King advance, The mystery of the Cross shines forth"

On that day, the realm of France received on parchment a stupendous accession. The fertile plains of Texas; the vast basin of the Mississippi, from its frozen northern springs to the sultry borders of the Gulf; from the woody ridges of the Alleghenies to the bare peaks of the Rocky Mountains,—a region of savannahs and forests, sun-cracked deserts, and grassy prairies, watered by a thousand rivers, ranged by a thousand warlike tribes, passed beneath the sceptre of the Sultan of Versailles; and all by virtue of a feeble human voice, inaudible at half a mile.[3]

Though he had accomplished the goal he had set for himself so many years before, at La Chine, when his Indian visitors told of a great river in the west, his quest was far from complete. Indeed, he had long known that

La Salle Claiming Louisiana for France, April 9, 1682, *by George Catlin, painted in 1847–48.* (PAUL MELLON COLLECTION, © 1997 BOARD OF TRUSTEES, NATIONAL GALLERY OF ART, WASHINGTON, D.C.)

the river emptied into the Gulf of Mexico. Now he'd simply proved it, a required step toward the grand plan of colonizing the delta and using the Mississippi to string together Forts Prudhomme, Crèvecœur, St. Louis, and the others that would surely follow.

But was he really on the Mississippi? The fact is, La Salle didn't know. In a letter later written in his own hand, possibly to Abbé Bernou, he spoke candidly about his predicament. The letter is known as the Chucagoa Fragment, for parts of it are missing. In the extant parts he discusses the idea that the Ohio was merely a tributary of the Chucagoa. Bolstering the notion that he had descended not the Río del Espíritu Santo but some other river was the discovery that he had not entered the gulf through a bay, as shown on the Spanish maps. (A few years later, in 1686, the name Bahía del Espíritu Santo would be given both to Mobile Bay, to the east, by Enríquez Barroto and Antonio Romero and to Matagorda Bay, to the west, by Alonso de León.)

La Salle wrote, "The course of the Mississippi during the last 120 leagues was exactly the route of the Escondido. This is what makes me maintain that we were near Mexico and therefore in another river than the Chucagoa from which the Spaniards took such a long time to reach Mexico. . . . If all the maps are worthless, the mouth of the River Colbert [Mississippi] is near Mexico."[4]

Weddle says, "La Salle still referred to the Escondido as the Mississippi because he still believed, until he actually arrived there, that the two were the same; then he was unbelievably slow to acknowledge his error."[5]

The Escondido, as shown on Nicolas Sanson's 1657–62 map of the gulf, is the first stream northwest of the present-day Rio Grande (then called Río Bravo), far to the southwest of the Mississippi. But the 27 degrees north latitude of its mouth matched La Salle's erroneous sightings, corroborating his misconceptions, as did meeting Indians in possession of Spanish muskets, daggers, and coats of mail. What seemed real was not, and he formed conclusions that would later come back to haunt him, binding his fate and those of his colonists.

Now he did the only thing he could, and that was to paddle home, upstream, slowly, at less than half the speed he'd descended. The thought is that he did so with urgency, though I see in his face the sadness of leaving, for where else could he call home? Not France, which he'd forsaken fifteen years earlier. Not his Montreal seigneury, which had been sold off to pay for the expedition. Perhaps he felt an attachment to Fort Frontenac and Mademoiselle d'Allonne, or to Fort St. Louis on the Illinois River, but I think his heart was here in the South, on the river, fixed on a picture of his colony springing from the canebrake.

The Algiers Lock mercifully opened, allowing us to escape the ships of the Mississippi. Suddenly we were transported into the bayous, the narrow waterways choked with water hyacinth and water lilies, the trees strung with Spanish moss. There were no levees on the Barataria Waterway to speak of and the houses were built on stilts. Near the bank was a graveyard, whose cadavers, we surmised, were surely soaking below water level.

At Rosethorn Park we pushed through the water lilies to the ramp, only to be chased out by a queue of bass boats waiting to launch. There was little choice but to move on down the waterway. We stopped at a chemical dock but there was no phone. Cochiara's Marina professed to have no slips; Joe's Landing claimed to be fully booked. Nearly out of gas, we came to the last stop before the Gulf of Mexico, Lafitte, Louisiana. The proprietor of Lafitte Harbor Marine, Mel Guidrick, rented us a slip, then gave us a ride back to the south side of the Mississippi, near Gretna, where he put us on a bus for New Orleans. We got off at Tulane University and hailed a cab for West End, arriving there at nine. Stanton Murray had left our car in front of his office, as promised. I felt like I was already home. We ate softshell crab at Robear's, then retired to a hotel on the Causeway. We had wheels, mobility, and clean, hot water.

That evening, for the first time in weeks, Steve watched television—a karate movie called *Savate* starring Jean-Claude Van Damme. A *Blood Sport* imitation. We were back. "Civilized." Mesmerized. Hypnotized. Corroded, cooked, and clean. Back to Nintendo, Flintstones, the Simpsons, and Jean-Claude Van Damme. Steve lapped it up, but for a time, there on the river, he hadn't even missed the Wow Zone.

In the morning, Steve complained of an earache. Since we had swum daily in the river and had no idea of its pollutants, it was surprising we hadn't all been afflicted long before now. Given the heat, which made swimming a practical necessity, it was a good thing we hadn't known what we were into: alachlor, a chemical that controls weeds among the fields of soybean, corn, and cotton, and atrazine, used on corn, sorghum, and sugarcane, both classified by the Environmental Protection Agency as "probable" and "possible" carcinogens. Dichlorodiphenyltrichloroethane, or DDT, though banned twenty years ago, still shows up in the river sediment. Insecticides have an affinity for the muck, clinging to it, surfacing when churned up by flood or propellers. Same with PCBs. Then there is the square-mile, sixty-foot-high pile of gypsum (a fertilizer by-product) south of Baton Rouge, contaminated with phosphoric and sulfuric acid that washes with the rains into the river. Small consolation that it's nastiest below Baton Rouge, where we had immersed ourselves only once.

At a clinic the physician's assistant wrote a prescription. No antibiotics in pre-America; you just died. Afterward we picked up and installed the trailer rollers ordered from Skipper B Trailers, then drove across the bridge back to Lafitte. A shrimper lent me his wrench so I could change the spark plugs. We wanted to see a bit of the bayous, and stick with La Salle to the end.

Steve and Mel Guidrick fished from the marina docks, the latter showing Steve how to use his wrist to flick the lure. They caught a few nice bass and some small catfish. Mel said there was an alligator in the basin, which Steve claimed to see when no one else was looking. He switched to shrimp for bait, sold at every convenience store and marina for two dollars a pound.

At Mel's suggestion, we dined that evening at a local Cajun restaurant called Bouttee's: Crawfish pie, shrimp, French fries, air-conditioning. Steve called Andra from the pay phone and talked for nearly an hour. He told her that every day we ate cookies for breakfast, never washed our underwear, and never showered. We spent the night at another motel in which, ironically, there was no cold water. Ate breakfast in the dining room, where there were no place settings and no patrons. Just an old Cuban woman who fetched our food from another building.

We returned to the boat and replaced the fuel filter, which was water-logged. With a hose, I cleared the engine intake and depthsounder transducer, both covered with the adhesive mud of the river. To clean the hull, the store clerk recommended a chemical called AlumaBrite, which she said was the only product that could remove the brown stain of the Mississippi. Shrimpers use it, she said, but you'd better wear rubber gloves.

At midday we motored out through the grassy bayous to Bayou St. Denis. This was the delta proper, where each year the river dumps 230 million tons of sediment. We anchored in six feet. Steve fished. Adria nursed a stomachache—Bouttee's crawfish pie and the Cuban woman's breakfast both were suspect—and napped. I read. Steve caught two sheepsheads and a skate. When Adria awoke we ran for an hour down an alley of red and green daymarks to Grand Isle, where the bayous give way to the gulf. Just to the east was the right arm of the Mississippi, where I'd hoped to come out. We'd missed Head of Passes, Pilottown, and the La Salle memorial, all of which I lamented. But we'd also missed eighty miles of oil stations, bulk carriers, and monotonous revetment. In a way, it was fitting: Neither I nor La Salle had come out where we thought. Yet we now cruised the same water that La Salle paddled 313 years ago, looking back north at the same yellow-brown grass, grown on the alluvial deposits of the great river.

In the pass we were surrounded by feeding dolphins, jumping, chasing, flashing in every direction. The water sparkled with sunlight. We took off our clothes and dove naked into the clear saltwaters of the gulf, more than 1,400 miles from Starved Rock.

CHAPTER 16

# Homeward

*What you hope for*
*Is that at some point of the pointless journey,*
*Indoors or out, and when you least expect it,*
*Right in the middle of your stride, like that,*
*So neatly that you never feel a thing,*
*The kind assassin Sleep will draw a bead*
*And blow your brains out.*

—Richard Wilbur, "Walking to Sleep"

We left Lafitte at sunset and crossed the Mississippi into New Orleans just as the city lights winked on. The route east out of New Orleans is over the long Interstate 10 causeway that crosses the channel connecting the gulf and Lake Pontchartrain. This channel was the alternative entry suggested by the Industrial Canal lockkeeper. We never would have made it. Not without more fuel, navigation instruments, or local knowledge of the shoals and bayous that spread across the delta in a labyrinth of white water and dead-ended channels.

Easier to go this way, on the freeway. Yet it was strange to again see *Pearl* through the rearview mirror, following like a dog at heel.

We passed a Ford F-350 double cab.

Steve said, "Dad, what does that remind you of?"

I grimaced.

"Dad, why didn't you look where you were going?"

Before reaching Slidell, he fell asleep in the backseat, cushioned on the beanbag. I carried him to our motel room.

In the morning we pushed on to Gulfport, where we had arranged to leave *Pearl* at Stanton Murray's satellite yard.

The heat was unbearable. Nearby, a group of campers sat on their gear waiting for an excursion boat bound for the wildlife refuge at Ship Island. At that moment, fresh from *Pearl* and the river, I could not conceive of anything I'd rather do less.

Steve fished, because *there* was the water and *here* was his rod.

The small Johnson outboard was removed from *Pearl*'s transom and stowed in the car trunk. I expected to take a bath on the boat and hoped at least to recoup the expense of the backup motor. The remaining gear was stuffed on top of it until at last the boat was empty. Empty, that is, except for the rows of red polyethylene gas jugs.

Adria peered at them over the gunwale.

"What about these?"

"Leave 'em."

"That's a lot of money."

"Where would we put them?"

She allowed as how there simply was no more room in the car, and besides, they smelled of gasoline.

Perhaps they would be an incentive to a prospective buyer, proof that we had done the river.

We took photos of each other standing next to *Pearl*, feeling as though we were abandoning a good dog to a new home. She had done her job well and we were sad to leave her. All the same, I was relieved not to tow her 1,300 miles home to Rhode Island. Neither the car, nor I, could take it.

There, at the boatyard, we left her to an uncertain fate, our *African Queen*, baking in the hot sun.

Interstate 59 cuts diagonally northeast through eastern Mississippi and into Birmingham, Alabama. Somewhere along the way a billboard welcomed us to the home of the civil rights movement. The whites had found a way to turn the sins of their fathers into tourist dollars.

We left Adria at an aunt and uncle's apartment in Huntsville. They were out of town but had hidden a key under a planter. Adria looked as though she felt halfway home, off the river, off the road. Feeling like a trespasser, too close to my past, I did not tarry.

Steve required a good bit of coaxing to bid his sister a proper farewell and I grew angry with him, as if all he'd learned had been left on the river.

Under way again, he behaved perfectly the rest of the ride home. Perhaps all he had wanted was his father to himself.

We made the long run up the Shenandoah Valley, to the east the Blue Ridge Mountains, to the west the Appalachians, the mountain barrier that for a hundred years during the seventeenth and early eighteenth centuries pinned the English colonists to the seaboard; had France acted more quickly and effectively, La Salle might have succeeded in establishing French sovereignty in the heart of America.

*Parlez-vous français?*

It was Labor Day weekend and many of the motels were full. Our last night on the road was spent at a small family motel high on a hill. No Visa, no MasterCard, no cable TV. In the dark, Steve swam in the peeling concrete pool, but a chill had come over the hilltop and he did not stay long. In the morning, I put on my shorts and T-shirt as I had every day for a month. But when I opened the door the valley was filled with a cold fog and I stepped back inside. I changed into long pants and shirt. It felt good.


On La Salle's return upstream, the Quinipissas and Coroas, who had been friendly during his earlier visit, now attacked. They were repulsed, but La Salle was not so fortunate when at Fort Prudhomme on the Chickasaw Bluffs, he was stricken with an illness—probably a stroke—that laid him low until July. He sent Tonti ahead, and the two were not reunited until September, at Michilimackinac. He intended to sail at once for France, but there were rumors that the Iroquois were again ready to ravage the Illinois, and so they returned to fortify Starved Rock. Responding to promises of protection by the French, more than four thousand Illinois were assembled about the palisades. On receiving news that Frontenac had been replaced by La Barre as governor, that the latter had sent a group to take over the fort, and that La Salle's enemies were denigrating him in Quebec and Paris, in the spring of 1683 he left Fort St. Louis to see what he could salvage.

In France, he could not have hoped for a better reversal of fortune. The minister Colbert was dead, but his son and successor, Jean-Baptiste Colbert, Marquis de Seignelay, was sympathetic to La Salle and presented his case well to the king. Fort St. Louis was restored to him, and more, he was provided with three ships, one an outright gift, and a navy escort to return to the Mississippi delta. This generosity owed much to the efforts of Abbé Bernou and Abbé Renaudot, the two men who were in the vanguard of the effort to place La Salle on the Mississippi prior to Jolliet.

The French idea was to fortify the Gulf Coast with soldiers, then march on New Spain and seize the silver mines there. La Salle, apparently going along with this plan, at least for a time, claimed he could field an army of nearly twenty thousand Indians for the campaign.[1] The scheme appealed to Seignelay's desire to flaunt his rebuilt navy to the Spanish. Some biographers, particularly those who think La Salle had a crazy streak, say that he was seduced by the two abbés into accepting this plan, a far-fetched escapade that was totally out of character. Others disagree, contending that the plan was hatched before his return to France.

In fact, there was momentum at court for just such an incursion. France and Spain were at war. Diego de Peñalosa, a Spanish count and former governor of New Mexico deposed by the Inquisition and living in France, several times petitioned Louis XIV to invade New Spain. Minister Seignelay developed a plan to enlist pirates to supplement the invasion. None of these schemes was implemented, but it is clear that they were not hatched solely by a demented La Salle. Indeed, it is probable that La Salle's opposition was a factor in their being abandoned.

Still, the king was caught up in the feverish excitement for the Americas. La Salle's flotilla was comprised of four ships: the *Joly*, a thirty-six-gun warship commanded by Tangeguy le Gallois de Beaujeu of the Royal French Navy; the *Belle*, a six-gun frigate; the *Aimable*, a 300-ton store ship; and a 30-ton ketch to carry supplies as far as Santo Domingo, where the expedition would take on freshwater and some buccaneers as reinforcements.

Good help was hard to find. France was at war and the best soldiers were occupied. Dubious crew were recruited, many lacking the essential skills. They joined a few merchants, volunteers, some women and children, and, naturally, a few priests. On board the three ships the head count was about three hundred.

On July 24, 1684, the small fleet set sail from Rochelle. Nothing went right. Captain Beaujeu and La Salle, whom the veteran naval officer called "a burgher lately enobled," quarreled over control. Beaujeu wrote to a friend: "I believe him [La Salle] to be a very honest man from Normandy, but they are no longer in fashion."

Pirates captured the ketch. At Santo Domingo, the men became debauched and some contracted syphilis. Others died of fever. To reprovision, La Salle borrowed money from two members of his company, Pierre and Dominique Duhaut, an unfortunate act with unforeseen consequences. He did not retain as guides any of the Caribbean pirates, but did consult them: None had ever seen his river. The coast, they believed, was inhabited by "wretched savages who lived on roots."[2]

When they rounded Cape San Antonio, at the western end of Cuba, and sailed for the delta, La Salle's earlier troubles with position followed him like a shadow. Robert Weddle, who has done much to explain the nature of these errors, wrote, "La Salle's geographical conjecture fixed the destination not as the true Mississippi River but as an obscure, largely hypothetical river mouth appearing on various maps of doubtful authenticity as the Río Escondido. The name was both ironic and prophetic: it truly was 'the hidden river.' "[3]

Not only were La Salle's latitudes incorrect, but also the longitudes could only be guessed at. Navigators employed a technique called latitude sailing. They sailed to the desired latitude on one side of the intended destination, then proceeded along the latitude east or west until they simply ran into their desired position. In La Salle's case, they reached their latitude west of the delta and sailed along it until they hit the coast of Texas, four hundred miles distant. If they had seen the mouth of the Mississippi, they wouldn't have been able to recognize it, so low is the land and devoid of distinguishing features. Nor would they have expected to see it so far to the east. Because of his original misconceptions, he expected to find the mouth of the Mississippi to be located at the bow of the gulf, which is where he ended up. Instead of finding the Mississippi, however, they found Aransas Pass, the channel connecting the gulf and Corpus Christi Bay, and the river that feeds the bay—the Nueces, the stream indicated for years as the Río Escondido. Give La Salle credit—he found the Escondido, the river he thought he wanted. Indeed, he practically sailed right to it. The only problem was, it wasn't the Mississippi.

One look and it was evident that he had made a huge mistake. Some biographers fault Captain Beaujeu for missing the mouth of the Mississippi, which they say he should easily have found if he'd simply rounded Florida and hugged the coast. Others note that La Salle had total control of the flotilla's course, including navigational matters (which angered Beaujeu no end). One biographer, Céline Dupré, asserts that La Salle had erred in his latitude at the delta and, to further confuse both himself and the captain, had intentionally placed the mouth of the Mississippi much farther to the west, nearer New Spain, solely for the purpose of convincing the king that a raid on Spanish silver mines was feasible. Weddle, however, makes it quite clear that La Salle was responsible for locating the river and that he was misled not by recklessness but by accidents and limitations he could not have been expected to recognize.

Lost and frustrated, the flotilla backtracked to the east. La Salle ordered the ships to anchor off Matagorda Bay about eighty miles southwest of present-day Galveston. The settlers were put ashore on a beach. The local Karankawa Indians could not be befriended and were a constant threat, springing from bushes to murder unwary crew. Alligators, rattlesnakes, and dysentery also took their toll. Anxious to be rid of Beaujeu, La Salle permitted him and the *Joly* to sail home. With him went the engineer Jean-Baptiste Minet, whose map of the bay would later prove invaluable in the search for the lost ships and colony. Minet also kept a journal in which he accused La Salle of rejecting all suggestions: "I saw a man who had made a mockery of the Court and was making a mockery of us. . . . This is a man who has lost his mind."[4]

The *Aimable* ran aground attempting to enter the bay. The colony, reduced to 180 persons, had only the *Belle* on which to escape, should it come to that. If La Salle was distraught by this fate, he was not about to surrender himself to it. To conceal themselves from Spanish ships, La Salle moved the colony up Garcitas Creek, which discharges into the head of the wide bay. While the others built a crude palisade, also dubbed Fort St. Louis, La Salle continued his search for the lost river, first to the west, then to the east.

He left the *Belle* in the hands of a small crew. One night, the pilot and several others decided to spend the night ashore and were butchered in their sleep by Indians. Not long after, other crew went ashore to fill water casks and were stranded, because the ship's mate, drunk on communion wine, chose to light not a lantern but a candle, which, predictably, blew out. Days passed, and the mate did not stop drinking until he ran the *Belle* onto a sandbar. Only a few small items, some gold, and La Salle's papers, were salvaged. The expedition was stranded.

Already La Salle had journeyed west to the Rio Grande and east to the piney woods and Caddoan Indian villages along the Red River, yet had not found the fatal river. Each time he returned to Fort St. Louis on

The unfortunate Adventures of the Sieur de la Salle.

*A woodcut from Louis Hennepin's* Nouvelle Découverte, *published in 1698, shows the Belle landing at Matagorda Bay. Clearly the artist was not present at the scene as there are no mountains on the coastal plain of Texas, nor was it possible to bring the ship so close to land.* (COURTESY OF THE BURTON HISTORICAL COLLECTION OF THE DETROIT PUBLIC LIBRARY)

Matagorda Bay he had fewer men—some deserted, some died. With the ships sunk and the colony dwindling, his only recourse was to seek help in New France, the closest outpost of which was his fort on the Illinois

River. He was determined to succeed, and had it not been for the retribu-
tions of his men who felt themselves wronged, he would have. Sixty-eight
days and 250 miles to the east, he came to the end of his trail.

What he himself did not foment, bad luck did. On an earlier excursion,
Dominique Duhaut and several others had been given permission to
return to the fort. They never arrived. Pierre Duhaut, Dominique's
brother and himself the target of La Salle's vitriol for previously having
gotten separated from the rest of the party, never forgave the leader. In his
absence, Pierre had tried to incite a mutiny, which Henri Joutel, a trusted
aide and chronicler of the expedition, only temporarily suppressed. Meanwhile, another of the minor officers, Barbier, had on an outing met several
Indians, who fired muskets into the air. Barbier, like a good Texas
rancher, shot first and thought second, killing one of their number. Unbeknown to him, the Indians were returning to the fort one of La Salle's
men who had become lost. That man, quite possibly Dominique Duhaut,
was slain by the Indians in revenge.

Well into their desperate journey, La Salle and his men crossed the San
Jacinto River. His nephew, the hot-headed Moranget, was sent to an
Indian village to trade for horses. There, the chief informed Moranget that
his tribesmen had been victims of the whites' treachery, to wit, the Barbier
incident, and had killed the Frenchman they had first sought to aid. Pierre
Duhaut may by this means have construed his brother's death and assembled its cause. His brother's fate sealed, so was La Salle's.

Near the Trinity River, La Salle dispatched the surgeon Liotot,
L'Archevêque, the ex-buccaneer Hiems (variously referred to as Hiens
and James), the faithful Nika, and Pierre Duhaut to fetch a cache of corn
he'd hidden on a previous foray. They found the corn spoiled. On their
return, Nika shot two buffalo, and the men stopped to butcher them.
There they camped for the night. The next day, La Salle grew worried
and sent Moranget, Marle, Pierre Meunier, and his servant, Saget, to learn
the cause of the delay. When they came upon the camp, Moranget was
enraged to find that Liotot, Hiems, and Duhaut had eaten the marrow-
bones and other savory parts to which, according to woodland custom,
they, as the killers of the animal, were entitled. On the surface tempers
cooled, and as it grew late, Moranget made his bed. He slept next to Nika
and Saget. In their slumber, Liotot axed the three of them.

The next day, March 19, 1687, La Salle came looking. As he walked
through the Texas hill country, he was accompanied by the friar Anastase

*The Sieur de la Salle unhappily assasinated*

La Salle's death in East Texas, a woodcut from Louis Hennepin's Nouvelle
Découverte, *published in 1698. La Salle, about to be shot, talks with Father
Anastase Douay over the bodies of Saget, Nika, and Moranget, while the
assassin Duhaut rises up from the bushes. The event took place well inland;
the sea and ships in the background are the artist's fancy.* (COURTESY OF THE
BURTON HISTORICAL COLLECTION OF THE DETROIT PUBLIC LIBRARY)

Douay, who later wrote, "All the way, he spoke to me of nothing but matters of piety, grace and predestination; enlarging on the debt he owed to God, who had saved him from so many perils during more than twenty years of travel in America. Suddenly, I saw him overwhelmed with a profound sadness, for which he himself could not account. He was so much moved that I scarcely knew him."

Soon, however, he recovered. As they approached the murderers' camp, La Salle saw two eagles circling in the sky ahead. He fired two shots, which alerted Liotot, Duhaut, and the others, who then rushed to lay an ambush. At the bank of a river, L'Archevêque stood to reveal himself. La Salle asked where was Moranget. L'Archevêque did not answer. La Salle cursed him, and moved forward menacingly. Duhaut, hidden in the bushes, shot La Salle at near point-blank range. He died instantly.

"There thou liest, great Bashaw! There thou liest!" Liotot cried. The corpse was stripped and dragged into the bushes, left there for the carrion eaters.

Parkman wrote:

> Never under the impenetrable mail of paladin or crusader, beat a heart of more intrepid mettle than within the stoic panoply that armed the breast of La Salle. To estimate aright the marvels of his patient fortitude one must follow on his track through the vast scene of his interminable journeyings, those thousands of weary miles of forest, marsh, and river, where, again and again, in the bitterness of baffled striving, the untiring pilgrim pushed onward towards the goal which he was never to attain.[5]

The epilogue is sad.

With Father Douay the murderers returned to camp. La Salle's brother, the cowardly Abbé Jean Cavelier, took one look at the sullen face of Douay and knew that La Salle was dead. He fell to his knees before Duhaut, begging that he be spared. L'Archevêque found Joutel some distance off and informed him of La Salle's death. Joutel was for several minutes confused, afraid that he, too, might be killed. Reassured, he returned to camp, where Duhaut told him that he bore no more grudges.

Hiems, who had been off negotiating with the Ceni Indians for horses, returned with two deserters: Rutre, a Breton sailor, and a Frenchman named Grollet. Accompanying them were about twenty Indians. Hiems

*L'Archevêque, who summoned La Salle to his death, and Grollet, a deserter, drew this picture of a ship on parchment, put a message on the back, and sent it via an Indian emissary to the Spanish force that was hunting them.* (J. P. BRYAN COLLECTION, UNIVERSITY OF TEXAS ARCHIVES)

yelled at Duhaut to give him his pay, as Duhaut had killed his master. Duhaut refused. Without a moment's hesitation, Hiems shot him dead at four yards. Rutre then shot Liotot, who lived long enough to say confession. Despite Abbé Jean Cavelier's pleas, Liotot was put out of his misery with a pistol to the head. The Indians were mystified by the violent nature of what they perceived as greetings.

Later, after taking to the woods, L'Archevêque and Grollet wrote a desperate message on the back of a painting of a ship on a piece of parchment (probably the *Joly*) and sent it via Indian emissaries to the Spanish, requesting rescue and forgiveness. Their prayers were answered.

Joutel, Abbé Jean Cavelier, another nephew of La Salle's named Colin Cavelier, and four others loyal to La Salle headed east. Eventually they made their way to the Mississippi, thanks to Indians who gave them horses. The Sieur de Marle drowned in the Red River, but the other six succeeded in making their way to Montreal and thereafter to France. Abbé Cavelier had no funds for the passage. To obtain a loan, he told Tonti at

Fort St. Louis at Starved Rock on the Illinois in spring 1688 that La Salle still lived. Only in France did Abbé Cavelier announce his brother's death. Had Tonti not been lied to, it is conceivable that he might have had time to rescue the pitiful remnants of Fort St. Louis in Texas.

Indeed, Tonti already had desperately descended the Mississippi in search of La Salle. At the river's mouth, in 1686, he had waited in vain. Despairing of his master's fate, he left a letter with an Indian chief, instructing him to give it to the white man who came on the "house that walked on water." Then he turned back to Illinois. When he learned of the assassination, he declared in despair that La Salle was "one of the greatest men of his age."

In 1690, "when Le Moyne d'Iberville entered into the mouth of the Mississippi to found a new colony for France, an aged Indian chieftain in a coat of blue French broadcloth carefully handed over the letter to the visitors."[6]

On learning of La Salle's death, Tonti did try again, in 1689, to reach the survivors. Dashing again down the Mississippi and up the Red River, he came within about eighty leagues of Fort St. Louis before learning from the Nabedache Indians of the presence of a Spanish army, Alonso de León's, in the area. News also came that the seven Frenchmen left by Joutel (Hiems and the others) may have been killed. Deserted by all but one Frenchman, reluctantly Tonti turned back.

Word of the existence of the French colony reached Spanish authorities in 1685 by way of several deserters, notably Denis Thomas, who had deserted La Salle at Santo Domingo and joined the pirates Michel de Grammont and Laurens de Graff. They all were apprehended following the rape and pillage of Campeche on July 6, 1685. Their confession launched a massive search for the French thorn in the heart of New Spain. The first Spanish effort to pluck the thorn was to search the entire Gulf Coast between Florida and Mexico. During the cruise, many of the earlier misconceptions about the numerous rivers were at last corrected. But their investigation was difficult, in part because they had no way of knowing that La Salle had confused the mouth of the Mississippi with that of the putative Río Escondido—actually, the Nueces. Instead, the Spanish searched for the equally mythical and elusive Bahía del Espíritu Santo.

Two ships, the *Nuestra Señora del Rosario* and *Nuestra Señora de la Esperanza*—"the two ladies"—commanded by Martín de Rivas and Pedro de Iriarte, anchored off Pass Cavallo, the channel into Matagorda Bay, on

April 3, 1687. Canoes were sent into Matagorda Bay, and there was found the wreck of the *Belle*, the fleur-de-lis on her poop still visible, heeled and sinking. Later the Spaniards found flotsam of the *Aimable*, including its rudder. Had they moved farther up the bay, they might have found what Weddle calls the "maimed and misfits" still alive at Fort St. Louis. But they moved on and so missed the last of the French.

The end for them came during the winter of 1688–89, when on hearing that La Salle had died, the Karankawa, with whom the settlers thought they had made peace, surprised them and slaughtered all save five children, four of whom belonged to the Talon family. It remained for General Alonso de León's land army to find the fort. En route he captured a deserter named Jean Jarry, " 'tatooed like a Chichemeco' and venerated as king by his Indian hosts."[7]

On April 22, 1689, the army at last sighted Fort St. Louis. Under a gray sky, they inspected the six buildings, the larger made from ship timbers, the smaller built of poles and plastered with mud, the roofs covered with buffalo hides. A rain fell on the garden of endives and asparagus. Only three skeletons were found,

> . . . one a woman's, shot in the back with an arrow. It was probably Juan Bautista Chapa—the one member of the expedition with known literary talent—who that evening by firelight memorialized the woman and the "sad and fateful site" of her death in an elegy of rhymed couplets:
>
> > *O beautiful French maiden fair*
> > *Who pressed sweet roses to your hair*[8]

Several days later, the Spaniards found the letter from L'Archevêque and Grollet, expressing their desire to live among Christians. León's soldiers liberated them from the Tejas Indians. During the return march to Mexico, they found fourteen-year-old Pierre Talon (left with the Indians by La Salle to learn their language) and twenty-year-old Pierre Meunier. The Spanish treated them well, prompting the boys to reveal that the other children lived with the Karankawa. On the west side of Matagorda Bay, León ransomed three of the five, but only after a dispute in which four Indians were killed. Two remained behind with the Karankawa, who wept to see their other adopted children taken.

As if the destruction of La Salle and all he had won or striven for was still not complete, his amour, Mademoiselle de Roybon d'Allonne was taken that same year by Iroquois Indians and held captive for several years. The governor of New York helped secure her freedom; she in turn aided him in making a peace treaty with the Indians. Eventually she wound up back in Montreal, where she sought permission to trade on her land at Fort Frontenac. Making her case required a voyage to France, where her petition was successful, on the condition that she also farm her land. Before she could act, however, she died in 1718, in Montreal, at the age of seventy-two.[9]

Years ago, an acquaintance sent me a magazine clipping of an ad paid for by the Business Publication Audit of Circulation Inc. It was a cartoon of La Salle landed in Texas, a sword driven through his chest. The caption read: "René Robert Cavelier de La Salle led an expedition across the Atlantic in 1684 to colonize New Orleans. Unfortunately, his campaign failed. He missed New Orleans and landed in Texas. His faulty sense of direction was not overlooked by his followers who eventually killed him." The headline read: "The right campaign in the wrong place can kill you."

My estimation of La Salle changes with the time of day, the light of day, the mood I'm in. Many of the shortcomings attributed to him by the Jesuits, competing traders, and small-minded bureaucrats were real. By his own admission, he suffered from an inability to win the devotion of his own men. Excepting Tonti and Joutel, they just couldn't get excited about his vision, couldn't see how their toil contributed to the grand scheme. And he was so highly moralistic: no women, no rum, no fun.

Others saw him as crazed, manic-depressive, alternately zealous and self-pitying.

The historian Hubert Howe Bancroft wrote of the last trip, "La Salle aided the destruction of the party by his utter unfitness for colonization. It is not easy to conceive how intelligent writers have exalted a man of such utter incapacity into a hero."[10]

Also no fan of La Salle's, Céline Dupré resented his portrayal as a hero, demoting him to "a mere case for psychoanalysis." He scorned La Salle for his "failure in Texas," blaming an "idealistic mind" for the "exaggerated dimensions of his dreams." Dupré grudgingly concedes the importance of his discovering the Lower Mississippi, and acknowledges La Salle's "almost superhuman strength, tenacity and courage" during his "perpetual comings and goings." And at the last, he cannot resist noting that, given the grisly nature of La Salle's death, the explorer's persecution complex was not "completely misguided."[11]

The French historian and Jesuit missionary Pierre Charlevoix (1682–1761) philosophized that it is the fate of all great men to possess both virtues and defects, leading alternately to their success and destruction: "Hence the very different portraits that are made of them, no one of which is a likeness."[12]

Marquis Childs, less caring of personalities perhaps, wrote kindly that La Salle was ahead of his time in viewing the New World not as an "opulent prize" to be "seized" for the sole purpose of filling the king's coffers. His quest to peel away the mystery of America, Childs said, became an obsession, "almost a kind of madness. Or so they thought at Versailles, seeing this stern, hard-bitten man from out of the wilds."[13]

Robert Weddle is succinct in his conclusions: "The La Salle colonization attempt is significant as the first real European penetration of the Texas–Louisiana Gulf shore since Narváez and Soto and as the very first settlement attempt between Mobile Bay and the Río Pánuco. Its impact on Spanish efforts to explore and colonize the region was immediate, and its influence on history has endured these three hundred years."[14]

I saw some of these same consequences in my own father's career, who also landed in Texas and was ultimately ridden out of office by the natives, to wit, an irascible regent to whom he could not bear allegiance.

President Lyndon Johnson, who in 1973 was retired and living on his nearby ranch, had arranged for his papers to be housed in the LBJ Library on the University of Texas–Austin campus.

Father, whose autobiographical interests had been reduced to the binder of analects, wrote, "One night, the Johnsons came to the University President's house for a small dinner. Pat and I met them at the door. Before I could speak he drew himself up to his considerable height and intoned: 'Mr. President.'

"I was taken aback and managed to utter: 'That is my line, Sir.'

" 'No,' he continued. 'Mr. President, I have been in politics a long time and know that every organization should have only one leader. As far as the University of Texas is concerned, you, sir, are the president. I shall not offer you any advice, but I am ready to give it if you ask for it. I shall not intrude on your campus, but am ready to come at a moment's notice if called.'

"It was an act, maybe, but darned impressive. I can only say that he lived up to his stated strategy.

"The time did come when I called him. I was sponsoring a Congress of Black Professionals in Higher Education in the hopes of recruiting some to work at the University. Word soon reached me that a number of the regents were most unhappy with the project. I called up the President, explained the situation to him, and asked if he would be willing to open the congress.

" 'I'll do better than that,' he replied. 'I'll deliver the keynote speech.' And that he did. When the Congress opened, his real concern with minority development set a tone muting potential attacks by the African-American delegates on the University for its tardiness in recruiting from their race. More than that, in the middle of his remarks, he stopped and issued an endorsement of me and of my role in organizing the Congress. His gesture of support silenced my critics and I was able to continue to try to increase the participation of ethnic minorities in the University as long as he lived."

Unfortunately, LBJ didn't live much longer, suffering his second heart attack two days later and dying January 22, 1973.

My father also fell victim to coronary disease and underwent triple-bypass surgery in June 1974. He returned to work just eight days after the operation. Without Johnson's protective umbrella or the strength to fight, on September 24 he was fired by the chancellor, at the behest of the regents, who acted largely at the request of one of their own, Frank T. Irwin. Lady Bird Johnson, a regent, abstained.

The dismissal changed him, that and the bad heart and the Parkinson's. Though he returned for a number of years as a professor in the LBJ School of Public Affairs, coteaching a course with Barbara Jordan, and assumed the presidency of the American Forestry Association, which conferred upon him the Gifford Pinchot medal, it seemed he knew he was nearing the end of his trail, too.

I thought of him a lot during that long drive home from the Gulf. He had the same kind of ambition as La Salle, the goal-setting drive, the nervous energy, trying to be everywhere at once. Like a river. Mostly I remembered the good, much of which was spent in the wilderness, or at least my perception of it: sleeping inside the giant sequoia, diving on the Japanese wreck off Papeete, hiking through forests so thick it seemed they would never yield.

Another memory came to me, from a time when I was five. Father taught then at the University of Minnesota in St. Paul, and each summer was spent at the Forestry School's research station on Lake Itasca, to which in 1832, Henry Schoolcraft at last traced the elusive headwaters of the Mississippi River.

Here, on its south shore, a small stream runs out of the lake, here where even a young boy might leap the stream and his father say, "Tell your friends you've jumped over the Mississippi."

Later, in the fall, after our return from the river, Steve brought home an assignment for the annual all-school pageant: Each second-grade student was to select a state to study and to represent on stage.

"Which did you choose?"

"Mississippi."

"Why?"

"I bet I'm the only kid in my class who's been down the Mississippi River."

"I bet you're the only kid in Rhode Island who's been down the Mississippi. Heck, probably in the whole United States!"

Steve looked puzzled, grappling with the proportions of things.

"Dad? Do you think I'm the *only* kid in Pennfield School who's caught a catfish on the Mississippi?"

# *Epilogue*

In July 1995, just as I was assembling my plans to follow La Salle's route down the Mississippi, the wreck of the *Belle* was found in Matagorda Bay. I did not learn of this until my return to Rhode Island in September. My mother sent a clipping from the *Austin Statesman American*. Barto Arnold, at forty-five years of age and in the seventeenth year of his search, had at last won the lottery.

As soon as it could be arranged, I flew to Austin.

"Where did you find it?" I asked Barto.

"Right where Minet showed it anchored. In Greens Bayou."

Technology had changed more than a little since the 1978 search. Instead of the $70,000 microwave radar positioning system used earlier, Barto fixed the location of the various anomalies with a yachtsman's-grade differentially corrected Global Positioning System, accurate to about three meters. Superior technology at a fraction of the price. Readings from the proton precession magnetometer and GPS were fed into a laptop computer at the rate of one per second. All the gear was carried aboard a survey boat, nothing on land to worry about. The skipper ran back and forth across the bay for a month, after which thirty-nine anomalies were selected for further investigation.

The survey vessel anchored over the site of the most promising anomaly. A swimmer entered the water and towed the magnetometer back and forth until the strongest return was pinpointed. Then the scuba-diver teams went in. Visibility, as usual, ranged from zero to one foot. No protruding remains were seen or felt.

Old organic materials, such as the wooden frame of a ship, are rare in the warm gulf waters of Texas. The use of crude, aggressive implements to uncover delicate remains would be self-defeating. So again, Barto employed the prop wash deflector to blow away the sand.

"Shortly after beginning digging," Barto said, "the archaeologists noted the first finds. A few loose boards were uncovered. This confirmed a man-made cause for the magnetic anomaly, but being organic, they suggested the possibility of a modern site.

"The next artifacts were a few cast-lead shot of small size. This suggested a historic shipwreck site, but they could date from early historic times to mid- to late nineteenth century. Still this site began to look interesting. Then the scuba-dive team brought up a buckle of copper alloy (bronze). The design of the buckle suggested a date for the site prior to the nineteenth century, and the crew began to be very interested indeed.

"The second dive team surfaced to report the finding of a large object, mostly buried in encrusted ballast and stiff clay."

One of the divers, an archaeology student from the University of Florida, was animated. He'd found something exciting. This time it was no joke, no Lone Star beer can.

"The object," Barto wrote in his report, "had readily discernible lifting handles known as dolphins that are characteristic of early cannon. The muzzle and cascabell were also identifiable although encrusted and mostly buried. The project director took down the third dive team and confirmed that the object was a cast bronze cannon with ornate decorations faintly visible beneath the encrustation. Taken together with the Spanish and French references to the general area where the *Belle* was lost, this cannon strongly suggested that we had found La Salle's ship."

Barto determined that the cannon had been in storage, and therefore was missed by the Spanish expedition that had sighted the grounded *Belle* and salvaged its deck cannon and rigging. "They would definitely have salvaged this gun if they had seen it."

Other parts of the ship began to emerge: frames that had formed the hull structure, casks, a copper caldron, the stub of the mast. There was even a human leg bone.

Mapping of the site continued for several days, after which the crew covered the wreck with clean sand. For this summer, time had run out. Just an estimated 1 percent of the wreck had been recovered. The next summer, Barto would build a cofferdam around the wreck, pump out the water, and jump in with trowel and brush. In the meantime, round-the-clock security was retained to thwart treasure hunters. Barto returned to Austin to announce his discovery, one that would make his career. Of similarities between La Salle and himself, he said, "We're both nuts."

Mother and I drove to Corpus Christi to see the cannon and the other few artifacts being worked on at the Corpus Christi Museum. She and I hadn't spent any appreciable time alone together in more than thirty years. This was a strange realization; always there was Father or the children.

Nearing the coast, the land in certain seasons becomes wet and marshy. Easy to see why the Spanish didn't want it, why the miserable occupants of Fort St. Louis couldn't wait to leave. Outside town, seen across the bayous where always the solitary egret stands, oil refineries were an incongruity. But coastal Texas is nothing if not oil country.

We took a room on the beach, near the World War II aircraft carrier *Lexington,* then drove downtown to the museum. On the grounds were replicas of Columbus's ships, the *Niña, Pinta,* and *Santa María,* built in Spain and sailed transatlantic for the five hundredth anniversary of the admiral's voyage. In the main hall, the principal exhibit was devoted to shipwrecks, though there was nothing yet of the *Belle.*

Resident archaeologists Toni Carrell and Donald Keith showed us to the conservation lab where the several staff worked to save and preserve the recovered articles. At a bench, a technician worked under a bright lamp polishing hawk bells, which the French traded to the Indians. In practice, they were used by falconers, who tied together pairs of bells whose tones were a half tone apart, so their sound would carry farther. Many of the wire ties were still intact. On the opposite side of the room was a large tray filled with a solution of acid and charged with low-voltage

*At the Corpus Christi Museum, the archaeologist Donald Keith examines the bronze four-pounder cannon discovered in 1995 at the wreck site of the* Belle, *at the bottom of Greens Bayou in Matagorda Bay.*

electrical current to remove the salts from a sword hilt. Stabilized and displayed in small wooden cases were brass pins, glass beads, and rings, one decorated with an *L*, presumably signifying King Louis XIV. A considerable number of pewter plates had the initials *LG* scratched on the back, most likely belonging to the Sieur Le Gros, the unfortunate merchant who died, if not from a rattlesnake bite, then from Liotot's wretched amputation of his leg. And there were a number of ceramic pieces, pitchers and jars, remarkably preserved.

In the storeroom, which ran the width of the museum and where shelf after shelf held trays of all manner of artifacts both ancient and modern, in a corner on a cart lay the *Belle*'s four-pounder cannon. It was cast bronze, superior to the more common iron cannon. The tube worms, shells, and clams that had encrusted it had been mechanically removed, then the piece had been treated in the electrolytic acid solution. The bronze surface was a goldish brown, smooth and ornate with the fleur-de-lis clearly engraved as well as the raised crests and name of Le Comte de Vermandois, King Louis XIV's illegitimate son, who had been named admiral of France in 1669 at age two. I touched it and I did not die or turn into a toad. Touched it and touched something La Salle probably had touched. After so many years and so many miles, I beheld tangible evidence of his existence, as if before now his story had been nothing more than fable.

That evening Mother and I ate dinner at a seafood restaurant on the second floor of a building in downtown Corpus Christi, from where we could see out over the gulf. On the horizon, the lights of a few oil rigs and shrimp boats. A tamer, safer world; still the sea can kick, navigators can become lost, people can perish. With each book, each journey, each interview, over and over I kept replaying La Salle's story, harboring the hope that this time it might work out differently, that he might sail directly to the mouth of the Mississippi, the river of his dreams. It was the same with Peter: In the months and years following his death, I would dream of him, waking on a similarly impossible hope, that he yet lived.

On the drive back to Austin, Mother and I talked of many things, of ancestors and family and mostly of things that were.

I related some of my concerns about Steve, his high energy, strong will, reckless curiosity, the effect on him of our TV culture and the work the river—the work pre-America—had done to change that. She did not have any answers, nor did I expect her to. Perhaps I told her simply to share something of my life, to make more intimate this rare visit alone together.

Later, at her home, I drew down for her a box from a shelf in the garage. In it were some of Father's papers. Mother did not find what she was looking for, but among the sheets was one of his analects I had not seen before. In it he told of his mother, the imperious German. His four older brothers had left home, and his geologist father was often absent, in his study thinking about the moon. Sometimes, mother and son clashed.

One day his mother invited several ladies to lunch. My father, yet a lad, was obliged, much to his dismay, to sit with them. Grandmother smiled and said, "Steve, please pass the bread plate."

*At a cost of several million dollars, a cofferdam was constructed around the wreck of the* Belle, *which sank in Matagorda Bay, Texas, in twelve feet of water, in 1686.*

*Once the water was pumped out of the area enclosed by the cofferdam, archaeologists began cleaning and cataloging timbers and artifacts from the* Belle's *remains. A complete skeleton was found in the bow.*

He smiled. "Yes, Mother." Then he removed all the bread and passed her the empty plate.

I remembered Steve at the Marina de Gabouri, tossing his hamburger bun like a Frisbee onto my plate, and the connection between grandfather and grandson was consoling if not downright comical.


In December 1996 I returned to Texas, drove to the coast, and chartered an aluminum pontoon boat, optimistically named the *Spoonbill Express*, to take me to *Belle*. The cofferdam stood alone in the bay, with a tin roof and a crane arced over it. As the boat approached, the sound of generators overwhelmed the racket of the outboard motors. I climbed a short ladder to the viewing platform and peered anxiously over the guardrail. There, below, carved from the mud, lay the skeletal remains of La Salle's ship. Workers sprinkled water on the burlap bags that kept the wood moist. In the still life one could make out a coil of rope here, a cask there. In the bow, a guard said, a human skeleton had been found. "Found a cask right next to him," the guard said. If there were any justice, I thought, the body would be that of Tessier, the pilot who got drunk every day on the wine reserved for Mass. But Tessier was one of the lucky six who made their way upriver and back to New France, and the name of the skeleton's owner is unknown.

Up Garcitas Creek, the foreman of the Keernan Ranch in Victoria County found eight cannon at the site of Fort St. Louis. Why Kathleen Gilmore and the earlier diggers hadn't found them was anybody's guess. A local man said, "It's just plain luck they didn't find these cannons, because they weren't very far from them. I guess they just didn't use a metal detector."

In the gulf states, big-city newspapers ran photos of the *Belle* on their front pages. *Smithsonian* magazine called it "the most important shipwreck ever found in North America." Three hundred years following his death, La Salle, at last, was getting his due . . . albeit for his failures.


There remained for me but one more piece of ground to visit—the death place of La Salle. Alone I drove north and east in search of it.

Historians have variously placed La Salle's death site anywhere from the Brazos to the Neches rivers, using accounts by Joutel, Abbé Jean Cavelier, and Father Douay to figure the terrain. Counting rivers as it were, though the picture is muddled by semantic disputations regarding the use of the terms "river" versus "creek," in reference not only to present-day Texas but to the streams' size and appearance three hundred years ago, and to what the French would have considered a *rivière*.

An early theory postulated a site near Navasota, Texas, about fifty miles north of Houston; indeed, there is today a bronze statue of La Salle in Navasota's downtown. I stopped to take a look, there in the small park, the Navasota Auto Company in the background, a red Texaco fuel truck belonging to C. J. Godbold parked next to it. I ate lunch at the La Salle Restaurant on Washington Street; the placemat was a map of La Salle's journeys, and in its four corners were cartoons of major events in his life: trading furs in Canada, discovering the mouth of the Mississippi, establishing the first European settlement in Texas, being murdered by his own men. Unlike the stone statue at Indianola, the one in Navasota is more realistic, showing La Salle wearing leggings and his famous crimson coat, the coat still very much out of place.

Most sources name a spot on the Trinity River, seventy-five miles to the east, but this, too, seems to be merely guesswork. E. W. Cole, in a 1946 article published in the *Southwest Historical Quarterly*, determined that the ambush took place on the east bank of Larrison Creek, several leagues from the Neches River.

At this point I realized I would not be able to stand on the edge of Larrison Creek or any other and be confident that this was where Duhaut rose up and shot his master dead, that this clump of mesquite approximated the bush under which La Salle's naked corpse was kicked into eternity. The best I could do was to view all four candidate rivers, the Brazos, Navasota, Trinity, and Neches, which I did in my rental car, gliding for a hundred miles along the state roads in air-conditioned silence. Each river looked much like the others, as does everything in east Texas—the flat, red earth, oak and elm ranging into the distance, the water, bordered by pecan and walnut, flowing up from the aquifer, here and there a snowy egret frozen like an angel in the desert.

Here my story fades to its denouement. There is, I am afraid, no climax other than reaching the gulf and seeing the *Belle*. No epiphanies to draw back the clouds. For La Salle, and me, it was the end of the line.

When I had been back home but a day, Lee Politsch called to learn whether I had found in the *Belle* artifacts any clues to the Ellington Stone.

I tried to sound hopeful, telling him I'd given the museum archaeologists a photograph of the stone and a brief description. He seemed a trifle disappointed, but he's used to that. With cannons and a ship coming up out of the earth, why not a twin to the stone?

The good news, he said, was that Art Griep, brother of his old friend Bob Griep, had been analyzing the Ellington Stone and discovered an interesting future: A line drawn at right angles to another line drawn through the I in IHS to the center of the cross forms a 40-degree angle with the staff of the cross. The latitude of Quincy, Illinois, is 39 degrees 57 minutes.

"A coincidence?" Lee asked.

"No," I said, deciding not to make an impertinent remark about Erich von Däniken. More, I was afraid that when my work on La Salle finishes, I will lose track of Lee, another good person, for no good reason, floating out of my life.

There is one more thing to tell.

In the spring following our trip down the Mississippi, Steve played Little League baseball. At the first game, I was asked to coach third base. My counterpart from the other team was John MacDonald, whom I had neither talked to nor seen since buying *Pearl*. Naturally, he was curious about our trip and the fate (performance) of his former boat.

After I had brought him up to date, he said, "Did you know that just after you bought *Pearl*, your *oma kuna* died?"

"I did know that. Read it in the paper on the way out of town."

"Her mate died, too. Both washed up on the beach. Turns out she'd laid her eggs there. The gulls picked them off on their run into the surf."

I told him I wasn't surprised, that the *oma kuna* hadn't really worked for me. Certainly not in Elkhart, when I stabbed the outboard through the grille of a Ford F-350.

"But that's not the end of the story! My daughters found a baby turtle hidden in seaweed, one the gulls missed. We took it home and released it on the Sakonnet River, where we first saw your *oma kuna*. That, my friend, is life. Brings everything full circle. From the dead there is life. And besides, no one ever said your *oma kuna* would work on land. You didn't have any trouble on the water, now, did you?"

"No, it was wonderful."

"See?"

Yes, I see.

Later, I told Steve. It was the weekend and we'd all gone fishing at a mountain lake. We'd parked near a bridge and climbed down a bank so that we could cast into the quick-flowing current that ran underneath. Steve nodded that he understood about the dead turtles and the baby that was saved, but he did not say anything.

He got up from the rock on which we were sitting and climbed the bank to the road. Then moved over to the bridge, resting his arms on the railing. A mess of shiners filled the bucket. Each one he swung over toward me, dangling from the rod so that I, below, could unhook it and reload the bait. The shiners were small, about three to four inches. Then he caught a nice-looking perch, big enough for the pan. I put on another worm and he went after another, but that was the only perch he would catch that day.

Andra and I drank coffee and watched him, marveling at how quiet and serious he could be about fishing. Suddenly a small bird landed on the rail next to him. Steve kept fishing, glancing down at the bird, then at his line. Back and forth, slowly, as if both were of equal interest. Then with one hand—and I swear this is true—he reached over and began to pet the little bird, stroking it three times from the head to the tail. Slowly he removed his hand, gripped the rod, and looked out at the water. The bird sat there another minute, then flew away.

Shortly, Steve reeled in the hook and slid down the embankment.

"I'm ready to go," he said.

Andra said, "Steve, you just petted a wild bird. That's pretty amazing."

"You don't see that too often," he answered quietly.

"What about these fish?" I asked.

"Throw back the shiners," he said. "But I'd like to keep the perch."

"You going to eat it?"

"Yup."

We were halfway back to the car when suddenly he turned around. I followed him down to the lake. He took the perch in his hand and held it underwater, watching the gills open and close.

"I think he'll be all right, Dad."

He released the perch, and we watched it wend its way toward deeper water.

"That sure is a beautiful fish," he said.

# Notes

## Chapter 1: An Idea of Pre-America

1. Hernando de Soto was the first European to lay eyes on the Mississippi, in 1541. In 1655, Pierre Esprit Radisson and Sieur des Groseilliers (christened Médard Chouart) may have ascended the Mississippi from Prairie du Chien to Lake Pepin, Minnesota; and Father Claude Allouez is credited by the historian John Gilmary Shea with visiting the headwaters in 1670. Also, Father Nicolás Freytas claimed in 1661 to have marched with Diego de Peñalosa, then governor of New Mexico, from Santa Fe to the Mississippi. That he preceded Jolliet and La Salle to the river, or was first to mention its Algonquian name, is generally discredited.

2. Francis Parkman, *La Salle and the Discovery of the Great West* (Boston, 1869), p. 143.

## Chapter 2: The Place of the *Griffon*

1. Marquis Childs, *Mighty Mississippi: Biography of a River* (New York, 1982), p. 16.
2. Edgar Allan Poe, "A Dream Within a Dream" (1827).
3. Francis Parkman, *La Salle and the Discovery of the Great West* (Boston, 1869), p. 132.
4. Ibid., p. 110.
5. Walt Kelly, 1970 Pogo cartoon used in a 1971 Earth Day poster.

### Chapter 4: Westward

1. Francis Parkman, in *La Salle and the Discovery of the Great West* (Boston, 1869), says it was Adrien's better-known brother, Louis (p. 16); Timothy Severin, in his book, *Explorers of the Mississippi* (New York, 1968), says it was yet another sibling, Lucien (p. 112). Jesuit scholar Jean Delanglez, in *Mid-America* (January 1945), makes a strong case for its being the elder Adrien, a fur trader, in whose footsteps Louis followed.

2. Anka Muhlstein, *La Salle* (New York, 1994), p. 43.

### Chapter 5: Starved Rock

1. Francis Borgia Steck, *The Jolliet-Marquette Expedition, 1673* (Quincy, Ill., 1928), p. 133.

2. An earlier and more direct route from Montreal to the northern lakes, via the Ottawa River and Lake Nipissing, led to Georgian Bay of Lake Huron. But a ship such as the *Griffon* could not follow that route, which may explain La Salle's investigation of the Detroit River.

3. Céline Dupré, *Dictionary of Canadian Biography* (Toronto, 1966), p. 174.

4. Ibid., p. 175.

5. It also is to be remembered that neither La Salle nor Jolliet "discovered the Mississippi," since they had been preceded at the least by Soto, and possibly by Pierre Radisson and Sieur des Groseilliers, Father Claude Allouez and Father Nicolás Freytas. As Henry Schoolcraft noted of the river in Julius Chambers, *The Mississippi River* (New York, 1968), p. 12, it had "the remarkable feature" of being " 'discovered' in sections, separated by long intervals of time." The Indians, of course, knew about it all along.

6. Dupré, op. cit., p. 175.

7. Francis Borgia Steck, *Marquette Legends* (New York, 1960).

8. Ibid., p. 70.

### Chapter 6: Dwellers on the Threshold

1. Herman Hesse, *Siddhartha* (New York, 1951), pp. 136–37.

2. Francis Parkman, *La Salle and the Discovery of the Great West* (Boston, 1869), p. 205.

3. Before the Illinois Waterway, the I & M Canal surmounted the Chicago Portage, connecting Lake Michigan to the Illinois River. Opened in 1848, it was sixty feet wide at the bank, thirty-six feet wide at the bottom, six feet deep, and ninety-six miles long. Use of the canal and its fifteen locks had already declined by 1854, by which time railroads offered faster transportation. The Illinois Waterway opened in 1933.

### Chapter 7: Broken Hearts

1. Francis Parkman, *La Salle and the Discovery of the Great West* (Boston, 1869), p. 154.

2. Ibid., p. 155.

3. Judith Franke, in her book *French Peoria and the Illinois Country* (Springfield, Ill., 1995), says (p. 73), "In France, 'Crèvecœur' was a family name, a place name, and the name of a military victory. It is likely that the fort was named after one of these." Her reasoning is that "it is now felt that La Salle's mood at this time was not one of despair."

4. Ibid., p. 75.
5. Parkman, p. 175.
6. Ibid., p. 180.
7. Ibid., p. 180.

## Chapter 8: The Wreck of the *Griffon*

1. *Quimby's 1994 Cruising Guide* (St. Louis, 1994), p. 67.

## Chapter 9: The Keeper of the Stone

1. Letter from Madeleine Cavelier, niece of La Salle, to a government official: "As soon as I read your letter, Monsieur, I sought a safe opportunity for sending you the papers of Monsieur De La Salle. There are maps which I have attached to these papers which serve to prove that in 1675 Monsieur La Salle had already made two journeys on these explorations, for there was a map which I am sending you in which mention is made of the place which Monsieur La Salle reached near the River Misipi, another place which he calls the River Colbert, etc." Pierre Margry, *Découvertes et établissements,* Vol. 3, pp. 416–17.
2. Francis Parkman, *La Salle and the Discovery of the Great West* (Boston, 1869), p. 25.
3. John Brinckerhoff, Jackson, *A Sense of Place, a Sense of Time* (New Haven, 1994), p. 3.
4. IHS is a representation of the Greek letters ΙΗΣ, an abbreviation of ΙΗΣΟΥΣ. IHS was used as a monogram for the sacred name of Jesus. This romanized form also has been thought to abbreviate *In Hoc Salus,* "in this cross is salvation."

## Chapter 10: The Great River

1. Julius Chambers, *The Mississippi River* (New York, 1968), pp. 4–5.
2. Letter from Weddle to the author, October 12, 1996.
3. Willard Price, *The Amazing Mississippi* (New York, 1963), p. 5.
4. Chambers, op. cit., p. 79.
5. Francis Borgia Steck, *Marquette Legends* (New York, 1960), p. 54.
6. Roderick Nash, *Wilderness and the American Mind* (New Haven, 1967), p. 138.
7. Anka Muhlstein, *La Salle* (New York, 1992), p. 145.
8. Patricia Galloway, an associate editor of *La Salle, the Mississippi and the Gulf* (College Station, Tex., 1987), p. 17, notes that there are a total of eight complete or partial accounts of the 1682 expedition.
9. Muhlstein, op. cit., p. 146.
10. Chateaubriand, *Oeuvres complètes* (Paris, 1837), Vol. 12, p. 109.
11. Pierre Margry, *Découvertes et établissements,* Vol. 2, p. 173.

## Chapter 11: To the River Calmer Than Air

1. Rev. August Reyling, *Historical Kaskaskia* (St. Louis, 1963), p. 8.
2. Ibid., p. 12.
3. Tom Weil, *The Mississippi River* (New York, 1992), p. 235.

4. Ken Lewis, "La Salle: Expedition II," *Mariah* (August–September 1978).

5. Robert S. Weddle, *The French Thorn* (College Station, Tex., 1991), p. 4.

6. Weddle emphasizes that La Salle's belief that he had entered a separate river system is based not on Spanish documents but on the "Chucagoa fragment" in Pierre Margry, *Découvertes et établissements,* Vol. 2, pp. 196–203. "The point is," says Weddle in a letter to the author of October 12, 1996, "that what he saw of the Mississippi conformed to none of the maps. There was no bay at the lower mouth, and the river flowed east-southeast in its lower reaches, rather than straight south. Examining the maps for a river that did fit his observations, La Salle settled on the Escondido, which some maps showed to be the same as the Magdalene."

### Chapter 12: Surrendering to the Stream

1. Mark Twain, *Life on the Mississippi* (New York, 1961), p. 119.

2. Tom Weil, *The Mississippi River* (New York, 1992), p. 315.

3. Jean Delanglez asserts that La Salle had with him on his descent of the Mississippi an abbreviated version of Vega's account, adapted by the translator Pierre Richelet. Robert S. Weddle, *The French Thorn* (College Station, Tex., 1991), p. 309.

### Chapter 13: Death of the Pilot's Mother

1. Shaun Morey, *Incredible Fishing Stories* (New York, 1994), p. 38.

2. Francis Parkman, *La Salle and the Discovery of the Great West* (Boston, 1869), p. 307.

3. Ibid., p. 309.

4. Ibid., p. 314.

5. Ibid., p. 318.

6. Ibid., p. 278.

7. Ibid., p. 279.

8. John Bierhorst, ed., *In the Trail of the Wind* (New York, 1971), p. 132.

### Chapter 14: The Fires of the Natchez

1. Tom Weil, *The Mississippi River* (New York, 1992), p. 385.

2. Mark Twain, *Life on the Mississippi* (New York, 1961), p. 22.

3. *USA Today* (August 25, 1995), p. 12A.

4. Jane Smiley, *Harper's* magazine (January 1996), p. 63.

5. Francis Parkman, *La Salle and the Discovery of the Great West* (Boston, 1869), p. 281.

6. Ibid., p. 284.

7. Robert S. Weddle, *The French Thorn* (College Station, Tex., 1991), p. 4.

### Chapter 15: Deliverance

1. Robert S. Weddle, *La Salle, the Mississippi and the Gulf* (College Station, Tex., 1987), p. 55.

2. Weddle says in *The French Thorn* (College Station, Tex., 1991), p. 5, "Quite likely the explorers, in following the widest channel, already had failed to notice an earlier division

and proceeded into the one leading to the North Pass. The branches they explored, therefore, were departures from the river's principal eastern distributary, not the three passes that are most obvious on a present-day map." This is not surprising, as there are channels everywhere, and even today, in many areas of the delta, it is difficult to determine which are the principals.

3. Francis Parkman, *La Salle and the Discovery of the Great West* (Boston, 1869), p. 286.

4. Weddle, *French Thorn,* p. 10.

5. Letter from Weddle to the author, October 12, 1996.

## Chapter 16: Homeward

1. Anka Muhlstein, *La Salle* (New York, 1994), p. 176.

2. Robert S. Weddle, *The French Thorn* (College Station, Tex., 1991), p. 17.

3. Ibid., p. 15.

4. Ibid., p. 23.

5. Francis Parkman, *La Salle and the Discovery of the Great West* (Boston, New York, 1869).

6. Timothy Severin, *Explorers of the Mississippi* (New York, 1968), p. 182.

7. Weddle, *French Thorn,* p. 72.

8. Ibid. p. 76.

9. Muhlstein, op. cit., p. 230.

10. Hubert Howe Bancroft, *History of the North Mexican States and Texas,* Vol. 1 (San Francisco, 1889), p. 396 n.

11. Céline Dupré, *Dictionary of Canadian Biography* (Toronto, 1966), p. 183.

12. Ibid., p. 183.

13. Marquis Childs, *Mighty Mississippi: Biography of a River* (New York, 1982), p. 9.

14. Robert S. Weddle, *La Salle, the Mississippi and the Gulf* (College Station, Tex., 1987), p. 13.

# *Index*